# JAPAN

*Through Writers' Eyes*

# JAPAN

*Through Writers' Eyes*

*Edited by*

ELIZABETH INGRAMS

ELAND

First published in 2009 by Eland Publishing Ltd,
61 Exmouth Market, London ECIR 4Q
Reprinted with revisions, 2014

Editorial Content © Elizabeth Ingrams 2009

All extracts © of the authors, as attributed in
the text and acknowledgements

ISBN    978 1 906011 08 6

Cover photograph: Courtyard of the Meiji Temple,
Tokyo © Werner Bischof 1951
Map © Reginald Piggott
Typeset in Great Britain by Antony Gray
Printed in Spain by GraphyCems, Navarra

We should like to thank
The Great Britain Sasakawa Foundation
for its support in the publication of this work

The Great Britain
SASAKAWA
FOUNDATION
グレイトブリテン・ササカワ財団

# Contents

# Acknowledgements

I would like to thank the following institutions for their encouragement and support: Mike Barrett and Stephen McEnally of The Sasakawa Foundation; Barnaby Rogerson, Rose Baring and Fran Sandham, of Eland Publishing; Professor Yozaburo Shirahata and Yukiko Okuno of Nichibun International Research Centre for Japanese Studies, Kyoto; Susan Meehan at the Daiwa Anglo-Japanese Foundation; Greg Irvine at the V & A Museum; Izumi K Tytler, Yuki Kissick, Rie Williams, Hitomi Hall at the Nissan Institute; Julia Turney at Japan–UK 150. I would also like to thank the following individuals for their enthusiasm, advice and support: Joan Anderson, Lesley Downer, Andrew Gebert, Irene Herera, Tobias Hill, Joanna Hunter, Koichi Kano, Chieko Maruyama, Roger Pulvers, Christopher Purvis, James Tink, Anthony Thwaite. This book is dedicated to my mother.

We would like to thank all of the authors for making this collection possible by allowing us to use their material, and gratefully acknowledge permission to reprint copyright material as follows:

Penguin Books Ltd for permission to quote from *The Roads to Sata: A 2,000 Mile Walk through Japan* by Alan Booth and from *The Narrow Road to the Deep North and other Travel Sketches* by Matsuo Basho, translated by Nobuyuki Yuasa; Donald Richie for permission to quote from his book *Tokyo Nights*; Anthony Thwaite for permission to use his poem 'On Dejima: 1845'; Georges Borchardt for permission to quote from *Modern Japanese Diaries: The Japanese at Home and Abroad As Revealed Through Their Diaries* by Donald Keene; Faber & Faber for permission to reproduce an extract from *A Pale View of the Hills* by Kazuo Ishiguro; Random House Inc. for permission to reproduce extracts from *The Lady and the Monk* by Pico Iyer, from *Naomi* by Junichirō Tanizaki, translated by A Chambers and from *Snow Country* by Yasunari Kawabata, translated by Edward G. Seidensticker; Salt Publishing for permission to use 'On the Island of Pearls' from *Year of the Dog* by Tobias Hill; Canongate for permission to quote from

*Hokkaido Highway Blues* by Will Ferguson; Lonely Planet for permission to use extracts from *Lost Japan* by Alex Kerr; Stanford University Press for permission to use an extract from *During the Rains* by Nagai Kafu, translated by Lane Dunlop; Marion Boyars Publishers for permission to quote from *Hiroshima Notes* by Kenzaburo Ōe, translated by Toshi Yonezawa; Sheil Land Associates Ltd for permission to use an extract from *The Nobility of Failure: Tragic Heroes in the History of Japan* by Sugawara No Michizane, translated by Ivan Morris; The Random House Group for permission to use an extract from *On the Narrow Road to the Deep North* by Lesley Downer and to quote from *The Sound of Waves* by Yukio Mishima, translated by Meredith Weatherby; Patt Barr for permission to use an extract from her book *The Coming of the Barbarians*; Continuum International Publishing Group for permission to quote from *Mitford's Japan* by Algernon Bertram Mitford; Global Oriental Ltd for permission to use an extract from *The Silver Drum: A Japanese Imperial Memoir* by Setsuko, Princess Chichibu, translated by Dorothy Britton; Tuttle Publishing for permission to reproduce material from *Okinawa: the History of an Island People* by George Kerr, *Shimoda Story* by Oliver Statler and *Ten-foot Square Hut and the Tales of Heike* by Kamo no Chōmei, translated by A. L. Sadler; The University of Chicago for permission to use an extract from *Japanese Inn* by Oliver Statler; New Directions Publishing Corp. for permission to reprint extracts by Princess Nukuda from *Women Poets of Japan*, edited by Kenneth Rexroth and Ikuko Atsumi; HarperCollins Publishers for permission to use an exerpt from *Japanese Pilgrimage* by Oliver Statler; James Kirkup for permission to use an extract from his book *These Horned Islands*; Angus Waycott for permission to use an extract from his book *Sado: Japan's Island in Exile*; University of Washington Press for permission to quote from *A Year in the Life of a Shinto Shrine* by John K. Nelson; Kodansha International Ltd. for permission to use an extract from *The Bells of Nagasaki* by Takashi Nagai, translated by William Johnston; Oxford University Press for permission to use an extract from *The Samurai* by Shusako Endo, translated by Van C. Gessel.

# Introduction

Japan is a country that was for centuries so cut off from the Western world that in Europe it was considered to be the stuff of legend. Coincidentally the Japanese too thought their country to be legendary. The Land of the Rising Sun was founded by the deities Izanagi and his sister (and wife) Izanami, and the contemporary Imperial line is said to descend from the Sun Goddess, Amaterasu. A sense of unbroken lineage is crucial to the identity of the Japanese, so it is no wonder that the country is still treated with respect if not awe by the modern-day Western adventurer.

This anthology gathers together some of the most resonant and powerful voices among Japanese and Western writers, under the heading 'literature of place'. The poetic myths of sacred Mount Fuji and of the exploits of courtiers in the seventh century Buddhist capital of Nara are taken from one of the oldest extant anthologies of national poetry, *Man'yōshū*. Included here are the first sixteenth-century European reports of Kyūshū and Kyoto by Jesuits Francis Xavier and Joao Rodrigues, expressing their admiration of the 'new found' Japanese civilisation. The Edo period (1603–1867) is still considered a time of backwardness by the West, but some of the best works of Japanese literature were written then, whether in Ōsaka, the centre of enterprise and mercantilism – in the tragedies of Chikamatsu Monzaemon and the humourous stories of Ihara Saikaku – or in Edo itself, by Matsuo Bashō, who managed to combine prose and poetry, *haibun*, into some of the greatest travel accounts of all time. His journey through the northern interior of Japan was followed in recent years by Lesley Downer. She relives the experience, finding that much of the romance of his journey has not faded with time.

As the novelist Junichirō Tanizaki wrote of Japan in 1933, 'the changes that have taken place since the restoration of 1867 must be at least as great as those of the preceding three-and-a-half centuries.'

After the Americans arrived during the 1850s and 1860s, foreign diplomats witnessed the drama of Japan's transformation, including Dutch, British and Americans – Townsend Harris, Henry Heusken, Sir Rutherford Alcock, Sir Ernest Satow, A. B. Mitford and the diplomat's wife, Mary Crawford Fraser.

A little later on in the late nineteenth and early twentieth centuries 'orientalist' literary giants such as Rudyard Kipling and Pierre Loti shared a palpable excitement at 'discovering' the closed-off islands, especially the beauty of the women and the arts and crafts in Kyoto and Nagasaki. Alongside these are the responses of Japanese novelists such as Higuchi Ichiyō, Natsume Sōseki and Tanizaki who reflected on the harsher social reality of Japan, while extolling the wonders and satirising the dangers of the Western culture which had landed wholesale on their shores.

The book is divided geographically, and Tokyo offers the greatest variety of descriptions, having been the seat of both shogunate and Imperial power for over four hundred years. The views of the shogun's castle and the Imperial Palace by foreign guests afford us both reverential and light-hearted glimpses of the changing nature of the Japanese power structure and its attitude towards foreign visitors. The city of Kyoto is more fascinating and also more impenetrable to outsiders, and the insights of recent foreign residents Nicolas Bouvier, Pico Iyer and Alex Kerr are invaluable to understanding the city.

In the mountains of Gifu and Nagano, Bashō's early exploration takes us on a tour of the perilous peaks, while writers and school teachers of the nineteenth century, Shimazaki Tōson and W. E. Griffis describe the shock of the new as ancient ways gave way to a more open society.

The islands of Shikoku, Kyūshū, and the hinterland of Chūgoku are also rich in literary history, coloured by reports from governors of remote provinces such as ninth century Ki Tsurayuki passing through the stormy Inland Sea towards Kyoto, as well as self-styled exiles such as nineteenth-century Japan specialist Lafcadio Hearn, and, in the post-war period, Donald Richie. At the extremities of Japan, there are early reports of poetry, song and sub-tropical hospitality on the islands of Okinawa, and in Hokkaidō, brown-bear hunting with the indigenous Ainu.

Modern-day voices bear witness to the horrors of war and the romance of everyday life – Takashi Nagai, working at a Nagasaki hospital, saw the A-bomb drop in 1945; Chizuko Oyasato was a girl who escaped at the hands of the Americans during the battle of Okinawa also in 1945; and Rey Ventura, working as a Filipino migrant labourer in downtown Yokohama during the recent boom years observes the *yakuza*.

This is not a comprehensive literary anthology or survey, nor is it intended as a guide book: it is simply a collection of some of the best travel writing (or in the case of Marco Polo and Gulliver, fictitious travel writing) related to the main cities and regions of Japan. The aim is to provide some inspiration to explore a country full of treasures, whether literally or through the powers of the imagination.

ELIZABETH INGRAMS

# Editorial Note

I have not tried to regularise the spelling of Japanese words and names, as these are sometimes spelt differently in different periods. Similarly the styling of the extracts has been kept intact. I have used the most up-to-date or sympathetic translations, but have had to rely on what is available.

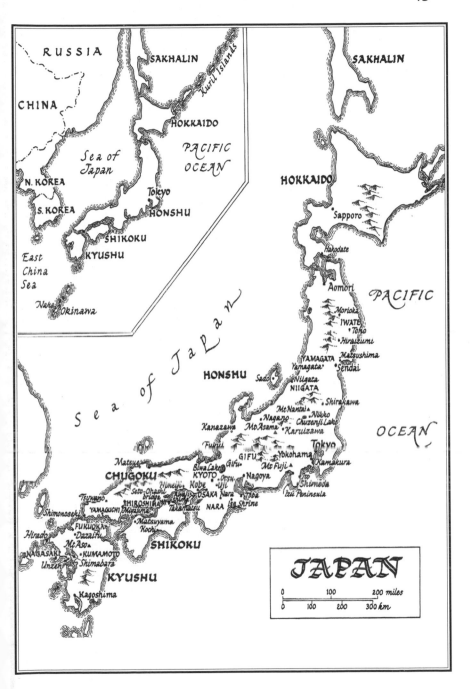

# 1

# Tokyo

## EDO PERIOD (1603–1867)

A cloud of cherry blossoms:
The bell, – is it Ueno?
Is it Asakusa?

MATSUO BASHŌ

The village of Edo, present-day Tokyo, was just a little fishing port in 1598 when Tokugawa Ieyasu (1543–1616) came upon Edo castle rising out of the Musashi plain. He was looking for a fortress that was far away from the imperial centre at Kyoto, from which to establish his domain. After his predecessor and rival *daimyo* or lord, Hideyoshi, died, Ieyasu went into battle at Sekigahara in 1600, against the rival guardians of the five-year-old heir to the throne, Hideyori. His victory established him not only as the *bakufu* (regent of the government), but he also took the title *shogun*, or military ruler (also known as *taiku*, tycoon), because he was a descendant of the Minamoto, the first shoguns who had ruled from Kamakura.

Ieyasu set up Edo as an eastern capital to rival Kyoto. And, as at Nara and Kyoto, there was a Chinese geomantic design at work in its conception. There is a river – the Sumida – for the Cyan Dragon in the east; an ocean – Edo (present-day Tokyo) bay – for the Vermillion Bird in the south; a White Tiger, a road – the Tōkaidō – to the west, and finally mountains for the Dark Warrior to the north. As you navigate modern-day Tokyo's intricate underground and overground systems, place names conjure these traces – names such as Tora-nomon, or tiger gate.

Ieyasu, followed by his son Hidetada (1579–1632) started their city project by building Edo castle with the help of the lords who had switched sides to support them during the battle of Sekigahara (1600). The castle was built in a spiral design; the *honmaru*, or castle keep, spiralled past the dwellings of the *daimyo*, right down to the merchants and townsmen, who were kept outside the palace gates.

Tokugawa Ieyasu's Edo project laid the foundations for a unified Japan under his family's military dictatorship. This system was to last for two hundred and fifty years, and all the *daimyo* of Japan were subjected to the will of the Tokugawa. There were different categories of feudal lords, including *fudai* (hereditary lords), *tozama* (outside lords who had won their status through siding with Ieyasu at the battle of Sekigahara) and *rōnin*, or masterless warriors, samurai dispossessed from their titles. The *bakufu* used a Confucian class system of *shinōkōshō*: samurai, farmers, artisans and merchants, in descending order.

The Tokugawa's greatest concern when they were establishing their regime were the powerful *tozama daimyo*, many of whom came from Kyūshū, which had been the first part of the country to engage with Europeans when the Portuguese arrived in 1543. After the Shimabara Christian rebellion in 1638, Hidetada cut off relations with foreign countries, which was partly a way of ensuring that these feudal lords did not become too powerful through outside assistance. The Tokugawa also operated a *sankin kōtai* hostage system of 'alternative attendance' at government whereby the *daimyo* had to travel between Edo and their rural fiefs, leaving their women and children in Edo, and ensuring that they spent at least three days per month in audiences with the shogun. They were closely watched by an elaborate system of *metsuke* or spies. Under a complicated system of increasing privileges, the closer you were to the shogun, the greater the privileges you enjoyed. The economy relied on rice production and also arts and crafts, with different *daimyo*'s regions specialising in different products – such as silk and porcelain.

Ieyasu started his city project by filling in parts of the river Sumida on the inlet to the sea and building a bridge, the Nihombashi (literally, 'Japan Bridge'), outside the castle moat. Nihombashi was home to the Japanese Mint during the Edo period and later became the location of the Bank of Japan. The great novelist Junichiro Tanizaki also prided himself that his birthplace was nearby, for this was the heart of the Low City, the *shitamachi*, in both the Edo and Meiji periods. Nihombashi Bridge, from which all distances were once measured is, however, now hidden under an expressway.

The Japanese still refer to the Edo period, from the time the foreigners were banned from Japanese soil (1638–1868), as the time of *taisei*, peace and tranquility. To enforce this peace, shoguns themselves relied on a highly regulated system. Not only were Japanese not allowed to travel abroad, but it was also difficult to travel within their own country. However, not all travel was prohibited and Buddhism was tolerated by the shoguns so monks were allowed to make pilgrimages. This was the way in which one of the world's most famous literary travel diaries was written.

Matsuo Bashō (1644–94) was born Kinsaku, the son of a poor samurai who earned his livelihood by teaching writing. He befriended a young heir who was also a poet – Sengin. When the poet died aged twenty-five in 1666, Bashō ran away to Kyoto, and studied the Chinese and Japanese classics. For a time he was caught up in the witty style of composition, the playful style epitomised by the poet Sōin (1605–1682). A merchant, Sugiyama Sampū, was a great admirer of Bashō and built him a small house in Fukagawa just east of the river Sumida. The poet wrote:

> I planted in my garden
> A stock of Bashō
> And hated at once
> The shooting bush-clovers.

He took the poetic name Bashō (which means banana plant) from then on, and was also introduced to Zen by the priest Bucchō. At that time, travel was dangerous and few people even thought of taking to the road for pleasure or as a pastime – so really Bashō was casting away earthly attachments when he made the first journey, which he wrote up as *Records of a Weather Exposed Skeleton*, (1684), followed by *Records of a Travel-Worn Satchel* (1687) and eventually *The Narrow Road to the Deep North* (1689), among others. The latter is seen as unique among his travel diaries because it shows such a great literary unity, in terms of the mixture of prose and haiku poetry known as '*haibun*' in Japanese. Bashō travelled the Oshukaidō and the Hokurikudō, the Northern roads, in the space of six months, but these roads wound through mountainous passes that were not usually travelled. It was not at all certain that any one who travelled these roads would return safely. Bashō's journey is, therefore, according to Nobuyuki Yuasa, a feat of both literature and life, the shape of the journey 'like two halves of a circle', and the whole thing representing 'a study in eternity'.

Traditional arts such as Kabuki theatre and *ukiyo-e* painting thrived during the Edo period. Famous artists like Hokusai (1760–1849) and Hiroshige (1797–1858) also travelled, sometimes painting scenes of the barrier gates through which every traveller had to pass along the main roads. Hiroshige painted the fifty-three stations of the Tōkaidō, and the sixty-nine stations of the Kisokaidō (the Nakasendō). The Kabuki dramas of the time often centred on stories of travellers being ambushed on the way, while *Jippensha Ikku* (*Shank's Mare*) by Ihara Saikaku describes a hilarious pilgrimage from Tokyo to Ise.

One of the more outstanding shoguns was Tsunayoshi Tokugawa (ruled 1680–1709), famed as a scholar and poet, who promoted tolerance during an age called the Genroku period (see Ōsaka chapter), which saw the flowering of art and literature. Japan was still to all intents and purposes a closed country, and Japanese ships were effectively prohibited from sailing abroad. Nevertheless, two Dutch ships per year were permitted to land in Nagasaki Bay. Like the local lords, the Dutch captain, the *Opperhoofd*, was required to attend to the shogun in Tokyo every year.

One Dutch ship visiting Japan at the time contained the German doctor and traveller Engelbert Kaempfer (1651–1716), who arrived as a physician to the Dutch embassy in Nagasaki in 1690. He stayed in Japan for two years and wrote secret reports on the country despite censorship.

Although the Edo period is known as Pax Tokugawa, a time when the manufacture of gunpowder was forbidden, with a focus on the arts of Japan (*bun* – culture as opposed to *bu* – war) there were still tensions simmering beneath the surface. In 1701, Lord Asano was insulted by

Lord Kira at a shogunal reception at Edo castle and drew his sword, an offence for which he was punished with an order to commit ritual suicide or *seppuku* following which the shogunate confiscated Asano's lands. But since his forty-seven retainers were left masterless *rōnin* on account of what seemed to them to be an injustice, they rose up to take their revenge on Lord Kira, whose head they presented to their dead lord's tomb in Sengakuji temple in Tokyo before turning themselves in to the authorities. The shogun did not know what to do, since their action was in line with Confucian ideals of loyalty to their lord, while at the same time disrupting the peace at Edo. In the end they were ordered to commit *seppuku*. The event was the subject of Chikamatsu Monzaemon's (1653–1725) Kabuki play *Chūshingura* (The Tale of the Forty-Seven Rōnin) and occupied pages and pages of Edo commentary. It is one of the most extreme examples of the vendetta of samurai who stood up for their murdered lord. As Oliver Statler describes the spirit of *bu* – way of the warrior – still survives within Edo Japan.

Gulliver, in Jonathan Swift's novel *Gulliver's Travels*, goes to Japan in 1709 and lands at Uraga (just by Yokosuka on the Sagami peninsula) and proceeds to Edo to be received by the shogun before taking ship from Nangasak (Nagasaki). In Gulliver's day, Uraga was an anchoring place for barges, where they were inspected before being allowed to enter Tokyo Bay. Gulliver cleverly avoids the *fumie* or ritual stamping on the crucifix, which all Dutch traders had to perform in return for trading rights.

The literate samurai classes, through their own studies during the Edo period, started to see a contradiction in the Confucian code of loyalty to one's parents and sovereign, which the shogun promoted. They saw that the shoguns had usurped power from the Emperor and promoted the Imperial cause through the study of ancient writings, such as the *Nihon Shoki* and the *Kōjiki* as opposed to Chinese classics. At the same time, Russian and American ships started to dock in the bays around Japan in the 1850s. Some of the influential Japanese were ready for a move away from the shogunate, which had after all left them with no navy with which to defend themselves against foreign invasion. The first visit of an American to Edo castle is described by

Henry Heusken, assistant to the American commander Commodore
Perry, in 1857.

The shockwaves that followed the arrival of foreigners in Japan
with the opening of the treaty ports were first felt in Shimoda, then in
Hakodate and Nagasaki, where the warships of the Americans had
been based. During the so-called Summer War of 1866, the *bakufu*'s
forces were embroiled in sustained fighting and were finally
outgunned by the superior modern weaponry of the anti-Tokugawa
alliance of Southerners (Tosa, Choshu, Satsuma *daimyo* and their
allies) keen to see the Emperor brought to power in Edo. Meanwhile
in Edo and the neighbouring region of Kanto there was a popular
uprising triggered by fears that Japan was on the brink of colonial-
style domination by foreigners, especially as foreign powers, Britain
and France, were siding with Emperor and shogun respectively. The
defeat of Yoshinobu Tokugawa's forces revealed many of the cracks in
the *taisei*, the great peace which had lasted since the time of Ieyasu.

In the relative calm that followed the storm, the *bakufu* set about
various reforms, one of which was to centralize the structure of the
Tokugawa government. Military reforms and indeed loans were
overseen by French diplomat Léon Roches, but in 1867 Yoshinobu
accepted the Tosa clan's proposal that he step down formally from his
position as *bakufu*. However the Satsuma and other *daimyo* continued
with plots and disturbances and, during the following year, 1868,
Southern forces started to head towards Kyoto, home of the Emperor.
Hearing of this, Yoshinobu Tokugawa could do no other than order
an advance; the result was a defeat at the battle of Toba-Fushimi.

The end of the Tokugawa regime is often written about as a
peaceful transition, but heavy losses were sustained on both sides. At
the battle of Ueno on 4th July 1868, a force of 2,000 of the shogun's
troops took on the Southerners and were slaughtered, whilst in Aizu
Wakamatsu in Tohoku, and Hakodate in Hokkaido, the fighting
between forces loyal to the shogun and those of the Emperor took on
tragic proportions, with Takeaki Enomoto and, under his command
Toshizo Hijikata and a force of 3,000, attempting to set up the
republic of Ezo against the Emperor's forces in Hakodate until their
defeat in June 1869. In the end, the Tokugawa castle was given up and

the Emperor Mutsuhito (Meiji) shifted his court from Kyoto to the city now known as Tokyo and revealed his face to the Japanese public for the first time.

**Bashō** from *Narrow Road to the Deep North and Other Travel Sketches*

Days and months are travellers of eternity. So are the years that pass by. Those who steer a boat across the sea, or drive a horse over the earth till they succumb to the weight of years, spend every minute of their lives travelling. There are a great number of ancients too, who died on the road. I myself have been tempted for a long time by the cloud-moving wind – filled with a strong desire to wander.

It was only towards the end of last autumn that I returned from rambling along the coast. I barely had time to sweep the cobwebs from my broken house on the River Sumida before the New Year, but no sooner had the spring mist begun to rise over the field than I wanted to be on the road again to cross the barrier-gate of Shirakawa in due time. The gods seemed to have possessed my soul and turned it inside out, and roadside images seemed to invite me from every corner, so that it was impossible for me to stay idle at home. Even while I was getting ready, mending my torn trousers, tying a new strap to my hat, and applying *moxa*[1] to my legs to strengthen them, I was already dreaming of the full moon rising over the islands of Matsushima. Finally, I sold my house, moving to the cottage of Sampū for a temporary stay. Upon the threshold of my old home, however, I wrote a linked verse of eight pieces and hung it on a wooden pillar. The starting piece was:

> Behind this door
> Now buried in deep grass,
> A different generation will celebrate
> The Festival of Dolls.[2]

1 The dried leaf of *artemisia moxa*, is used in a treatment known as moxibustion applied to the skin in small quantities and ignited.
2 The festival of dolls is celebrated on March 3rd. It is sometimes called the Festival of Peach blossoms or the Girls' Festival.

It was early on the morning of March the 27th that I took to the road. There was a darkness lingering in the sky, and the moon was still visible, though gradually thinning away. The faint shadow of Mount Fuji and the cherry blossoms of Ueno and Yanaka were bidding me a last farewell. My friends had got together the night before, and they all came with me on the boat to keep me company for the first few miles. When we got off the boat at Senju however, the thought of the three thousand miles before me suddenly filled my heart, and neither the houses of the town nor the faces of my friends could be seen by my tearful eyes, except as a vision.

> The passing spring
> Birds mourn
> Fishes weep
> With tearful eyes.

With this poem to commemorate my departure, I walked forth on my journey, but lingering thoughts made my steps heavy. My friends stood in line and waved good-bye as long as they could see my back.

**Oliver Statler** from *Japanese Inn*

*The master of the Inn observes the course of the vendetta.*

One of their number, disguised as a rich merchant of Kyoto, was taking lessons in tea ceremony from a certain master who also tutored Kira. He learned that there was to be a tea ceremony at Kira's early in the morning on December 6 and so, confident that Kira would be at home on the night before, the league scheduled the attack for the night of the fifth.

On the second day, they met for last instructions. A month before, there had been fifty-five of them. Now there were forty-eight. They signed their final pledge, vowing that they would act as a team, each to perform his assigned part in the plan.

Then came the news that Kira's party had been postponed till the afternoon of the fourteenth. The fourteenth was the monthly anniversary of their lord's death, and so they rescheduled their attack for that night.

On the fourteenth, in the midst of one of Edo's rare snowstorms, the senior members of the group met at the temple of Sengakuji. They paid homage at Asano's grave and then reviewed their tactics. They would split into two groups: one, under Oishi, would attack Kira's main entrance; the other, under the nominal command of Oishi's son Chikara, assisted by an elder, would attack the rear gate. They decided on passwords, agreed that Kira was their first and last target, and dispersed to meet again that night.

At their inns throughout the city, each of the men, announcing that he had to make an urgent visit to Kyoto, paid his bill and bid farewell to his landlord. Each of them stopped by the room of the eldest member of the league for a final cup of sake. Some of them took time for a leisurely supper of noodles.

At the rendez-vous they dressed from the skin in new clothing, for they were undertaking not merely a battle but a rite. First, underwear of white padded silk, soft and warm; then a coat of mail, a padded kimono of black silk with the wearer's crest, trouser-like *hakama*, leggings, gauntlets, helmet and finally a mantle and hood of black and white. A few followed an ancient battlefield custom: each of these traditionalists burned incense in his helmet so that if the enemy took his head they would find it sweetly scented.

At two o'clock in the morning they set out, marching silently through deserted, snowy streets. There were forty-seven now, for there had been one more defection. Of Asano's more than three hundred retainers, the burden of revenge fell on these forty-seven.

Near Kira's mansion they split, one group to the front, one to the rear. Slipping silently through the snow, they overpowered the gate-keepers huddled over charcoal in their huts.

The main gate was strong. They made no attempt to force it, but scaled it with ladders. The rear gate they battered open. They were inside.

Some screened the garden to prevent anyone fleeing to seek help. The rest burst into the house.

As the attack began, Oishi dispatched runners to tell the neighbors what was happening. The masters of two of the mansions were home in their fiefs; their caretakers chose to ignore the attack. In the third house the master was in residence; he ordered his men out, had lanterns lit in his garden, and calling for a chair, sat there himself, ready to cut off any of Kira's men who might try to escape into his compound; he stationed one of his men at the top of the wall to shout the progress of the attack.

Some of Kira's men fought and died that night, but more, including Kira's son, dropped their swords and ran. The attackers slashed their way to Kira's room, found his bed warm but empty. As resistance died they scoured the huge house. An hour slipped away. They began to fear they had lost their quarry.

Then some of them broke into an old hut, used to store charcoal in the back yard. Two men came out fighting but were overcome. A spear thrust wounded a third. He came out wielding a short sword, was downed with another spear thrust. The body bore an old scar across the back. Asano's sword had put it there. Kira had been found.

Whistles sounded the signal. The man who had killed him severed the head and wrapped it in Kira's kimono. They assembled in the courtyard and by a roll call confirmed that none was missing. It was nearly dawn.

Before the main gate of the ravaged house they planted a declaration. It told how Asano had been driven to attack Kira; how he had been properly condemned; but how, since he had been prevented from killing his enemy, his retainers had been obliged to take up arms, 'for it is impossible to live under the same heaven with enemy of lord or father'.

Then they marched to a nearby temple, the fit helping the wounded. They were refused admittance but they waited at the gate, half-expecting an attack from Kira's relatives, half-expecting that some of Kira's family or retainers might wish to offer parting words to their lord. No one appeared. They moved to the river and boarded a ferry which took them along the bay to the pine shrouded shore below the temple of Sengakuji.

At Sengakuji they carefully washed Kira's head and placed it before Asano's tomb. Then each man in turn kneeled there, burned a pinch of incense, and bowed in prayer that his lord's spirit might now find peace. When their ceremony was finished the abbot called them into the main hall of the temple. He welcomed them and gave them a temple breakfast of rice gruel.

Two of the group were dispatched to report their vendetta to the shogunate's inspector general. That dignitary received them sympathetically, heard them out, and then hurried to advise the council.

The men waited that day at Sengakuji. At nightfall they were ordered to report next morning to the inspector-general. There, all next day, they were questioned, and finally told that pending a decision in their case, they would be detained in the mansions of four *daimyo*. The shogun, who had been so swift to dispatch their master, was now moving carefully.

Each of the *daimyo* went out of his way to show that he was honoured. The lord to whom Oishi and sixteen others were assigned sent a palanquin for each man, and an escort of 750 samurai, including all of his principal retainers. And he greeted and praised each of his wards personally though it was after two in the morning before they reached his house.

Later Oishi described their reception in a letter to Kyoto. He went on to tell how their host had begun immediate construction of special rooms for them, how he had provided new clothing, lavish food, sake and tobacco. Meanwhile the shogunate was racking its brain. By the feudal code, their action should have been praised, but it was obvious that this would encourage organized resort to force.

Every major official studied the question, every scholar at the government's disposal wrote a brief probing the moral issues at stake.

The debate raged all the way through January while the country held its breath.

The final solution was regarded as saving face for everybody. The forty-seven Ako *rōnin* had conducted an unauthorized vendetta although their lord had received only due punishment for misconduct. They ought therefore to be punished as criminals. But in consideration of their loyal spirit they would be allowed to commit suicide.

Chikamatsu Monzaemon wrote the only Kabuki play fit for a samurai's family to see, and its name *Chūshingura* has become the popular title for the whole story.

**Jonathan Swift** *from Gulliver's Travels*

We landed at a small port-town called Xamoshi,[3] situated in the south-east part of Japan; the town lies on the western point where there is a narrow strait leading northward into a long arm of the sea, upon the north-west part of which, Yedo,[4] the metropolis stands. At landing I showed the custom-house officers my letter from the King of Luggnagg to his Imperial Majesty. They knew the seal perfectly well; it was as broad as the palm of my hand. The impression was, a king lifting up a lame beggar from the earth. The magistrates of the town, hearing of my letter, received me as a public minister; they provided me with carriages and servants, and bore my charges to Yedo, where I was admitted to an audience, and delivered my letter, which was opened with great ceremony, and explained to the Emperor by an interpreter, who then gave me notice of his Majesty's order, that I should signify my request, and whatever it were, it should be granted for the sake of his royal brother of Luggnagg. This interpreter was a person employed to transact affairs with the Hollanders; he soon conjectured by my countenance that I was an European, and therefore repeated his Majesty's commands in Low Dutch, which he spoke perfectly well. I answered (as I had before determined), that I was a Dutch merchant, shipwrecked in a very remote country, from whence I travelled by sea and land to Luggnagg, and then took shipping for Japan, where I knew my countrymen often traded, and with some of these I hoped to get an opportunity of returning into Europe: I therefore most humbly entreated his royal favour to give order, that I should be conducted in safety to Nangasac:[5] to this I added another petition, that for the sake of my patron the King of Luggnagg, his Majesty would condescend to excuse my performing the ceremony imposed on my countrymen of *trampling upon the Crucifix*, because I had been thrown into this kingdom by my misfortunes without the intention of trading. When this latter petition was interpreted to the Emperor, he seemed a little surprised, and said, he believed I was the

3  Uraga bay near Tokyo      4  Edo      5  Nagasaki

first of my countrymen who ever made any scruple in this point, and that he began to doubt whether I was a real Hollander or no; but rather suspected I must be a CHRISTIAN. However, for the reasons I had offered, but chiefly to gratify the King of Luggnagg, by an uncommon mark of his favour, he would comply with the *singularity* of my humour, but the affair must be managed with dexterity, and his officers should be commanded to let me pass as it were by forgetfulnesss. For he assured me, that if the secret should be discovered by my countrymen, the Dutch would cut my throat in the voyage. I returned my thanks by the interpreter for so unusual a favour, and some troops being at that time on their march to Nangasac, the commanding officer had orders to convey me safe thither, with particular instructions about the business of the Crucifix.

On the 9th day of June, 1709, I arrived at Nangasac, after a very long and troublesome journey. I soon fell into company of some Dutch sailors belonging to the Amboyna, of Amsteram, a stout ship of 450 tons. I had lived long in Holland pursuing my studies at Leyden and I spoke Dutch well. [...] Before we took shipping, I was often asked by some of the crew whether I had performed the ceremony above-mentioned? I evaded the question by general answers, that I had satisfied the Emperor and Court in all particulars. However a malicious rogue of a skipper went to an officer and pointing to me, told him, I had not yet trampled on the Crucifix; but the other, who had received instructions to let me pass, gave the rascal twenty strokes on the shoulders with a bamboo, after which I was no more troubled with such questions.

**Engelbert Kaempfer** from *History of Japan*

*The City of Jedo* [6]
Thursday March 29th, the presents for the shogun were taken to court, accompanied by the deputies of the senior commissioners and Settsu no Kami. At court they were, as usual, arranged in orderly

6 Edo

fashion, each on a special little wooden table, and lined up in the large audience chamber, where his majesty will inspect them. We followed, a rather poor-looking procession, wearing black silk coats as European robes of honor or ceremonial garments. We were accompanied by three house stewards of the Nagasaki governors, as well as our *dōshin*, or deputy leader, two Nagasaki city messengers, and the interpreter's son, all of them proceeding on foot. We three Dutchmen as well as the junior interpreter were on horseback, riding one behind the other; the horses were being led by servants holding the bridle and walking on the right side of the horses. Horses were also mounted from the right in this country. Previously horses were led by two men, but this has now been discontinued. After that followed the captain in a *norimono* and the old interpreter in a basket. Our personal servants walked at the side and followed as far as they were permitted.

After quarter of an hour we reached the first castle fortified with ramparts and solid walls. There we crossed a large bridge adorned with brass knobs, spanning a river with many boats, which seemed to be moving in a northerly direction around the castle. The entrance was closed off by two strong gates, with a small guard post in between. As soon as we passed through the second gate and reached the square of the first castle, we had to pass a stately guard post on the right, where, however, the emphasis seemed to be on grandeur rather than strength. The guard post was adorned on the outside with beautiful awnings, tufts, and pikes and with gilded screens, lacquered guns, pikes, shields, each girded with two swords over his black silk robe. No sooner had we crossed this area, built up with the mansions of territorial lords (and leaving behind on our left yet another large and busy river), than we reached the second castle, fortified just like the first, but the gates and the great guard inside as well as the palaces seemed far more splendid. Here we left behind our sedan-chairs, horses and servants and walked across the square with our leader toward the *honmaru*, or shogunal residence. Then we passed a long stone bridge, went through bastions sealed off twice, and climbed about twenty paces up a winding road, which was sealed off on both sides with incredibly high walls in keeping with the lay of the land. We reached the great castle guard, called *hyakuninban*, meaning the guard of one hundred men (situated on the left at the end of the above-mentioned road, below the last gate leading to the residence). There we waited for an invitation to proceed, which was to come as soon as the shogunal councillors had arrived at the castle. Two officers of this guard welcomed us cordially and treated us to tea and tobacco. Both commissioners and Settsu no Kami also stopped to greet us on their arrival, quite apart from a number of courtiers unknown to us. In an hour's time the senior and junior councillors had entered the castle, going past us either on foot or carried in a *norimono*, and were called up and led through two splendid gates closing off a square. Walking through the second, we climbed a few steps and reached the forecourt of the residence.

This area situated between the last gate and the front of the shogunal mansion, was only a few paces wide and in addition to being crowded with courtiers and valets, was well manned with guards. Having climbed about two steps, we entered the shogunal mansion and proceeded into the first chamber to the right of the entrance. This is the usual waiting room for people who are to be received by the shogun or the councillors. The room is fairly high, but once the sliding partitions are closed, it is rather dark, since only very little light enters through a lattice high on the wall to a storage area on the right. But apart from that, the room was beautifully decorated with the ceiling, walls and sliding partitions all gilded. After we had sat there for more than an hour and the shogun had proceeded to his throne, both commissioners and Settsu no Kami entered and led the captain to the audience hall but left us behind. As soon as the captain appeared someone shouted in an exaggeratedly loud voice, '*oranda kapitan*' ['Hollanda Capitain'] to prompt him to step forward and pay his respects. Thereupon he crawled forward on his hands and knees between the place where the presents had been lined up and the high seat of his majesty as far as they motioned him. Crouching on his knees, he bent his head to the floor and then, like a lobster, crawled back in this very same position, without one word being exchanged. This short, miserable procedure is all that there is to this famous audience. Nothing else happens at the annual audience of the important territorial lords. After their names have been called and they have in similar fashion silently paid their respects to express their submission and obedience, they too must crawl out backward.

*Audience hall*

[...]

The audience hall with its one hundred mats is open to a small courtyard on one side, from where it receives its light. On the opposite side are two rooms, which open up in the direction of the courtyard. The first of these rooms is fairly wide and is used to seat the councillors when they receive lesser territorial lords, stewards, and emissaries. The other, or last, room is narrower, deeper, and one step higher than the common hall. The shogun sits at the end of this room on a floor raised by a few mats, with his legs folded under him. It is difficult to discern his shape there, because the full light does not reach this part of the room. Also the ceremony takes place too quickly, and the visitor has to appear with lowered head and must leave again without lifting his face to look at his majesty. But the silent presence of the councillors, aristocratic princes, gentlemen-in-waiting, and other high-ranking court attendants gives the event considerable grandeur.

[...]

As soon as the obeisances had been made and the shogun had retired to his usual chambers, we remaining three Dutchmen were also called and together with the captain were led through various chambers to an artistically carved and gilded gallery. After sitting there for a quarter of an hour, we were led through further corridors to a hall and invited to sit down. A number of tonsured courtiers (these are religious men, doctors, and kitchen attendants) arrived and asked our name, age, and other trifling matters. Gilded screens were soon pulled up, however, to rescue us from being surrounded and inspected by the swarms of court attendants passing by. During the half hour we were waiting there the court had proceeded to the rooms of the performance, to which we were led through some dark corridors. These corridors were lined by a single row of shogunal bodyguards, followed by other high-ranking courtiers in similar order, right along the length of the gallery and along the foreground of the site of the performance. They were all wearing ceremonial robes and were sitting on their knees and bending low.

It consisted of several rooms some of which opened up to a central area and some were closed off with blinds; each was fifteen mats wide, and each on higher than the next by the thickness of a mat in accordance with the rank of the occupants. In the central area the mats had been removed. It was therefore the lowest area, and we were instructed to be seated on the varnished floor boards that covered it. His Majesty and his wife were seated behind the blinds on the right near to us. I glimpsed the face of the latter twice when the blinds were bent and saw that it was brownish, rounded, and of beautiful shape, with black European eyes, full of fire and vigor. Judging from the proportions of her head, I imagined her to be a tall lady, about thirty-six years old. What I call blinds are hanging mats made of small, split, soft pieces of reed, with interwoven silk threads a span apart. They are painted for decoration and to make them less transparent. When the light behind them is covered up, one cannot make out people at a distance. Only the sound of his voice gave us an indication that His Majesty was present, even though he spoke only in low tones as if he did not want to be heard loudly. Women of the court and the invited princesses of shogunal descent sat behind the blinds in front of us at a distance of four mats. Here and there the joints or gaps in these blinds had been widened to permit a better view [...]

As soon as the commissioners had brought us to the gallery, we were greeted by a junior councillor and led to the central area described above. There we all had to show our submission in Japanese fashion with heads on the floor and crawling in the direction where they indicated his majesty to be present. The interpreter moved closer to enable him to hear better, and we others sat beside him in a row. After we had paid our respects, Bingo welcomed us upon instructions from the shogun. The interpreter listened to the words and repeated them to us. Thereupon the captain presented respectful compliments on behalf of his superiors and at the same time expressed his gratitude for the favour of being permitted free trade with Japan. Lying low on the floor, the interpreter repeated the above for the shogun to understand. Whatever the shogun said, Bingo had to receive from his mouth, and then pass it on to the interpreter. The latter passed it on to us Dutch-men. The interpreter could have directly received the words from the shogun and saved Bingo the trouble. But I believe that – still warm from the shogun's mouth – the words are considered altogether too exalted and sacred for this.

Then the farce began, but not before we had been asked a number of meaningless questions. For instance, each of us was asked in turn for our age and name, and since we were carrying a European ink-pot, we each had to write our name and pass it to Bingo, who passed the piece of paper together with the writing utensils to his majesty behind the blind. Our captain was asked: How far is Holland from Batavia?[7] Batavia from Nagasaki? Who was mightier, the governor general of Batavia or the prince of Holland? I was asked: Which internal and external illnesses I considered to be the most serious and most dangerous? How I treated damage caused by cancer and internal abscesses? Whether I had not searched for an elixir of long life like the Chinese doctors have done for many hundred years, and whether our European doctors had discovered anything? I obliged them with the answer: Our doctors are still daily searching for a medicine to preserve people's health to a ripe old age. He asked: Which of them was considered the best? Answer: The latest was always considered the best until experience indicated otherwise. Question: Which was the latest? Answer: A certain alcoholic spirit which when used moderately has the effect of preserving the body's fluids and reviving and strengthening a man's vital spirits. Question: What is it called? Well aware that things esteemed by the Japanese all have long names, I replied: Sal Volatile Oleosum Sÿlvii. The name was written down behind the blind, and I had to repeat it several times. Question: Where and by whom was the spirit discovered? Answer: In Holland by Professor Sylvius. Questions: Whether I knew how to prepare it? The captain ordered me to reply in the negative, but I answered: Yes, of course! But not here! Could the spirit be obtained at Batavia? Answer: Yes! Thereupon the shogun asked that a sample be sent on the next ship.

7  present-day Indonesia

The shogun had first been seated next to the women at some distance in front of us, but now he moved to the side as close to us as he could behind the blind. He had us take off our *kappa*, or ceremonial robes and sit upright so that he could inspect us; had us now stand up and walk, now pay compliments to each other, then again dance, jump, pretend to be drunk, speak Japanese, read Dutch, draw, sing, put on our coats, then take them off again. During this process I broke into the following song [...]

At the demand of the shogun we had to put up with providing such amusements and perform innumerable other monkey tricks. The captain, however was excused so that the light of authority of our superiors, whom he represented, would not be blemished. Moreover, his poised demeanor made him an unlikely candidate for such impositions. After we had been drilled for two hours – albeit always after courteous requests – tonsured servants served each of us with small Japanese dishes on separate little tables; instead of knives we were given two small sticks. We ate just a little. The remains had to be taken away by the old interpreter, carried with both hands in front of him, by him who hardly had the strength to drag his feet. Thereupon we were told to put on our coats and take our leave; we complied immediately, and this brought the second act to a close. Our guides returned us to the waiting room and took their leave. It was already the third hour after noon, and we still had to present our gifts to the senior and junior councillors as listed above under March 25th. We left the *honmaru* on foot, greeted the officers of the great guard in passing, and did the rounds on foot

**Henry Heusken** from *Japan Journal 1855–1861*

*December 7 1857*

At nine o'clock in the morning, we set out en route to the Imperial Palace.[8] First comes Shinano no Kami, Governor of Shimoda in *norimon* with his retinue, then Mr Harris preceded by the flag of the

8 Heusken means the shogun's castle when he refers to the Imperial Palace

United States and followed by his retinue, then myself, then Wakana Myosaburo, Vice-Governor of Shimoda, all in *norimons*.

The sky was most serene. After skirting the walls of the second enclosure for about twenty minutes, we cross the moat and entered the enclosure through a double gate forming a square in the walls of the enclosure. After passing over another moat and through another gate, we find ourselves within the last enclosure in the true Imperial castle.

This enclosure is much more picturesque than the others, having been kept in a splendid condition. The walls are adorned with entirely white, three storied pagodas. Where the walls protrude and along them, there are plastered galleries. All this together with the trees provides a most picturesque effect.

At this gate all of us leave our horses, *norimons*, flags, etc., with the exception of the Ambassador who remains in his *norimon*. After having reached the fourth bridge, the Ambassador also leaves his *norimon* and after having passed through four other gates flanked by walls, we reach a courtyard in which the Imperial Palace stands.

Once at the entryway we exchange our soiled shoes for others and climb a staircase of seven steps. We are received in a kind of vestibule by the two Ometsuke,[9] Tamba no Kami and another one who precede us into an antechamber. About eight feet above the floor the panelling is carved in openwork representing trees, flowers, parrots, etc.

Here the Commissioners came to pay their respects and to offer their services. One of the dignitaries carries kindness so far as to ask the Ambassador if he does not wish to visit the men's room. Thereupon we are shown into the great hall of the Palace. The ceiling, which is thirty feet high, is supported by wooden pillars. We are then led into an audience room in order to see it and to rehearse what we are to do. Then we return to the hall and are offered chairs behind a screen.

Finally the Taikun is on his throne. We hear people make the sound so well-known throughout the world in order to enjoin silence.

The two Ometsuke come to inform us that everything is in readiness. They precede us, then comes Shinano no Kami, then the Ambassador, then myself carrying the letter of the President wrapped

9 Spies

in the American colours. On our right we pass a crowd of court nobles (about six or seven hundred) on their knees in court costume, which consists of a kind of square-shaped lacquer cap perched on the very top of the head, and of garments with very wide sleeves of hemp of a pale yellow colour. On the ample sleeves of their costumes they carry their coat of arms. They wear a black belt of white silk tied like the *rabat* of a Protestant minister, in which is their scimitar. They carry only one for this occasion. They wear trousers which, being twice as long as the leg, completely conceal their feet and the remainder of the trousers trails behind, giving them the appearance of walking on their knees. There reigned the most profound silence despite the great number of courtiers.

On arriving at the panelling which partitions the hall from the chamber where His Majesty can be seen, the two Ometsuke fall upon their knees as does Shinano no Kami. Making a half turn to the right we find ourselves facing His Majesty. Shinano no Kami precedes us, dragging himself on his knees; then the Ambassador follows him, walking normally and bowing; he ascends one step, proceeds the length of two mats, bows a second time, and a third on the fifth mat, where he halts. On his right are the five members of the Great Council, on his left five other dignitaries all on their knees. Otherwise there was no one who could rejoice in seeing His Japanese Majesty.

From the place occupied by the Ambassador the floor rose another step; at the rear of this chamber on a platform about three feet high, His Majesty, the Taikun of Japan, was seated on a kind of stool; but the place where he was so dark and remote that I could hardly see him, the curtain hanging from the ceiling hid his face. Those who were on their knees could see him very well, but for us, standing erect, it was more difficult.

Then the Ambassador delivered his speech saying that he appreciated the honour of having been chosen by the President to carry a letter to His Majesty, and the honour of being appointed Plenipotentiary to His Majesty's Court, and that it was for him his greatest pleasure and finally in English:

May it please Your Majesty, in presenting any letters of credence

from the President of the United States of America, I am directed
to express to Your Majesty the sincere wishes of the President for
your health and happiness and for the prosperity of your dominions.

I consider it as a great honour that I have been selected to fill the
high and important place of Plenipotentiary of the United States at
the Court of Your Majesty, and as my earnest wishes are to unite
the two countries more closely in the ties of enduring friendship,
my constant exertions shall be directed to the attainment of that
happy end.

Upon the conclusion, the Taikun seemed to stamp his feet three
times and answered in Japanese: 'Vergenoegd met eenen brief
gezonden met den afgezant van een verafgelegen gewest en tevens
met zyu gesprek. Eeuwig zal Gemeenschap gehonden worden.'

This is the Dutch of the interpreter, Moriyama Takichiro, and
means, 'Pleased with the letter sent with the Ambassador from a far
distant country, and likewise pleased with his discourse. Intercourse
shall be continued forever.'

At the end of that speech – in which there are no personal pronouns,
because the Taikun is too great to use the small word 'I' – I, who had
remained at the entrance of the Imperial chamber, came forward, and
making the compulsory three bows, I present the President's letter to
the Ambassador who opens it, shows the President's signature to the
Minister of Foreign Affairs, and hands it to him; he, in turn, puts it on
a small table before the throne. Then, the Ambassador takes his leave,
walking backward and observing the compulsory three bows.

[...]

The court of Japan is certainly not conspicuous for its luxury. Not
one diamond sparkled among the crowd of courtiers. A small gold
ornament on the handles of their swords was hardly visible. I have
seen the nobles of the Siamese Court trying to hide their savage
condition behind a barbarous luxury, covering themselves in gold,
and gems. But the simplicity of the Court of Edo, the noble and
dignified bearing of the courtiers, their polished manners which would
do honour to the most illustrious court, cast a more dazzling splendour
than all the diamonds of the Indies.

# MEIJI PERIOD (1868–1912)

In the days of old, a queer object known as Twelve Storeys reared itself over Asakusa. From wherever you looked there it was that huge, clumsy pile of bricks. From the roof of every house, from the laundry platform, from the narrowest second floor window, there it was, waiting for you. From anywhere in the vastness of Tokyo — the embankment across the river at Mukōjima, the observation rise at Ueno, the long flight of stone steps up Atago Hill, there it was, waiting for you, whenever you wanted it.

KUBOTA MANTARŌ

The Meiji period, the era of 'enlightened rule' was a time of rapid innovation; the pace of change surprised both Japanese as well as foreigners who witnessed it. It also caused unprecedented social changes among the Japanese themselves. For instance, mixed bathing was banned in 1869, while barbershops opened in the same year. The male population had their hair cropped for the first time. The Empress stopped blackening her teeth in 1873. On the political level too, Japan expanded its army and navy, under German and British tutelage respectively, waged war with China and won in 1894, gaining Taiwan, fought Russia and won in 1904 5, gaining Sakhalin, and started to expand into Korea and China as well. This was the era when the first industrialist families, such as Mitsui, Mitsubishi, Sumitomo and Yasuda, most of which are still names to reckon with, were given license to develop gold and silver mines and shipping dockyards, founding the first *zaibatsu* or financial cliques in Japan. Foreigners were also brought into the making of a new, industrialized Japan. This was the era of big ambitions and great careers.

Gōtō Shimpei (1857–1929), mayor of Tokyo at the turn of the century was known as 'the mayor with the big kerchief' – his career was huge, spanning Taiwanese colonial affairs, the South Manchuria railway as well as becoming the first director of homegrown NHK television. He asked architects, led by Englishman Josiah Conder

(1852–1920), to design buildings in Tokyo 'that would astonish the world'. These included the Rokumeikan, 'The House of the Cry of the Stag' – a state-owned lodging house designed on many floors for the cosmopolitan set – the brainchild of a Minister of Foreign Affairs, Inoue Kaoru (1836–1915). Conder, an *oyatoi*, or outside architect, also supervised the building of the still-standing Nikolai Russian Orthodox cathedral in Kanda, finished in 1891 after the design of a Russian professor. The above-mentioned Asakusa Twelve Storeys was also built on the advice of an *oyatoi*, William Barton.

Conder also designed the Marunouchi, beside the Imperial Palace, the district bought up by the Mitsubishi family enterprise at the turn of the twentieth century. It was rebuilt as London town, an abortive architectural endeavour which nevertheless left Tokyo with fine red-brick buildings such as Tokyo Station.

A great chronicler of this age was novelist Natsume Sōseki (1867–1916), who gently satirised the Meiji middle class, whom he portrayed as so keen to Westernise and buy Western goods that they occasionally forgot themselves and their own standards. His young student Sanshiro in the novel of the same name is a perfect satirist of the changing Tokyo, with its paranoia about foreign competition, while enjoying the remains of the floating world of Edo including the flower festivals.

But Sōseki also sounded a cautious note about the thrills and spills of progress: 'Sift civilization to the bottom of your bag of thrills,' he wrote in 1907, 'and you have an exposition. Filter your exposition through the dull sands of night and you have blinding illumination. If you possess life in some small measure, then for evidence of it, you go to an illumination, you must cry out in astonishment at what you see. The civilised, who are drugged with civilization, are first aware that they live when they cry out in astonishment.'

As Rudyard Kipling patronisingly predicted, when he visited Japan in 1889, Japan had become a 'little great power'. After the early successes of the Japanese Army, Emperor Meiji wanted Japan to join the world powers. Arthur Lloyd, who taught in the Naval College, visited in 1911, when Japan was expanding into other countries including Taiwan and Manchuria. He describes the spoils of imperial campaigns which were laid at the feet of the aging Emperor, who would die a year later.

As the Emperor lay dying, the wide plaza in front of the palace moat filled up with people silently praying. The funeral procession took place at night, the streets were covered in sand and the coffin, or catafalque, drawn by seven oxen took the Emperor to be buried in Kyoto. The heroine of *The Ginger Tree* by British novelist Oswald Wynd attends the funeral of the Emperor in 1912. The narrator compares it to Queen Victoria's funeral, as she sits watching from Hibiya Park on the edge of the Imperial Palace.

But many of the elements of old Edo did survive into the Meiji period. Tokyo was divided like Edo into High City (*yamanote*) and low city (*shitamachi*). In the *shitamachi*, all the houses were still made of wood and each area was divided into quarters. It was here that the *tatami* makers lived in *tamichō* as well as the carpenters, the *daiku* who lived in *daiku-chō* and quarters for chandlers, builders, greengrocers and so on. If you were especially skilled in your trade you would be a purveyor to the shogunate (or later, the Emperor). Every year during the Kanda festival, the *shitamachi* spirit still breaks out onto the streets – when the Shinto shrine of Kanda Myojin holds a festival known as *Tenka matsuri*. The diversity and the contradictory nature of Edokko, or 'child of Edo', spirit was captured by Futabatei Shimei in *Ukigomo* or *Drifting Clouds* in 1887.

Another survivor from the Edo period was the red-light district Yoshiwara in present-day Ningyōchō (or 'doll quarter'), just north of Yanaka, dates back to the sixteenth century when it became a licensed pleasure quarter. It suffered during the so-called Long–Sleeved fire in 1657, because many of the ladies tragically died, and much of the trade moved to Asakusa.

Higūchi Ichiyō (1872–96), one of Japan's great female novelists, describes the quarters in her novel *Takekurabe*, or *Growing up* (1895), paying homage to the vanishing world of Edo from which her family came. This was also the place where the Kabuki theatre thrived. The Ichimura-za and the Nakamura-za were located here and the Meiji-za was also built here. The Kabuki hero Benkei (see Kamakura chapter) still has a shrine in the area.

**Natsume Sōseki** from *Sanshiro*

*A walk through Hongō* [10]

Tokyo was full of things that startled Sanshiro. First, the ringing of the streetcar bells startled him, and then the crowds that got on and off between rings. Next to startle him was Marunouchi, the busy commercial centre of the city. What startled him most of all was Tokyo itself, for no matter how far he went, it never ended. Everywhere he walked there were piles of lumber, heaps of rock, new homes set back from the street, old warehouses rotting in front of them. Everything looked as though it were being destroyed, and at the same time everything looked as though it were under construction.

To Sanshiro, all this movement was horrible. His shock was identical in quality and degree to that of the most ordinary country boy who stands in the midst of the capital for the first time. His education could no more soften the blow than might some store-bought remedy. He felt a large chunk of self-confidence simply disappear, and it made him miserable.

If this violent activity was what they called the real world, then his life up to now had been nowhere in touch with it. He had been straddling the fence – and had fallen asleep there! All right then, could he end his napping today and contribute his share of activity? No, that was not likely either. He stood at the centre of activity now, but his life as a student was the same as before.

'I was going to walk through Hongō on the way home. Would you like to come along?' said Nonomiya.

Sanshiro accepted with pleasure. They climbed to the top of the hill where the nurse and the girl had been standing. Nonomiya paused to look at the red building through the green of the trees, and at the pond far below the cliff.

'Nice view from here, don't you think? See how just the corner of that building sticks out a little? From the trees. See? Nice, isn't it? Had

10  An area near Tokyo University in Ochanomizu

you noticed what a fine piece of architecture it is? The Engineering buildings aren't bad either, but this is better.'

Nonomiya's appreciation for architecture came as a surprise to Sanshiro. He himself had no idea which of the two was better. Now it was Sanshiro who replied only, 'Yes, yes.'

'And the – shall I say – the effect of the trees and the water. It's nothing special, but after all this is the middle of Tokyo. Very quiet don't you think? The academic life demands a place like this? Tokyo is so damned noisy these days.' Walking on, he pointed to the building on the left.

'Over here is the Mansion, where the faculty meets. Somehow they manage to get things done without my help. All I have to do is continue my life in the cellar. Research goes on at such a mad pace nowadays, you can't let up for a minute or you get left behind. My work must look like some kind of joke to other people, but I can see it from the inside, and I know my mind is working furiously – maybe a lot harder than all those streetcars running around out there. That's why I don't go away, even in the summer. I hate to lose the time.'

Nonomiya looked up at the broad sky. A meagre gleam was all that remained of the sun's light.

A long wisp of cloud hung across the sky at an angle like the mark of a stiff brush on the tranquil layer of blue. 'Do you know what that is?' Nonomiya asked. Sanshiro looked up at the translucent cloud. 'It's all snowflakes. From down here, it doesn't look like it's moving, but it is, and with greater velocity than a hurricane. Have you read Ruskin?'

Sanshiro mumbled that he had not.

Nonomiya said only, 'I see.' A moment later he went on,

'This sky would make an interesting painting, don't you think? I ought to tell Haraguchi about it. He's a painter you know.'

Sanshiro did not know.

They walked down the hill past the playing field and stopped in front of a large bronze bust. DR ERWIN BAELZ, PROFESSOR DER MEDIZIN, 1876–1902, the inscription read.

'How do you like this?' Nonomiya asked, and again Sanshiro could think of nothing to say.

They left through the side gate and walked alongside Karatachi

Temple to the busy avenue. The commotion there was horrible. The streetcars never stopped coming.

'Don't you hate those things? They're so noisy,' said Nonomiya.

Soon autumn was at its height, the season when the appetite quickens and a young man of twenty-three can in no way be tired of life. Sanshiro went out often. He walked around the University pond a lot, but nothing ever came of it. He passed the University Hospital often, but encountered only ordinary human beings. He went to Nonomiya's cellar to ask about his sister and found that she had left the hospital. He thought of mentioning the girl he had seen in the doorway, but Nonomiya seemed busy and he restrained himself. There was no hurry; he could find out all about her when next he visited Ōkubo. He left the cellar. Restless, he walked up one street and down another. Sanshiro walked as far as the Yakushi in Arai. From there, he decided to walk by way of Ōkubo and visit Nonomiya at home, but he took the wrong street near the Ochiai crematorium and ended up at Takata. He took the train home from Mejiro. On the way, he ate most of the chestnuts he had bought as a gift for Nonomiya, and the next day Yojiro came and finished off what was left.

Sanshiro was restless, but it was a light airy restlessness and the more he felt it, the happier he became. He had concentrated too hard on the lectures at first, until he could barely hear them well enough to take notes, but now he listened only moderately well and there was no problem. He thought about all sorts of things during the lectures. It no longer worried him if he missed a little. The other students did the same, he noticed, Yojiro included. This was probably good enough.

Now and then, as his thoughts wandered, the ribbon came to mind. That bothered him, ruined his mood. He thought of rushing out to Ōkubo. But thanks to the associative links of the imagination and the stimulus of the outside world, the feeling soon vanished. For the most part he was carefree. He was dreaming. The visit to Ōkubo never happened.

When Sanshiro was rambling about the city as usual one afternoon, he turned left at the top of Dangozaka and came out to the broad avenue in the Sendagi, Hayashi-chō. These days, ideal autumn weather made the skies of Tokyo look as deep as those of the countryside. Just to think that one was living beneath skies like this was enough to clear the mind. Walking out to open fields made everything perfect. The sense unwound and the spirit became as broad as the heavens. For all that, the body took on a new firmness. This was not the irresponsible balminess of spring. Gazing at the hedges to either side, Sanshiro inhaled Tokyo's autumn fragrance for the first time in his life.

The chrysanthemum doll show had opened at the bottom of Dangozaka two or three days ago. Sanshiro had noticed a few banners as he turned left at the top of the slope. Now he could hear only the distant shouts, the beating of drums and bells. The rhythms floated slowly up hill, and when they had dispersed themselves in the clear autumn air they turned at last into exceedingly tenuous waves. The waves stirred by these waves moved on as far as Sanshiro's eardrums and came to rest. All that remained of the noise was a pleasant sensation.

**Arthur Lloyd** from *Everyday Japan*

*The Palace of the Emperor*

In the very centre of Tokyo surrounded by moats and massive ramparts of stone, surmounted by gnarled pines which, in the old days of mediaeval warfare afforded an excellent shelter for the archers of the garrison, stands the Imperial Palace, consecrated, in Japanese eyes, by the constant presence of His Sacred Majesty. Before it lies an extensive space of turf, dotted here and there with pines, and occupying the whole area between the second and third or inmost, moat; and encircling it behind is another moat with many high banks, a favourite haunt of wild sea birds which live here in absolute security, knowing that no man dare touch them.

If your business takes you to the Palace you will enter the broad space, either by the modern bridge which leads from the city to the Palace along a wide road finished since the conclusion of the war with Russia, or else through one of the old fortified gates which flank it on

north and south, and are known respectively as the Wada Kura Go
Mon and the Sakurada Gate.

Inside the Maru no uchi, as this open space is called, you will be
struck by the strict simplicity that rules everywhere. The Maru no
uchi is but a big grass lawn fringed with stunted trees, yet it is grand by
virtue of its very simplicity, and we were able to judge of its dimensions
a short time ago when the returning army brought its trophies of guns
and other implements of war and laid them down here at the feet of
His Majesty.

There are two approaches to the Palace leading across the inner
moat. If (we will suppose it is New Year's Day, and that you have been
honoured with a command to attend the reception) you are a humble
rider in a *jinrikisha* you will go in by the gate on the left, past the
buildings of the Imperial Household department and so gain the side
door of the Palace. If you are higher up in the social scale, or drive in
a carriage, you will go in by the big double bridge known as the Niji
Bashi and so arrive at the front entrance of the Imperial residence.
You will be surprised to find it a one-storey house, but you will
nevertheless admire its simple elegance as you are ushered along
carpeted corridors to your waiting room. All day long his Majesty has
been receiving his New Year's visitors, and by the time your turn
comes, as a foreign employee of the Government, it will be 2pm but
the ceremony is not relaxed in its solemn strictness, weary though his
Majesty may be of bowing at the streams of persons that pass by in
slow moving procession. Presently your turn will come and you will
take your place with the rest and be ushered into the august presence.
You will advance a few steps, make three low bows, conscious that you
are doing it very awkwardly and back out at the opposite door to that
by which you came in. Your part of the ceremony is now over, and you
may go home and doff your swallowtail coat.

**Oswald Wynd** from *The Ginger Tree*

> *Sueyama Apartments,*
> *Surugadai, Tokyo*
> *September 14, 1912*

Emperor Meiji, the God, Aiko shouted, is dead. Last night, with two
million other people packed along the route, I watched the first stage
of his journey to the Imperial tombs in Kyoto. It was a pageant from
five hundred years ago and the people moving through it, silent, were
ghosts. Today the unreality remains, the capital completely shut
down, not a tramcar running, no clattering clogs, no factory hooters
to wake me. From the windows of my new flat, the view of roofs is
like grey waves rolling in against this hill, and the black bathhouse
chimneys, with no smoke from them, might be posts caught by a high
tide. The continuation of last night's clamped-down stillness is eerie
in daylight, and I wait for the reassurance of familiar sounds, something simple like the beancurd seller's horn, but hear nothing.

In a way, this reminds me of Queen Victoria's death. I was
seventeen when Edinburgh went into mourning for a monarch who
had ruled longer than any other in British history. Overnight colour
drained away from those stone streets as women went into black. It
was as though no one had ever realised that an old lady could not live
forever, and to all those who had expected somehow to spend their
days safely tucked under the quilt of her reign it was almost frightening
to have survived her. Mama was quite certain that the rule of the
flighty and probably immoral Prince of Wales, now so strangely king,
would soon see a rapid decline in standards of public and private
behaviour. The tears shed in our house, and all over Britain, were for
an irreplaceable mother figure. For months prayers in churches for
the new monarch held the only slightly veiled plea that in his great
mercy the Lord God of Hosts would not abandon us, or the Empire,
to a grim time of decay and collapse. It seems like similar prayers are
now being said in Tokyo temples where the gongs are silent today.
Like those suddenly bereft Victorians, the Japanese are in a kind of
shock at the thought of their great Emperor, the giver of the new

constitution, their guide through years of change and foreign wars, replaced by a son reputed to be half-mad.

I watched the procession from the relative luxury of a folding chair in the area in front of Hibiya Park reserved for the American Embassy and important US citizens including Bob Dale. I was on Emma Lou's ticket. She was too near the termination of her fourth pregnancy to have any wish to attend a funeral, even an Emperor's. Early September should have been warm, but it wasn't, there was a chill more than autumnal after rain, and by one in the morning, after we had been in our places for four hours, I could have done with my Peking fur coat which is still in service, though Emburi San hates to see me arriving at the shop without wearing it.

[…]

In Japan, drama of any kind never hurries and the Son of Heaven's funeral certainly didn't, it was well past midnight before the street lights, disguised as ceremonial lanterns went out, leaving not a lit window anywhere. Noise thinned and then died as though on order. The procession brought its own light, torches burning on pine resin, the men carrying them spaced out at about every hundred yards. The procession moved at about half a walking pace, footfalls completely deadened by the two-foot layer of silver sand laid over all the roads on the route. There was no clopping of hooves as the Imperial Cavalry came by, the horses held on tight rein but not snorting. The marchers on foot looked dressed for the *Noh* drama, in medieval robes with the flowing lines which said China, not Japan, all in white except for some of the headdresses. Banners had black characters on white, fastened top and bottom to white painted bamboo poles. Elaborate though all this was, it was also almost without pomp, the opposite of a state funeral circus in the West, as though here the object underlying pageantry was silence.

Then, in the distance, silence was broken. I felt a prickling on my skin. The sound was half groan, half creak and came spaced at something like thirty second intervals, growing louder, aggressive intrusion into an arranged stillness, a lament that held nothing plaintive, just the grim, uncompromising and somehow immediately recognisable voice of death. A cart moaned towards us, two-wheeled, simple design in unpainted wood, the Emperor's body housed under a curved roof, the coffin screened only by gently flapping side curtains. Pulling the cart were seven white oxen, one behind the other, seven heads waggling from side to side as thick legs went down with an almost timid caution into soft sand.

After the cart came priests, completely silent when I would have expected some kind of chanting, and behind them military and naval officers of high rank, four abreast but under a new discipline from that sand beneath their feet, unable to march. They were all in uniform and presumably bemedalled, but seemed to have been placed in a planned gap in torchlight which diminished them to shadows. We were kept in the dark for more than half an hour after the last of the torchbearers had rounded a corner, and we waited like that, comfortless, until the groaning faded and was gone. The disguised street lights came on, but in pairs and in no hurry, not really in any pursuit of death's procession, and for a long time there wasn't much movement amongst the crowds, no attempt to break through the looped rope barriers. When finally we were released, there wasn't much talk either. I doubt whether anywhere else in the world such a vast number of people have begun to make their ways home in such stillness.

**Futabatei Shimei** from *Drifting Clouds*

It is three o'clock in the afternoon of a late October day. A swirling mass of men stream out of the Kanda gate, marching first in antlike formation, then scuttling busily off in every direction. Each and every one of these fine gentlemen is primarily interested in getting enough to eat. Look carefully and you will see what an enormous variety of individual types are represented in the huge crowd. Start by examining the hair bristling on their faces: moustaches, whiskers, Vandyke beards, and even extravagant imperial Bismarck beards reminiscent of a Pekingese, bantam beards, badger's beards, meagre beards that are barely visible; thick and thin they sprout in every conceivable way.

Now see how differently they are dressed. Here is a dandy, a fashionable black suit purchased at Shirokiya set off by shoes of French calfskin. And now confident men, oblivious of the ill fit of their tweeds, worn with stiff leather shoes, trousers that trail in the mud like a tail of tortoise; suits bearing the indelible stamp of the ready-made clothes rack. 'I have a beard, fine clothing, what more do I need?' they seem to say. Glowing like embers on the fire, these enviable creatures swagger home, heads erect.

Now behind them come the less fortunate. Pitifully stooped, their hair gray, they stagger along with empty lunchboxes dangling from their waists. Despite their advanced years they still manage to hold a job, but their duties are so negligible they can easily work in old-fashioned Japanese clothes.

**Higuchi Ichiyō** from *In the shade of spring leaves*

### *The Yoshiwara*

It's a long way round to the front of the quarter, where the trailing branches of the willow tree bid farewell to the night-time revellers and the bawdy house lights flicker in the moat, dark as the dye that blackens the smiles of the Yoshiwara beauties. From the third-floor rooms of the lofty houses the all but palpable music and laughter spill down into the side street. Who knows how these great establishments prosper? The rickshaws pull up night and day.

They call this part of town beyond the quarter 'in front of Daion Temple'. The name may sound a little saintly, but those who live in the area will tell you it's a lively place. Turn the corner at Mishima shrine and you don't find any mansions, just tenements of ten or twenty houses, where eaves have long begun to sag and shutters only close halfway. It is not a spot for trade to flourish.

The menfolk do odd jobs at the less dignified houses. You can hear them in the evenings jiggling their shoe check tags before they leave for work, and you'll see them putting on their jackets when most men take them off. Wives rub good-luck flints behind them to protect their men from harm. Could this be a final parting? It's a dangerous business. Innocent bystanders get killed when there's a brawl in one of the houses. And look out if you ever foil the double suicide of a courtesan and her lover!

[...]

Customs here are indeed a little different. You won't find many women who tie their sashes neatly behind their waists. It's one thing to see a woman of a certain age who favours gaudy patterns or a sash stretched out immoderately wide. It's quite another to see these barefaced girls of fifteen or sixteen, all decked out in flashing clothes and blowing on bladder cherries, which everybody knows are used as contraceptives. But that's what kind of neighbourhood it is. A trollop, who yesterday went by the name of some heroine in *The Tale of Genji* at one of the third-rate houses along the ditch, today runs off with a thug. They open a lean-to bar, though neither of them knows the first thing about running a business. They soon go broke. The beauty begins to miss her former calling. Her assets are gone with the chopped-up chicken bones left from last night's *hors d'oeuvres*. Unlike the chicken however, our charmer can still return to her old nest. People around here, for some reason, find this kind of woman more alluring than your ordinary one.

A ferry – off to Boshu off to Izu?
A whistle sounds, a whistle.
Beyond the river the fishermen's isle,
And on the near shore the lights of the Metropole.

KITAHARA HAKUSHU

The end of the Meiji period and the beginning of the Taishō and Shōwa periods (1912–26) were years of intense industrialisation. This had its downsides, such as the rising price of rice, and ensuing disturbances, as the cracks in Japan's great modernisation began to show. Japan started to expand her interests on the mainland at the invitation of her European allies at the time – for instance in Russia, Japan joined the Allies to rescue the Czechs on the Transiberan route in 1918, staying in Russia for many years afterwards. At the Treaty of Versailles (which ended the First World War), Japan was granted the German concession in the Chinese province of Shantung. Japan had just been admitted to the League of Nations along with the other 'great powers' of the world and was in a position, under the leadership of Prime Minister Shidehara, to seek friendly relations with China once again and to use this opportunity to expand her interests in China and Korea. While the Emperor Taisho himself suffered from mental illness, the early teens and twenties in Japan were characterized by the new world of modern manners and sexual liberation, where '*moga*' and '*moba*' – modern girls and modern boys – might even, in a daring way, walk down the street hand in hand in Ginza. Tokyo also had taxis, jazz and taxi dancers.

Ginza, which means literally 'silver merchants' district', is the part of town where most of the new Westernised delights appeared. The area became noted for its willow trees and wide boulevards. Nagai Kafū took on the subject of the Ginza of the twenties in his novel *During the Rains*, which shows the relationship between a literary celebrity and a young geisha girl.

But this period, where the old world of Yedo still lingered, vanished after the Great Kantō Earthquake of 1923, which destroyed the whole of Yokohama and half the city of Tokyo, taking along with it the foreigners' settlement of Tsukiji, which Kitahara Hakushu mourns (above). This was where the first Western hospitals and schools were built, where tradesmen and scholars had settled in the Meiji period. Tsukiji is now famous for the fishmarket, which was moved here in 1931.

Setsuko, Princess Chichibu, the wife of Prince Chichibu, one of the brothers of the Emperor Shōwa was taken on a tour of the dead and wounded and herself sheltered in a sewage pipe in the uptown area of Aoyama. After 1923, many of the down-and-outs gathered at Asakusa Kannon Temple, whose vermillion pillars survived the fire.[11] Yasunari Kawabata (1899–1972) caught the atmosphere of Asakusa as a thriving downtown city hub in those years. Kawabata, who lived near Ueno Park, enjoyed the *va et vient* even during the small hours, as men from the Yoshiwara pleasure district were on their way home, while their geisha were on their way to pray. His novel conjures the anarchic and creative tension of the period of reconstruction after the disaster. Tokyo in fact rose from the ashes as a city of wide boulevards – only to be destroyed again in the 1940s. The upheavals of the early twentieth century sent shockwaves through everyone's lives, including that of Tanizaki, who was born in the *shitamachi* of Tokyo: 'The bones of my grandfather and grandmother have been moved twice', he wrote after he moved to Ōsaka after the quake.

Although, in the 1920s, some moves towards democratic freedoms were established (universal suffrage for males over the age of 25 was passed in 1924), there were also more disturbing developments. A Peace Preservation Law was passed in 1925 which effectively criminalized socialism, communism and other ideologies which might threaten the Imperial system. Special Higher Police were also installed as well as the *kempeitai*, Japanese Military Police, who were to be feared. The depression hit Japan earlier than elsewhere, with a banking crisis in 1927 when twenty-seven banks went into liquidation

11  One of Tokyo's most ancient temples said to be founded in 628AD from an image of the Kannon (Goddess of Mercy)

and small businesses suffered. But then, in 1929, Japan was affected by the collapse of the silk market in America and the suffering of the general public caused widespread anger. Young military officers became contemptuous of the industrial complexes, the *zaibutsu*, with their growing power which came from expanding Japanese interests abroad. Various assassination attempts and coups were made. In 1936 a military coup was squashed, but from that moment on the politicians were dictated to by the military as the country headed down what is known as the *kurai tanima*, the dark tunnel, towards war.

Meanwhile, Japan took more of an interest in China and Chiang Kai Shek's Kuomintang army threatened Japanese interests. This fuelled the nationalist cause and Japanese army officers took action by attacking and occupying Mukden in Manchuria and assassinating the Chinese warlord Chang Tso Lin. The future Emperor Showa (Hirohito) made a trip to Britain in 1921 and was photographed with the Prince of Wales. Not long after this trip, he was almost assassinated by a young man who pushed his way through the crowds at the Toranomon gate on December 27th, 1923. The title Showa meant Enlightened Peace, and the new Emperor assumed the throne on his father's death in 1926. Two Japanese Prime Ministers, Hara in 1921 and Hamaguchi in 1931, were also almost assassinated at this time. The economic and social volatility of Japan mirrored much of what was going on elsewhere in the world, especially in the West.

But the public was more educated and aware than ever, and newspapers took off in Tokyo – the largest Tokyo newspaper's circulation totalled a third of million, to compete with Ōsaka's *Asahi shimbun* and the *Mainichi shimbun*, each circulating about a million nationwide. The city was redesigned, with smaller quarters for the workers, euphemistically called *bunka jutaku* (the cultural dwelling place). At this time Shibuya was turned into a company town and the first subway line ran from Ginza while the Yamanote (hill top) circle line was built. All the fun of the roaring twenties in Europe found its way to Tokyo, with French style café names – *L'Automne*, *Combin*, *Mon Ami* – and cabarets and dancing girl shows sprang up in the Asakusa, with '*eruguro nansensu*' or 'erotic nonsense' dominating the interwar years as much in Tokyo as in Berlin.

Places of entertainment shifted gradually westwards, following a review house opening in Shinjuku in 1931 and the promise of a great Kabuki theatre in nearby Kabukichō. Thus the heart of Asakusa changed and the ruins of the place were a cause of great melancholy.

**Nagai Kafū** from *During the Rains*

*A literary celebrity becomes a detective*

At about this time, Kiyooka had been thrown over by a movie actress called Suzuko something or other, who, for a while, had served as a concubine. Since her theft by another man, he'd been searching for a replacement. Completely overwhelmed by Kimie's ardent attitude, as if she'd given herself up body and soul to his pleasure, he told her he would indulge her in any luxury she wished and that she was to give up being a waitress. But Kimie said that she meant to open up a café herself in the future and would like a little more experience. In that case, said Kiyooka, she should work on the Ginza. Making her quit her job at the Salon Lac after a month or so, he took her around Kyoto and Ōsaka for a couple of weeks. Upon their return, he got her a job at the Don Juan, one of the prominent cafés on the Ginza. Soon thereafter, the rainy season came to an end and it was summer. From midsummer to the days when the first autumn breezes began to blow, Kiyooka had no doubt but that he was loved by Kimie from her heart. One evening, however, on his way back from the theatre with two or three fellow writers, he stopped in at the café. Told by the other waitresses that Kimie, complaining of feeling suddenly unwell, had gone home early, he decided after parting from his friends to go by himself to her rented room in Honmura-chō and see how she was. As he set out, he saw a woman's figure suddenly emerge from the street along the Moat that he always turned into. Although it was not yet midnight, the houses along the one side of the alleyway had already shut their doors. Along the thoroughfare, where both pedestrians and trolleys had become spares, only a solitary taxi raced by. From a distance of about thirty feet, Kiyooka soon ascertained that the woman was wearing a whitish gauze silk-crepe kimono and a summer *obi* with a pattern of green bamboo. His suspicions aroused, he cut across the roadway. Keeping to the sidewalk along the foot of the embankment, he shadowed the woman. The woman, briskly and blithely passing in front of the police box, seemed to stop and be waiting for a trolley at the Ichigaya stand. Then, unexpectedly, she entered the gate of the Hachiman Shrine. Without looking behind her, she made her way up the Woman's slope on the left. Although more suspicious than ever, Kiyooka was determined to stay out of sight. Well acquainted with this neighbourhood and trusting to his man's fleetness of foot, he ran around the shrine compound and climbed the Sanai slope. Entering the shrine grounds form the back gate, he looked about. A man and woman were sitting close together on a bench at the bottom of the stone stairs of the main shrine, where a cliff overlooked the Moat and the Ichigaya Approach. Of course, theirs was only one of three or four benches, on each of which a couple was sitting rubbing shoulders in an illicit rendezvous. Kiyooka, thinking this an excellent opportunity and with a grove of cherry trees as his cover, gradually crept nearer. He wanted to eavesdrop on Kimie and also find out what sort of person her companion was.

Telling himself that no detective in any detective story had ever succeeded in his investigations as he had that night, Kiyooka, at that moment, in the excess of his surprise, had no time to spare for an outburst of jealous anger. The man, wearing what looked like a panama, had on a dark blue *yukata* without even a summer *haori* over it and held a walking stick. Although he did not appear to be particularly old, even by the dim light of the park lamp, the whiteness of his moustache stood out to the eye. Clasping Kimie around the waist under her *obi*, the man said, 'It certainly is nice and cool up here. Thanks to you I'm having some new experiences. I never thought that at sixty years of age I'd be meeting a woman on a park bench. Even now, I believe, there's a big archery range on the other side of this shrine. When I was young, I used to come and practice my archery there. Since then, its been decades since I climbed these stone stairs. Well now, where shall we go from here? Just staying here with you on this bench is fine with me. Ha ha.' Laughing, the man kissed Kimie on the cheek.

**Setsuko, Princess Chichibu** from
*The Silver Drum: A Japanese Imperial Memoir*

*The Great Kantō Earthquake*

The summer of 1923, after the usual fortnight with my best friend
Masako at the Kabayama's villa in Gotemba, I spent a while as usual
in Oiso at the Nabeshima villa with my grandmother, Marchioness
Nabeshima, my cousins, my elder brother and younger sister, and
Taka, having fun at the seaside. Then, when the summer holidays
were almost over and I still had some unfinished homework to do, I
returned to Tokyo. The next day, 1 September, was the day of the
Great Earthquake. There is no telling what would have happened to
me if I had not gone back to Tokyo, since the Oiso house was
completely destroyed.

My sister Masako wanted to stay in Oiso until the very end of the
holidays and stayed behind with Taka and we had no news of them for
almost a fortnight. We were beside ourselves with worry. Com-
munications were not what they are now, and since telephone lines
were down, there was nothing one could do.

Fortunately our relatives turned out to have survived, but many
people lost their lives, including classmates of mine, and countless
people were injured and lost their homes. The news that gradually
filtered through, was heartbreaking. We heard that the elder sister of
Princess Kan'in had been killed at her villa in Odawara. We were
terribly worried about Masako Kabayama in Gotemba and I shall
never forget the relief we felt when we heard that she was safe.

On the day of the earthquake I was in my room doing my homework.
I heard a roar that seemed to be coming up from the bowels of the earth
and suddenly the room started shaking up and down and sideways. I was
thrown out of my chair and rolled about, and remembering being taught
to get under a table in an earthquake, I grabbed the legs of my desk
and rolled under it. As I did so, the house started to collapse. I wasn't
scared so much as in a state of shock, so much so that I could not even
cry out for help, but simply waited until somebody came and rescued
me and took me outside. I was in such a daze I could scarcely think.

After the second big aftershock, we all took refuge in Prince Nashimoto's palace nearby. My mother's sister Itsuko was married to the Prince. The main building had not even lost a single tile, while the annex had only lost a few. Scary aftershocks continued intermittently, so we spent an uneasy night in a tent set up in a bamboo grove on the grounds. Bamboo groves have always been considered the safest places. Fires could be seen blazing in various directions, which seemed to be spreading. Prince Li – heir to the throne of Korea – and Masako, his Japanese princess, joined us in our refuge. Aoyama Avenue was said to be a sea of flames, and a great many people whose homes were burned, fled to the palace grounds.

Thinking back on it now, I realize it must have been because I was a child, but in spite of all the turmoil, I remember curling up in the tent, sharing a quilt with my cousin Princess Noriko, who was only two years older than I, and falling fast asleep as if I had not a care in the world.

We lived in a sewage pipe for a while afterwards, which was great fun as far as I was concerned. My father was chief of the European and American Affairs bureau of the Foreign Ministry and since people from the Ministry and others would doubtless be coming to see him, he felt he could not stay away from the house too long, so, escorted by a secretary from the Prince's household, we went home. Fortunately the house had escaped being burned, but it was uninhabitable. So we copied our neighbours and took shelter in the sewage pipes that workmen had left in the road – living like hermit crabs or snails!

Sewage construction happened to be underway in Tokyo just at that time, and all along the road where we lived, the pipes had been set out ready to be laid down. The pipes were large, and so there was no danger of them sliding into the cracks in the ground that might open with further earth tremors, nor would they break apart, since they were made of iron.

Pipes were lying in front of every house, so there were plenty to take shelter in. Lengths of cloth were hung at each end for privacy. Ours had a sheet of paper with Matsudaira written on it hanging at one end, but a man from the Foreign Ministry failed to notice the sign and went to the Nashimoto estate where he expected we would be. When Princes Itsuko Nashimoto heard an equerry say, 'I think they are still in the sewer pipe,' she was both alarmed and intrigued, wondering how on earth we would lie down to sleep. That night, escorted by two guards, it seems the princess, together with Princess Noriko, stole out incognito to see how we were faring. After satisfying themselves that all was well, they returned without saying a word to us. When we heard about it afterwards we agreed it was just like Princess Itsuko to do a thing like that.

By the time Masako and Taka had returned to Tokyo our house was more or less fit to live in; Taka suggested that I should tour the earthquake damage. What I saw made a deep impression on me which I shall never forget. It was a real eye-opener […]

On the day of the tour, they dressed me in a plain coarse cotton kimono and *tabi* (Japanese foot mittens) and clogs to protect my feet. The idea was not to wear Western-style clothes or anything too conspicuous but to resemble the ordinary children of the burnt-out area.

Taka and I – just the two of us – slipped quietly out of the house in Aoyama. We went via Kudan and Nihonbashi, finally walking as far as Ueno. It was hard walking in unfamiliar clothing and not being used to walking in clogs, I got very tired. It was hard going, and I marvel even now at my perseverance.

Most of the bodies had been cleared away, but there were some left, and I wanted to close my eyes, but instead Taka insisted that I fold my hands and join her in prayer for them. There was no sign of anyone in Nihonbashi, except for a few corpses still floating in the river. Harrowing scenes like that engraved themselves on my young mind. Although I was already familiar with tragic stories of the fall of Wakamatsu Castle, it had all faded into the past and seemed no more than a bad dream, whereas this was naked truth, something I was seeing with my own eyes.

My mother worried terribly, wondering if she had done the right thing to let me go; wondering if the impressions I would receive might not be too much for me; terrified for fear something awful might have happened to us. It was not until we arrived home safely some time after three o'clock that she was able to stop worrying.

That night, the horrors that I had seen did in fact keep me awake until the early hours.

**Yasunari Kawabata** from *The Scarlet Gang of Asakusa*

*The Piano Girl*

Even now, right now in modern Tokyo, just like in the old Edo picture books, he's still here, it's said – the bird-catcher: the copper-colour fittings on his tanned suede pouch, the pipe hanging from the agate fastener on the pouch strings, and the old-fashioned tobacco case filled with that sweet-smelling Kokubu stuff, mixed in with a few green stems to keep it from drying out – all dangling from his waist, and his white drawers, his black leggings, the white fingerless mittens, and a plain blue cotton kimono hiked up around his hips. The man who told me this is an inspector at the Metropolitan Police Office, not a person given to idle reminiscence.

But I am. I want to talk like they did back then in the old Edo days. Take this road. Yes, we ought to determine, my dear reader, if this road on which I am about to lead you to the hangout of the Scarlet Gang is the same road on which it has been said, in the old days of Emperors Manji and Kanbun, men with swords in white scabbards tucked into their leather *hakama*, all white right down to their steeds, travelled to and from the Yoshiwara while making their horsemen sing bawdy Komuro *bushi* songs.

Let's now suppose it's past three in the morning and even the bums are sound asleep, and I am here walking through the grounds of the Sensō Temple with Yumiko. Dead ginkgo leaves flutter down, and we listen to the crowing of the cocks.

'That's funny. It's chickens they keep at the Holy Kannon Temple.' Having said this, I freeze in my tracks. Four dressed-up young girls with very white faces are standing right in front of us.

Yumiko laughs: 'You'll always be a tourist. They're the Hanayashiki dolls.'

Then with the first gray of dawn, it's said that the bird catcher hunts out the little birds with his long pole. But this is something a late riser like me isn't likely to see.

And lately isn't prominently displaying the girls' picture forbidden even in the Yoshiwara, and so they put little photos in glass cases and you have to peer at them as though they were butterfly specimens?

And (another example) that musical instrument that blends the typewriter and the piano – we all know it as the 'Taishō koto' but now some enterprising shopkeepers are calling it the 'Shōwa koto'. That's how it is these days. Just no nostalgia for old Edo. Here, let me unfold it before you, dear reader, the newly revised 'Shōwa Map' drawn following the reorganization of the city after the shake-up of the 1923 Great Kantō Earthquake.

Look, right here the Asakusa motor bus runs along the asphalt road between Uguisudani in Ueno and the Kototoi Bridge. Walking north from the bus-stop in back of the Sensō, the Asakusa Kannon Temple, you see Umamichi-machi[12] is on the right and Senzoku-machi is on the left. Go on a bit, past the Kisakata Police Station on the left and the Fuji Elementary School on the right. Then, after the Sengen shrine, you pass the public market, then the Kamiarai Bridge, spanning the banks of the Yoshiwara canal. But before reaching the bridge, there is a certain alley . . . Well to say 'a certain alley' sounds like I'm beginning a real old-fashioned novel. The members of the Scarlet Gang haven't done anything that criminal. They're much less likely to prey on you than the local rickshaw pullers, and I could just as well write out the address.

'Mister! Hey, Mister!' A rickshaw puller calls out to you in Asakusa Park, in the Yoshiwara, thereabouts: 'You look like a guy who knows how to have a good time. How about something different for a change?'

An agreement is reached. The rickshaw man at once takes off his rubber-soled cloth boots, puts on his wooden sandals, tosses his rickshaw-man cap into the rickshaw, flags down a one-yen taxi, haggles the fare down to fifty sen, and off he goes with his customer. Each man has his own territory, secret (he never tells the others), where he keeps his woman, who, when things get tough, he sells off to passersby. It doesn't matter if she has a nine-year-old, a four-year-old, or is six months pregnant with the next.

But now, dear reader, if you happen to be interested in pilgrims'

12  *machi* is the word for a town or district of a city

votive stickers, then you've seen those stuck here and there on shrines advertising the Scarlet Troupe. The Scarlet Gang likes to call itself the Scarlet Troupe because it wants to think of itself as a theatrical group and harbours hopes of staging something spectacular – or what it would consider spectacular – in this small booth set up on a vacant lot. One young member has already started upon the Nakamise. She sells rubber balls while doing the Charleston.

## POSTWAR TOKYO (1945– )

> In the city with these clogged wounds
> International streets will appear soon,
> Rows of gay shops will grow,
> Tempting goods will brighten the windows.
> Under the hazy, blossom-laden sky
> New building goes on.
>
> JUN OKAMOTO

During the '*kurai tanima*' 'dark valley' years of the '30s and war years, Japan was taken over by an extreme Shintoist nationalist government, which led to the Pacific War. US General Curtis le May's policy of firebombing Japanese cities meant that, by March 1945, Tokyo was reduced to ashes and 100,000 people were left for dead. Across Japan, millions had already been left homeless and starving. The country was on its knees by the time the A-bombs exploded firstly over Hiroshima and then over Nagasaki in August 1945. After the unconditional surrender, General MacArthur, the Supreme Commander of the Allied Forces, took up his position in what is now the Dai-ichi Life Insurance building in Chiyoda ward, overlooking the destroyed Imperial Palace. This was taken as a symbol of the first time Japan had ever been occupied by a foreign power.

The Occupation was extremely painful, including the still contro-versial Tokyo trials, which sat for two years and resulted in seven hangings of war leaders including ex-Prime Minister Tōgō. However, the occupation also brought many benefits, such as demilitarisation and drafting of a new constitution which renounced 'the threat or use of force' as well as land and educational reform, although the US then went ahead and used Japan as a base for their military interests in Korea during the Korean War of 1950–2. The US still keeps a vast military presence in Japan including in Okinawa.

The ageing poet Edmund Blunden had taught in Tokyo in the 1920s and came back to lecture there as an educational advisor from 1948. He was invited to an Imperial poetry reading, held every New Year. These date back to the Heian period (794–1185). Perhaps because of his great age and experience, he could note both the good humour but also the exhaustion of the city.

The Occupation officially ended in 1952 with the formation of the LDP – Liberal Democratic Party – which governed Japan, and the country started to develop once again at an astounding pace. At the end of the 1950s Japan's economy had grown at twice the expected rate and in 1964, Japan officially joined the 'rich nations' club and the Organisation of Economic Development provided assistance to start the *shikansen* or bullet train. Tokyo hosted the Olympic Games in Kenzō Tange's Yoyogi National Stadium in 1964. But as with other nations, Japan suffered from the energy crisis during the 1970s and became famous for pollution, noise and political corruption as politicans cosied up to big business. One of the best chroniclers of the realities of downtown Tokyo, Nicolas Bouvier, came to Japan a number of times, setting up his home in Araki-cho, which was the underbelly of Tokyo in the 1970s. As he says 'the area is not marked on any map'. Not far from Ichigaya station just north-west of the Imperial Palace, it is one of the dilapidated places of the Yoshiwara area. Although Araki-chō does not feature much in guidebooks, around parks near Ueno or in Shinjuku station, or anywhere near a canal, you will find the homeless roaming.

The 1980s was the time when the famous bubble economy took off. During this time booming prices were fuelled by low interest rates and an expanding stock market, but the LDP clung on to power and Japan experienced a general rise in its standard of living.

Ginza is still a place to watch the fashionable crowds and Donald

Richie's *Tokyo Nights* is a glitzy, sparkly novel written about the bubble period of the 1980s, when Tokyo pulsed with more energy and frittered away more money than any other city in the world.

In 1989, Emperor Hirohito died, and his son, Prince Akihito, who was the first Emperor to marry a sweetheart of his own choosing, Shōda Michiko, was enthroned, ushering in the Heisei era (the time of Enlightened Peace). During the 1990s, Japan's Self-Defence forces were engaged for the first time in UN peacekeeping missions abroad, and in 1998 the economy was officially announced to be in a recession after several banks and institutions collapsed due to bad debts.

If you are going to Tokyo today, you are likely to go to Harajuku, Aoyama, Kabuki-chō or Roppongi where you will find Tadao Ando's Collezione building in Harajuku, Maki Fumihiko's Spiral Building in Aoyama, Richard Rogers' Kabuki-chō building and the Kohn Pederson Fox designed Mori Tower in Mori Minoru's Roppongi hills development. Roppongi was at first a military base after the war, a place for American 'Occupationaires'. It retains its multicultural flavour, with one of the first internationally recognised Japanese contemporary art museums, the Mori Art Building, located there. Roppongi is also a '*gaijin*' or foreigners' ghetto, filled with the sub-cultures of Japan. There are reggae venues, discos and *gaijin* bars as well as hostess clubs – more clubs open every year, and many employ foreign bartenders, from Drug Store that is open twenty-four hours a day, to the Rising Sun which caters to the British away from home in search of alternative kinds of love. Rika Yokomori's fictional creation, Saya, is a well-born Tokyo gambler's moll in *Tokyo Tango*, a portrait of the demi-monde scene that has developed since the 1980s in Azabu-jūban, a suburb of Roppongi.

**Edmund Blunden** from *Wanderings in Japan*

*A Party at the Palace*

Poetical competitions have pleased mankind at all times and in all countries, and even Apollo, god of the golden lyre, did not disdain them. They vary widely in kind and in importance. Sometimes they are private affairs, as when some of the English Romantic poets gathered to write sonnets on given subjects within a fixed time; the works of Shelley and Keats contain the results of some such occasions.

Sometimes the editors of newspapers or of other journals invite us to try for prizes with poems on announced themes. The prize poem at old universities is an institution which does not die, though possibly its winners no longer hold quite that place in literary history which they used to have. [...]

I come to the Eastern example of Japan, a land in which the writing of short lyrical poems has gone on so long and forms so pleasant a part of the life of one and all. It may be that the times we live in have reduced the number of these parties at which the men and women assembled vie in penning their *tanka* on the subjects proposed, or those which leave behind on the blossomed boughs of the garden their fluttering papers of verse for the breezes to judge as they will.

But the most illustrious of all the Japanese poetical competitions is still one of the institutions which decline to be upset by all our modernisms, and the New Year brings it regularly into the news – it is the Emperor's own poetry competition. The subject is selected as in past years by the Emperor; he and his family contribute their own treatments of it in the accepted verse form; thousands of his subjects produce theirs from all parts of the islands, and even a few Western writers (for it is permitted) send in their attempts. At length the day comes for the poetry party at the palace in Tokyo, when the multitude of copies of verses has been gone through and only a workable minority of them remains to be read aloud and judged, in the presence of the Emperor and before an audience of authors and others.

It was on a bright morning at the end of January that we found ourselves on the way round the ever enchanting moat, making for the

Palace as guests on this annual occasion. It seemed wrong, on an
occasion of fancy and sentiment, that we should be arriving in a car
(however beautiful and gentle voiced) at the tall towered gate, whence
one half expected several knights and one or two henchmen with
silver trumpets to appear in stately challenge. However the mild
policeman waiting there collected the pass and admitted the car; the
age of chivalry faded out; and we were at the modern steps rising to
the door of the Palace.

Friendly figures here took us up to the antechamber and explained
the order of the ceremonies which were to follow. Here already
gathered were twenty or more dignified persons mostly in Japanese
dress whom I assumed to be some of the literary specialists judging or
competing. I began to think of Wordsworth's lines:

> The high and gracious Muses shall accept
> Deliberately;
> For there was a seriousness in the air.

Before long we were guided into the long room in which the great
business of the day was to be transacted. At one end, a long screen and
several tables; before them, a table which I thought of, no matter if it
was really square, as a round table, for the judges and readers of the
poetry; alongside the rows of chairs for the poets who had got so far in
the competition; at the other end, the chairs for the rest of the
company. Three of these were occupied by foreign guests, and I had
the pleasure of sitting just below a finely coloured and delightfully
elaborate picture of trees and flowers and birds.

The Emperor entered, together with the Empress Dowager and
Princess Takamatsu; they occupied their several places, and with no
more than simple decorum, the party began. The characteristics of the
ceremony were silence (apart form the readings), stillness and slow
motion. The director whose function it was to deliver the manuscripts
in turn to the 'lecturer' and the little court of judges, or chorus of
chanters – for the poems were not only read but chanted – handled
each paper with reverent nicety. Such matters as poetry, the style
seemed to say are eternal; there can be no hurrying over them. It was
a long time before I saw on any face the relaxation of a slight smile,

and that I think was when one of the poets forgot that he should rise to his feet during the recitation of his own composition. How much I sympathized with his absent-mindedness.

The Emperor in his dark morning coat, the Empress Dowager in her purple velvet gown sat movelessly, impartially, as guardians of the treasure of poetry, while the readers intoned poem after poem. The voices and tones, as I felt, had a resemblance to the choral responses in which I was trained in a shadowy old church as a child. The exactness and the difficulty, in their style of poetry reading were not lost on us, though we could not gather wherein the differences were between poem and poem. These differences would be differences of touch and illustration, the form being the same through all; and I see I have not mentioned the subject, which was The Young Grass – the 'reviving' of happy nature. A Renaissance.

No commentary occurred – the poetry was left to speak for itself. This was in one view a Criticism Party, but the critics had done their work and (so to speak) had already withdrawn from the scene. This was, for the time, simply the Temple of the Muses. It may have been my desire, as a talkative student of literature, to hear an address from some notable veteran in this profession concerning the relation of poetry to the destiny of mankind – I surmised that, had we been meeting somewhere beyond Japanese boundaries, such an address would have inevitably been part of the proceedings.

But here – no, and I reflected that all the solemnities and traditional observances which I had been enabled to attend here in Japan, this undecorated and straightforward commemoration of poetry in the Palace itself brought me nearest to the particular quality of the Japanese mind.

It was not an archaic occasion, and the lacquered chairs with the golden chrysanthemums dappling their black frames were looking at me from modernized Japan – but here was the antiquity – here was the dignity, here the contemplation and intuition of Japan's earlier ages.

And now the poems of the Emperor, the Empress (whose indisposition had prevented her from taking her place at the high table), the Empress Dowager, and the Princess in her blossom-like Kimono, had been read. The Emperor was rising, and the quiet procession was passing out of sight. The ceremony for poets and poetry was over – but the ceremony for next New Year was already in preparation, and the next subject was decided.

We followed the others into the ante-chamber; were complimented with the clear and dulcet sake in the red lacquer saucer (and how well the dried cuttlefish goes with it!). Then, with a few merry words among our friends, we said our farewells, and returned to the usual tasks and tumults of the year 1950.

**Nicolas Bouvier** from *The Japanese Chronicles*

*Around Araki-chō*

Not easy to find a room here. A foreigner is obviously rich, he can travel. The serious agents offered me fifteen-room villas; the less serious ones also refused to believe that a foreigner could be interested in a room measuring four mats (4.6 square yards), and usually ended up offering me women. When they happened to have something, it was necessary to pay them up front, the *shikkin* (guarantee), the *ken rikin* (key deposit), and the *tesuryo* (commission), which equalled ten months' rent.

Better to search door to door and neighbourhood by neighbourhood through the biggest capital of the world, sleeping each night in a quarter with a different name – Akihabara, (the plain of autumn leaves), Yotsuya (four valleys), Ochanomizu (tea water), Nabeya yokochō (the crossroad of the pothole) – every day more exhausted but more enamoured of this sea of pug faces, oiled lanterns, laundries, tiny houses of gray wood leaning one against the other in the bitter iodized smoke of Japanese cooking. I tried this for seven days without success. On the eighth, the owner of the Poem Bar found something for me. I bought a straw mattress, a quilt, a small pillow filled with rice balls (all you need to move in here) and settled myself into the home of a night watchman in the Araki-chō quarter for a year.

*Chō* is a small quarter; *ki*, wood or tree; and *ara* is a type of berry. But there aren't any more berry trees in Araki-chō.

Sunflowers, bamboo, wisteria. Tilting, worm-eaten houses. Smell of sawdust, green tea, salt cod. At dawn from all sides, the ruffled song of roosters. Omnipresent advertising hideously incorporating the most beautiful writing in the world.

Araki-chō is, in sum, a forgotten bit of village within the city; in the past, four first-class geisha houses had made it famous. They had been burned down, like most of the others, leaving only a small 'school' to which a handful of suffering, fussy young women come, in feet bent from their high wooden shoes, to learn to play *shamisen*, to walk so each step is made up of twenty-six distinct movements, and to be at ease with both classic poetry and libertine innuendo. But today, the city's directory of geishas shows it to be at the bottom level – the very borders of gallantry – and the quarter has long since cast aside those memories. It is not marked on any map, and the taxi drivers who skirt its borders rarely even know its name.

Two very distinct mentalities can be seen in Tokyo. The southern and eastern parts of the city – home of barge owners, fishmongers, grocers and artisans, whose tools have not changed for a hundred years – have the *shitamachi* (low city) spirit. Cheeky and heartfelt. It is the *shitamachi* who applaud the sumo wrestlers with their chignons, who feed the gossip columns and sniff and sob over the drama of the Kabuki theatre. Who carry the flavour of the old folklore of Edo. The more well-to-do areas of the West and North have the *yamanote* (next to the hills) spirit – more bourgeois, studious, preserved. *Yamanote* are interested in the traditional arts: calligraphy, Noh theatre. They embrace the West, sitting under a hanging brass lamp to read European books, much in the spirit of the Meiji era.

Araki-chō is *yamanote* by geography and *shitamachi* in spirit, with an extra touch of rusticity. There are no foreigners there, and the only English words that have entered the local language are *kissu* (from kiss) which goes back to pre-war times, and *stenko* (from stinky), which is a word that is especially apt whenever rain floods the septic tanks (no sewage systems before 1970) or when the cesspool cleaners go on strike. Araki-chō is still in the bullseye of the huge target of 'Greater Tokyo' only six train stations from the Imperial Palace. You get off at Ichigaya station and for ten minutes follow a

canal sheltered by mastic trees where lovers paddle timidly in rented
canoes on a full moon evening. At the intersection of two avenues,
you reach a sake bar where a narrow alley carries you up to the
plateau of Araki-chō.

**Donald Richie** from *Tokyo Nights*

Bong went the clock and the Ginza flowed, six on a payday Friday
night, late spring, the sun just going down. The big Hattori clock
went pink in its tower and Mitsukoshi glowed; a rooftop Shinto shrine
gleamed once in the sinking sun and down below, the sidewalks
surged. The light went green, stopped, taxis revved, bikes roared,
and, squat before fancy Wako, the phone-board *pachinko*-like lit up.
Another bong, the last, and walkers ebbed like surf as buses, trucks,
the family cars, filled the street, red all ahead. One cordovaned foot
now safely on the curb, Hiroshi Watanabe heard the final stroke, cast
an eye on to the high clock, dodged a Honda, checked his Seiko,
rounded the Burger King, skirted the Dairy Queen, ran right past the
Cozy Corner and down an alley hung with bar signs as far as he could
see; then into a side street, sky pale, sun gone as the bar signs flicked
on, then in and under an old-fashioned *kamban* upon which was carved
Yamato – the name of Old Japan.

He ran down the stairs, past the fake Fabergé in its fancy nook, the
real Louis Seize commode reflecting in the foyer, and into the club
itself, empty but for its near-Empire chairs, tambour tables, pouffes, a
love-seat, shelf upon shelf of Johnny Walker Black, four golf trophies,
two stuffed fish – gifts of customers – a crystal chandelier and, under it,
Mariko Matsushita, showing impatience.

'So, you're finally here,' she cried.

'I hurried. Traffic. Payday.'

'Well, just catch your breath. Then: Payday. Don't I just know.
Cleaned out. These girls.'

'She glared at a closed back door behind which was the kitchen and,
presumably, the girls.

'Who's for him?' he wondered.

'A new one', I thought. 'Pretty. In a way. The way foreigners seem to like.'

Hiroshi's client (and friend, he often said) was due that evening back in Tokyo once more, buying, it was hoped, selling it was feared. And Mariko, madame and sole proprietor of the popular Yamato, was to have (Hiroshi paying) a small and intimate repast.

'Seeing all that one is doing, one would have thought one could have come a bit early. And a foreigner as well. So upsetting.'

'I am a bit early. I am an hour early.'

'It is so difficult, having to do everything by oneself. Is it raining out?'

'No. It is a beautiful spring evening. Why did you think it would be raining?'

'Spite. Everything else has gone wrong.'

She then put on a large and sorrowful face and told why. The cuisinart had broken, so no *miso* soup. Then three – three! – of the girls had called in sick (colds, though one a miscarriage for sure.) And then she got the estimate for the remodelling of the Yamato. Just a little Spanish colonial, she'd thought – and oh, Watanabe-san, I cannot tell you! Tears. Here he responded with practiced pats and she raised mascaraed eyes.

This was apparently why she had wanted his earlier arrival, so that he might hear particularly of the financial woes. Had one thought that perhaps there was more here than just owner and patron, one would have been correct.

I have heard cicadas even in the busiest streets, though they thrive best in the back alleys, where they ceaselessly emit that scarcely tolerable susurration which is like a shrill intensification of extreme heat.


**Rika Yokomori** from *Tokyo Tango*


It had snowed a lot that winter. I used to go slithering through the snowdrifts down the Usenzaka slope from Roppongi Station to Bogey's pad in Azabu Juban. It took me thirty minutes to get to

Roppongi on the Hibiya line, and after that it was a fifteen-minute walk. Azabu Juban had the same kind of raffish, easygoing atmosphere as Minowa, the district in Tokyo where I'd been born and bred, but it also had a certain vigour that Minowa could never match, and you could smell money in the air.

In the old days, Azabu-Jūban had been known as one of Tokyo's leading pleasure quarters. And nowadays, apart from the local shop-keepers, just about everyone who had lived there had something to do with the night world. Either that or they were wheeling and dealing in the financial or property markets. I guess there wasn't much difference between these people and the night birds who hung out near my home in Asakusa, but those living in Azabu-Jūban were in a higher league – hostesses from the glittering Ginza, Japan's Number One Nightstpot, and their menfolk. The amount of money floating around was different too. This was where the hostesses chilled out when they came off duty, so the place had something of the air of a backstage changing room for butterflies of the night. It had a buzz to it.

In the middle of Azabu-Jūban stood Bogey's regular coffee shop, the Edinburgh. During the daylight hours, the Ginza and Roppongi hostesses would hang out there, unmade-up brunching in sunglasses and shiny spats, each with her yapping little dog, of course. Their men would be sporting frizzy gangster perms and baggy bomber jackets and be clanking with thick 18-carat gold bracelets and Rolexes, devouring the sports papers and working the phones at the back of the coffee shop.

No doubt Bogey chose to make his base there because he liked the commonness and *nouveau riche* atmosphere, together with the rough humanity that rubbed off from its *demi-monde* associations. There were no ordinary folk here, no regular guys squeezing into over-crowded trains to get to their companies or government offices, earning the bread to support their suburban families. But that didn't mean Azabu-Jūban had lost out in the great game of life – far from it. The only people living there were the people who weren't regular but were nevertheless successful. They rented expensive condominiums and lived gaudy, glittering lives of leisure. Of course, the highly off-colour tone of the place didn't bother Bogey one little bit. He took to it like a duck to water.

# 2

# Yokohama

The Sacred Fuji, pale as pearl,
Is ruled across with telegraph wires.

WILLIAM PLOMER

Yokohama became an international destination after the Americans arrived in Japan in the 1850s. Phileas Fogg attempted to get to Yokohama when he was trying to cross the Pacific from Hong Kong to San Francisco in Jules Verne's 1872 novel *Around the World in Eighty Days*. Not long after Fogg, Isabella Bird came on the way to Edo in 1878. She was impressed by the very populous fishing port and the view of Mount Fuji from the sea took her breath away. Just ten years before, the new international port had been little more than a fishing village.

The city was one of the few places where foreigners could settle after the opening of the 'treaty ports' in 1858. The settlement, which was separated from the mainland by a bridge, flourished on the silk and tea trade, with a motley host of Europeans, bread bakers, photographers, ice cream makers, even a brewery, a newspaper office and the first railway engineers. Commodore Perry brought three hundred and fifty feet of track and a quarter scale model train to Yokohama to impress the shogun into negotiations. Sir Ernest Satow who was the official interpreter for the British legation describes the 'goldrush' community of those days, where a mix of English, Japanese and Malay was spoken and the rough traders who arrived were closely watched by sometimes corrupt Japanese officials, and there was an atmosphere of distrust on all sides. Events often took a violent turn and in 1862 the foreign embassies, who were meant to be housed in vacated monasteries in Edo, returned to Yokohama after some violent attacks.

A few of the landmarks from this era are still standing including

Christchurch, the church founded in 1862, the Akarenga, a warehouse and the *gaijin bochi*, the foreigners' cemetery where some 4,500 people from forty countries are buried, including Edward Morel, chief engineer on the Yokohama railway, and Charles Richardson, the merchant whose death in 1862 sparked a war between Britain and the Shimazu clan (see Kyūshū chapter). The first railway in Japan was built between Yokohama and Shinagawa in 1872.

Yokohama became a centre for the movies during the Taishō era, with theatre company Shochiku establishing a cinema studio in 1920 in Kamata. It was here on Yokohama bluff that Junichirō Tanizaki learnt to dance the foxtrot along with fashionable young dandies. The cosmopolitan nature of the port continued into the early years of the twentieth century as Japan sought alliances with disaffected Chinese in order to advance her interests there. Sun Yat Sen, head of the Kuomintang army and Chiang Kai Shek, his fellow Marxist, studied in Tokyo in 1907 and retreated here after an unsuccessful bid to take over Shanghai in 1911. You can visit Yokohama Big World Museum to find out more about Japanese Imperial 'East Asia Co-prosperity sphere' ambitions in the 1920s. The entire city of Yokohama was destroyed in the 1923 earthquake and was rebuilt, only to be destroyed again in several US air raids in May 1945. The Chinese are now established in their own Chukagai or Chinatown, while the new migrants of the 1980s and '90s come from further afield. They inhabit the *motomachi* or downtown streets and Filipino novelist Rey Ventura's novel *Adopted Son* is a rare, luminous account of a hermetic 'illegal' foreign community who prop up the Japanese economic miracle. If you walk around Yokohama you will see signs of great Japanese wealth, from the carefully built Sankei-en, built by Tomitaro Hara (1868–1938), a silk trader more commonly known as Sankei Hara, while Mitsubishi tycoon Minato Mirai has built the eponymous Minato Mirai 21 development complex in line with the futurist landscaping of the city.

**Sir Ernest Satow** from *A diplomat in Japan*

*Yokohama Society, official and unofficial*

The foreign community of Yokohama of that day was somewhat extravagantly described by an English diplomat as 'the scum of Europe'. No doubt there was a fair sprinkling of men who, suddenly relieved from the restraints which social opinion places upon their class at home, and exposed to the temptations of eastern life, did not conduct themselves with the strict propriety of students at a theological college. That they were really worse than their co-equals elsewhere is unlikely. But in a small community where the actions of everyone are semi-public and concealment is not regarded as an object of first-rate importance, the vices that elsewhere pass unnoticed become prominent to the eyes of those who are not exposed to the same temptations. There were also not a few who came there without much capital to make a livelihood, or, if possible, something more, and hastened to the attainment of their object without being troubled with much scruple. And the difficulty which soon presented itself of obtaining a sufficiency of native coin in exchange for the silver dollar of Eastern commerce was the cause of extravagant demands being presented to the Japanese Treasury. But the compromise eventually arrived at, by which the merchant had to buy his *ichibu* [Japanese currency] in the open market, while the official obtained the equivalent of his salary, and often much more in native coin nearly weight for weight of his 'mexicans' [silver dollars] was to the minds of all unprejudiced persons a far greater scandal. Detractors said that the advantages thus given to Ministers, Consuls, sailors and soldiers was a bribe to induce their compliance with violation of treaty stipulations to the 'prejudice of their non official countrymen', but this is unfair. It was the result of false theories as to the nature and function of money, and personal interest worked against a conversion to views more in accordance with the principles of political economy.

[...]

A few words may be devoted to describing the Yokohama society of those days. There were few ladies in the settlement. Japan was a long way from Europe, with no regular steam communication, and the lives of foreigners were supposed to be not very safe at the hands of the arm-bearing classes. The two great China firms of Jardine, Matheson and Co and Dent and Co were of course represented. The latter came down with a crash a year or two after my arrival. Fletcher and Co another important Shanghai firm had a branch, and so had Barnet and Co, both now long forgotten. Most of the remainder were Japan firms, amongst whom Aspinall, Cornse and Co, Macpherson, Marshall and Co were the foremost English and Walsh, Hall and Co the leading American firms. Germans, French and Dutch were considered of 'no account'. Money was abundant or seemed to be, everyone kept a pony or two, and champagne flowed freely at frequent convivial entertainments. Races were held in the spring and autumn and 'real' horses competed in some of the events. A favourite Sunday's excursion was the ride along the Tōkaidō to Kawasaki for tiffin and back again toward the evening. Longer outings were to Kanazawa, Kamakura and Enoshima; but anyone who had ventured as far as Hachiōji or Hakonē which were beyond the Treaty limits was regarded as a bold, adventurous spirit. The privilege of travelling beyond a distance of 25 miles from Yokohama was reserved to the diplomatic representative of foreign powers, and Yedo could be visited only in the disguise of a member of one of the legations with the permission of its head. Such favours were regarded with extreme jealousy by those who were debarred by circumstances from obtaining them, and loud murmurs were heard that it was the Ministers' duty to invite his countrymen to the capital, and give them board and lodging, irrespective of the shape which their private relations with him might have assumed. Then and perhaps even yet, there existed a theory that public servants were practically the servants of the extremely small section of the public that inhabited Yokohama and when the servants failed to comply with the wishes of their employers they were naturally and rightly abused – behind their backs.

So strong was the hostility excited in the breast of the English, Scotch and Irish portion of the community by the unlucky phrase 'scum of Europe' that no member of either legation or consulate of their country was allowed admittance into the Yokohama Club, composed chiefly of British merchants; and this feeling lasted until the year 1865 brought about a permanent change in the representation of Great Britain. The excuse for such relations between the British residents and one who ought to have been the leader of the small society, is to be found in the comparative youthfulness and ignorance of the world which characterised the former. The experience of men and manners which saves the dwellers in Little Peddlington from believing that others are deliberately plotting to inflict insults on them is seldom attained before middle life, especially when Little Peddlington happens to be located in an Eastern land, where the mind's growth comes to a standstill and a man's age is virtually to be reckoned by the years actually spent in the mother country. For all purposes of mental and moral development the time passed on the opposite side of the world must be left out of the calculation.

It was agreed in the Treaties that Yedo should be the residence of the foreign diplomatic representatives, and four Buddhist monasteries had, in accordance with Japanese custom, been assigned to the representatives of the four chief powers – Great Britain, France, Holland and the United States. Sir Rutherford Alcock occupied Tōzenji in the suburb of Takanawa, M. de Graef van Polsbrock lived in Chōji a little nearer the city; then came Saikaiji, the residence of M. Duchesne de Bellecourt; and Mr Harris had settled down at Zempukuji in Azabu. But a series of alarming occurrences had caused the European portion of the diplomatic body to transfer their quarters to Yokohama, and the American Minister alone held out, declaring his confidence in the good faith of the Japanese Government and their ability to protect him. In September of 1862 he had already been replaced by General Pruyn, who followed the example of his predecessor, until eventually driven out of the capital by a fire which destroyed his house, whether purely accidentally or maliciously contrived. The English legation in 1861 had been the object of a murderous attack in which the Secretary, Mr Laurence Oliphant, and Mr G. C. Morrison were wounded. The assailants were principally retainers of the *daimyo* of Mito, but others belonging to various clans were concerned in the affair and some of these are still living. Sir R. Alcock had consequently removed to Yokohama, where the strong guard placed by the Japanese government at the entrances to their own and the foreign men-of-war in the harbour offered sufficient guarantees for safety. On his quitting Japan for a term of leave early in 1862, his *locum tenens* Colonel Neale, not believing in a danger of which he had no experience, brought the legation back to Tozenji. But he had no sooner installed himself there than an event occurred which led him to change his opinion. This was nothing less than the murder of the sentry who stood at his bedroom door and of a corporal on his rounds, at the hands of one of the Japanese guards, in revenge of an insult offered to him, it is said, by the youngest member of the staff, a heedless boy of fifteen or sixteen. So the British Legation packed up their archives and hastened back to Yokohama, where they installed themselves in a house that stood on the site of the present Grand Hotel. This building belonged to an Englishman named Hoey, who was murdered in his bed in 1870, apparently from motives of private revenge. The foreign consuls were all stationed at Yokohama with the exception of the American consul, Colonel Fisher who remained at Kanagawa, the town mentioned in the treaty. Mr Harris it is said, would never admit that Yokohama could be rightfully substituted for Kanagawa, and would not permit his consul to reside there. He even carried out his opposition so far as to declare that he never would countenance the change of settlement, and carried out his vow by leaving Japan without having set foot in Yokohama.

**Junichirō Tanizaki** from *Seven Japanese Tales*

*Yokohama*

There was indeed something dreamlike about walking along this quiet, almost deserted street lined with massive Western-style buildings, looking into show windows here and there. It wasn't garish, like the Ginza, even in daytime a hush lay over it. Could anyone be alive in these silent buildings, with their thick gray walls where the window glass glittered like fish eyes, reflecting the blue sky? It seemed more like a museum gallery than a streeet. And the merchandise displayed behind the glass on both sides was bright and colourful, with the fascinating, mysterious luster of a garden at the bottom of the sea.

A curio-shop in English caught his eye: ALL KINDS OF JAPANESE FINE ARTS: PAINTINGS, PORCELAINS, BRONZE STATUES . . . And one that must have been for a Chinese tailor: MAN CHANG DRESS MAKER FOR LADIES AND GENTLEMEN . . . And also: JAMES BERGMAN JEWELRY. . . RINGS, EARRINGS, NECKLACES . . . E & B CO. FOREIGN DRY GOODS AND GROCERIES, LADIES' UNDERWEARS . . . DRAPERIES, TAPESTRIES, EMBROIDERIES . . . Somehow the very ring of these words in his ear had the heavy, solemn beauty of the sound of a piano. Only an hour by streetcar from Tokyo, yet you felt as if you had arrived at some far-off place. And you hesitated to go inside these shops when you saw how lifeless they looked, their doors firmly shut. In these show windows – perhaps because they were meant for foreigners – goods were set out on display in a cold, formal arrangement well behind glass, quite unlike the ingratiating clutter of the windows along the Ginza. There seemed to be no clerks or shop boys at work; all kinds of luxuries were on display, but these dimly lit rooms were as gloomy as a Buddhist shrine . . . Still that made the goods within seem all the more curiously enticing.

**Rey Ventura** from *Underground in Japan*

*Filipino Sunday*

On Sunday morning, Kotobuki looks like what it is – home to the dregs of Japanese society. Among the litter, the coffee cans and chopsticks, the vomit and urine, it's not unusual to find a day-labourer lying in the street beside his empty sake bottle. Some of the bars never close, and a day's drinking might begin at seven, indoors or out – in the Korean run bar, or in the street by the open braziers. It's a rough place – the mention of Koto is enough to make your Japanese friends alarmed – but it has some merits. This is the part of Japan where I can greet an old man on the street and be greeted in return. Koto scared the Japanese, but it's the only place where I am not scared.

It's a question of territory: Koto belongs to a series of overlapping groups. Korean-Japanese-run small shops and bars and a few cheap inns. We Filipinos provide the illegal workforce, and although there may be a few individual Pakistanis or Latinos, if a Pakistani group tries to form, we'd see them off. The communists have a base here as well, with their labour unions and the surprising thing is that this is the only place where I have not seen them clash with the Yakuza.

The Yakuza themselves – the subordinates, that is, not the *oyabun* – will be around on Sunday, keeping an eye on things: the betting shops, the pachinko parlours, the snack bars. They're in their casual clothes and they're amused at the way we always get dressed up on Sundays. They call out to ask where we're going. Church? Oh yes, they say, you're Christians aren't you? That's why. And then they make the sign of the cross, or try to. They must have picked that up from mafia films.

'We're going to church,' we say, 'to ask God's blessing, so we don't get arrested.' And we make the handcuff sign, placing our wrists together at an angle.

'There are police over there,' they say, pointing to the box.

'Don't worry,' we reply, unimpressed, 'they're our friends.' We know 'how to ride' the Yakuza, we say to ourselves; we know 'where to tickle' them. They're not our friends, exactly, but there is a coincidence of interest. Sometimes Filipinos will do errands for them, in the crack business for instance or as number runners. I knew one man who got so close to the Yakuza that he used to copy their look, with crinkly hair and dark glasses, but I never heard of a Filipino actually joining up. Nor did I ever hear of trouble between us and the Yakuzas in Koto. But there was a price for this. If we were short changed by their associates on our wages, we never complained, and when we joked with them on the streets, we knew just how far we could go.

[…]

The church, the Sacred Heart Cathedral, stands in the Yamate district, a wealthy area of foreign-occupied bungalows and the congregation at the English language service is two thirds Westerners – Americans and Europeans – one third Filipino, and because I was in the habit of turning up late I often had to stand. Indeed I could sometimes hardly get in.

I used to arrive late because to me the service was more important for social than for spiritual reasons. That wasn't true of most of the community. Most people – even the worst of the bully boys – had their own prayer books and sacred images, their gold crosses and religious texts carefully copied out by hand and stuck on the walls of their rooms. They kept their bibles either beside the bed or displayed in some prominent place, and the kind of Bibles they had were annotated by topic, so that you could look up a subjects such as 'confidence' or 'safety'. You would never place a Bible alongside other books on a shelf, or beneath anything at all. You might share a Bible but you would never lend it. If there was a fire, it would be the first thing you would try to rescue. If you lost your Bible, that would be a very bad omen, and it would be bad luck to be separated from it — for instance, by being put under arrest. But in that case, at least, you would always have your prayer book – wherever you were, you would always have in your pocket some money, a loved one's photo, a list of telephone numbers, a prayer book and in the case of most men – a knife.

# 3

# Kamakura

Shingo lit one of the cigarettes he had just bought. 'It has
the Buddha on it,' he said, handing the package to Fusako.
'Especially made for Kamakura.'

YASUNARI KAWABATA

Kamakura, now a UNESCO world heritage site, may finally gain its
rightful place on Japan's tourist map. After his ancestor had founded
the Moritomo tutelary shrine at Kamakura, Minamoto no Yoritomo
(1147–99) set up his capital at Kamakura following his defeat of the
Taira clan at Dan-no-Ura in 1185. Yoritomo wanted to murder
Yoshitsune, his younger brother for outshining him in popularity and
skill in that war and at court, but first he set his eyes on Yoshitsune's
mistress Shizuka Gozen, who was invited to dance for him. When
Shizuka danced out her love for Yoshitsune in defiance of Yoritomo,
he killed her and later, his brother.

Hōjō Masako, Yoritomo's wife, determined the fate of the shogunate after Yoritomo's death. Not only did Masako wear a sword and
ride into battle, but she ensured that her heirs, the Hōjō, rather than
Yoritomo's family, the Hiki, inherited the ruling line. She did this by
inviting her in-laws to dinner with her family and had the Hikis
murdered. Yoritomo and Masako built the temple of Tsurugaoka
Hachiman (the god of war), which stands at the end of one of the
loveliest arcades of cherry trees. This was the location for the famous
Kabuki play, *Shibaraku!* or *Wait a Moment!*, a great example of
bravura style. Written in 1697 by Ichikawa Danjuro, it is named after
the moment in the play when the hero halts an execution at the shrine.
Its treasure hall (*kokuhōkan*) contains abundant works of art from

the temples and shrines of the Kamakura period of the twelfth to fourteenth centuries.

During the thirteenth century, there was a resurgence of interest in Buddhism as well as trade with China; dozens of grand monuments were built in Kamakura as different branches of Buddhism attempted to establish themselves. Some of these temples are preserved in their original condition. The Zen sect was very powerful at this time in China and through the reestablishment of relations with the 'Middle Kingdom', many Zen priests visited and took up residence in Japan. Just near the Tsurugaoka Hachiman-gū shrine, the Rinzai Zen temple and convent of Jōfūkuji were built by Masako, Yorimoto's widow, in 1200 with the help of Eisai (1141–1215), a Chinese Zen monk. She then entered the convent after her husband's death.

The 1240s in Japan were a time of great religious fervour. The Amida Butsu, or 'Pure Land' sect of Buddhism, was on the rise. Otherwise known as Jōdo, this school was founded on the repetition of the name Amida Butsu over and over again. It was later to raise enough funds to cast a Daibutsu, a twelve-metre-high statue of Amida Buddha in 1292, one to rival the great Buddha at Tōdaiji in Nara. Hojo Tokiyori, the regent at Kamakura founded Kenchōji, in 1253, appointed Rankei Dōryū as its first abbot at that time.

But, during the 1260s, Japan was suddenly faced with a challenge it hadn't faced before, the invasion of a foreign power. The Mongols had already besieged and crushed Peking and in 1268 they sent ambassadors to the shogun of Japan at Kamakura. The Buddist priest Nichiren (1222–82), who had predicted the threat of foreign invasion, counselled Hōjō Tokiyori, the regent at Kamakura, with a famous treatise, the *Rissho Ankoku Ron, On Establishing the Correct Teaching for the Peace of the Land.* This was based on his comprehensive studies of all the available Buddhist scriptures. However, Tokiyori's son Tokimune (1251–84) decided to cut off the Mongol Ambassadors' heads on Enoshima beach when they sent representatives in 1275. Japan faced a Mongol invasion in 1274, and, after the slaughter of the islanders of Tsushima and Iki, about 100,000 Mongols landed in Kyūshū in 1281.

Zen was still in favour at court, and specifically Ryokan's Zen Buddhism. Engakuji temple was founded in 1282 at the order of

Tokimune, apparently as an act of gratitude to Mongaku, a Zen priest from China who had meditated his way through the threatened Mongol invasion, while his monks were all slaughtered. Mongaku trained Tokimune and his commanders in meditation and *bushidō*, or the way of the warrior. However, due to the superior gunpowder and weaponry of the invaders, the Japanese suffered huge losses. And although a *kamikaze*, a divine wind, finally carried off Kublai Khan's army of 150,000, they left a devastated Japan. The government of Japan erected a wall to keep the invaders out, and remained on a state of alert for thirteen years. The flower of Japan's chivalric warriors expected some kind of reward for their patriotic duty but found that the government's coffers had already been emptied and there was none forthcoming. The art of the time records the dire poverty, disease and the era of destructive civil war that followed.

Iso Mutsu was born Gertrude Passingham in Cambridge, England, (see authors' biographies) and wrote the first thorough guide to the Kamakura. Her travels took her to 'sacred' Enoshima, the island where the Mongols were beheaded, and Nichiren (see above) was saved from execution. She finds the island full of temporal delights, including the shells for which it is famed. Legend has it that the Goddess of Good Fortune, Benten, represented by shells, persuaded the dragon god to protect the island.

The area opposite Enoshima is known as the Shōnan coast, a Mecca for the Taishō era (1912–26) bourgeoisie who bought houses around Kamakura, and also for intellectuals such as the writers Natsume Sōseki (1867–1916), Junichirō Tanizaki (1886–1965) and Mori Ōgai (1862–1922), who came to stay to visit the beach and write. This is where the narrator in Sōseki's novel *Kokoro*, comes with Sensei, his mentor in life. The opening of the novel presents a vivid picture of beach life, from the middle class point of view. The experimentalism of this novel, which opens with Sensei, which means master or teacher, taking a swim at Kamakura, belies its serious melancholic nature. The title '*Kokoro*' represents the writer's search for 'the heart of things' in his intellectual relationship with Sensei, his personal relationships and also with his friendship with K, who commits suicide.

Tanizaki came to Kamakura in the 1920s and his novel *Naomi* shows the life of decadent luxury of the time. He became famous because he serialised the book in 1924 in the Ōsaka Asahi newspapers, titling the novel in Japanese, *Chijin no Ai* (*A Fool's Love*). It shows the progressive nature of popular culture between the First World War and the earthquake in 1923. A satirical tale of obsessional love; Naomi is a modern girl, neither shy nor naïve, who defies Japanese tradition in dress, etiquette and morality. The public outcry against the novel made it famous. Today however, beach life on the *taiheyō* or Pacific Ocean, is a less glamorous affair, quite different from *shōnan no imeji*, the image of Shōnan.

**Natsume Sōseki** from *Kokoro* or *The Heart of Things*

I always called him Sensei.[13] I shall therefore refer to him simply as Sensei, and not by his real name. It is not because I consider it more discreet, but it is because I find it more natural that I do so. Whenever the memory of him comes back to me now, I find that I think of him as Sensei still. And with pen in hand, I cannot bring myself to write of him in any other way.

It was at Kamakura, during the summer holidays, that I first met Sensei. I was then a very young student. I went there at the insistence of a friend of mine, who had gone to Kamakura to swim. We were not together for long. It had taken me a few days to get together enough money to cover the necessary expenses, and it was only three days after my arrival that my friend received a telegram from home demanding his return. His mother, the telegram explained, was ill. My friend, however, did not believe this. For some time his parents had been trying to persuade him, much against his will, to marry a certain girl. According to our modern outlook, he was really too young to marry. Moreover, he was not in the least fond of the girl. It was in order to avoid an unpleasant situation that instead of going home, as he normally would have done, he had gone to the resort near Tokyo to spend his holidays. He showed me the telegram, and asked

13 'Teacher' or 'mentor' in Japanese.

me what he should do. I did not know what to tell him. It was, however, clear that if his mother was truly ill, he should go home. And so he decided to leave after all. I, who had taken so much trouble to join my friend, was left alone.

There were many days left before the beginning of term, and I was free either to stay in Kamakura or to go home. I decided to stay. My friend was from a wealthy family in the Central Provinces, and had no financial worries. But being a young student, his standard of living was much the same as my own. I was therefore not obliged, when I found myself alone, to change my lodgings.

My inn was in a rather out-of-the-way district of Kamakura, and if one wished to indulge in such fashionable pastimes as playing billiards and eating ice cream, one had to walk a long way across rice fields. If one went by rickshaw, it cost twenty sen. Remote as the district was, however, many rich families had built their villas there. It was quite near the sea also, which was convenient for swimmers such as myself.

I walked to the sea every day, between thatched cottages that were old and smoke-blackened. The beach was always crowded with men and women, and at times the sea, like a public bath, would be covered with a mass of black heads. I never ceased to wonder how so many city holiday-makers could squeeze themselves into so small a town. Alone in this noisy and happy crowd, I managed to enjoy myself, dozing on the beach or splashing about in the water.

It was in the midst of this confusion that I found Sensei. In those days, there were two tea houses on the beach. For no particular reason, I had come to patronize one of them. Unlike those people with their great villas in the Hase area who had their own bathing huts, we in our part of the beach were obliged to make use of these tea houses which served also as communal changing rooms. In them the bathers would drink tea, rest, have their bathing suits rinsed, wash the salt from their bodies, and leave their hats and sunshades for safe-keeping. I owned no bathing suit to change into, but I was afraid of being robbed, and so I regularly left my things in the tea house before going into the water.

*       *       *

Sensei had just taken his clothes off and was about to go for a swim when I first laid eyes on him in the tea house. I had already had my swim, and was letting the wind blow gently on my wet body. Between us, there were numerous black heads moving about. I was in a relaxed frame of mind, and there was such a crowd on the beach that I should never have noticed him had he not been accompanied by a Westerner.

The Westerner, with his extremely pale skin, had already attracted my attention when I approached the tea house. He was standing with folded arms, facing the sea; carelessly thrown down on the stool by his side was a Japanese summer dress which he had been wearing. He had on him only a pair of drawers such as we were accustomed to wear. I found this particularly strange. Two days previously I had gone to Yuigahama and, sitting on top of a small dune close to the rear entrance of a Western-style hotel, I had whiled away the time watching the Westerners bathe. All of them had their torsos, arms, and thighs well-covered. The women especially seemed overly modest. Most of them were wearing brightly colored rubber caps which could be seen bobbing conspicuously amongst the waves. After having observed such a scene, it was natural that I should think this Westerner, who stood so lightly clad in our midst, quite extraordinary.

As I watched, he turned his head to the side and spoke a few words to a Japanese, who happened to be bending down to pick up a small towel which he had dropped on the sand. The Japanese then tied the towel around his head, and immediately began to walk towards the sea. This man was Sensei.

From sheer curiosity, I stood and watched the two men walk side by side towards the sea. They strode determinedly into the water and, making their way through the noisy crowd, finally reached a quieter and deeper part of the sea. Then they began to swim out, and did not stop until their heads had almost disappeared from my sight. They turned around and swam straight back to the beach. At the tea house, they dried themselves without washing the salt off with fresh water from the well and, quickly donning their clothes, they walked away.

After their departure, I sat down, and lighting a cigarette, I began idly to wonder about Sensei. I could not help feeling that I had seen him somewhere before, but failed to recollect where or when I had met him.

I was a bored young man then, and for lack of anything better to do, I went to the tea house the following day at exactly the same hour, hoping to see Sensei again. This time, he arrived without the Westerner, wearing a straw hat. After carefully placing his spectacles on a nearby table and then tying his hand towel around his head, he once more walked quickly down the beach. And when I saw him wading through the same noisy crowd, and then swim out all alone, I was suddenly overcome with the desire to follow him. I splashed through the shallow water until I was far enough out, and then began to swim towards Sensei. Contrary to my expectation, however, he made his way back to the beach in a sort of arc, rather than in a straight line. I was further disappointed when I returned, dripping wet, to the tea house: he had already dressed, and was on his way out.

## Junichirō Tanizaki from *Naomi*

Naomi was constantly begging me to take her to Kamakura. We went at the beginning of August with the intention of staying two or three days.

'Why does it have to be only two or three days?' she asked. 'It's no fun unless we go for a week or ten days.'

Her face showed her displeasure as we left the house. But I'd come back early from the country with the excuse that I was busy at work, and out of deference to my mother, I didn't want to risk my ruse being exposed. If I'd put it to Naomi in this way, though, she'd have felt humiliated. Instead I said, 'Try to be content with two or three days this year. Next year I'll take you for a longer stay somewhere else. All right?'

'But just two or three days . . . '

'I know, but if you want to swim when we get back, you can go to the beach at Omori.'

'I can't swim in a filthy place like that.'

'You shouldn't say things like that when you don't really know. Be good, girl. I'll buy you something to wear, instead. Didn't you say you wanted some Western clothes? I'll get some for you.'

Caught with the bait of Western clothes, she finally agreed.

In Kamakura we stayed in the Golden Wave Pavilion at Hase, an unremarkable inn for bathers. It makes me laugh to think of it now. There was no need to economize, because I still had most of my semi-annual bonus. Thrilled to be taking my first overnight trip with Naomi, I wanted to leave her with the most beautiful impressions possible: we'd stay in a high-class place and not worry about the cost. But when the day came and we boarded a second-class coach bound for Yokosuka, we were seized by a kind of timidity. The train was full of women and girls headed for Zushi and Kamakura, sitting in resplendent rows. In their midst, Naomi's outfit, to me at least, looked wretched.

As it was summer, of course the women couldn't have been particularly dressed up. But when I compared them to Naomi, I sensed an unmistakable difference in refinement between those who are born to the higher classes of society and those who aren't. Though Naomi seemed to have become a different person from the café girl she'd been, there's no concealing bad birth and breeding. And if this is what I was thinking, she must have felt it even more. How pitiful it looked now, that muslin kimono with the grape design that had made her seem so stylish. Some of the women sitting around us were wearing simple summer robes, but their fingers glittered with gemstones and their luggage was luxurious; everything bespoke their wealth and station, while Naomi had nothing to show but her velvety skin. I can still remember how she hid her parasol self-consciously under her sleeve. And well she might – though the parasol was brand-new, anyone could see it was a cheap item, worth no more than seven or eight yen.

At first, then, we'd pictured ourselves staying at the Mitsuhashi Inn, or even at the Kaihin Hotel. But when we approached the buildings, we were so intimidated by their magnificent gates that we walked up and down the Hase road two or three times until we finally found ourselves at the Golden Wave Pavilion, a second or third class establishment, by local standards.

There were too many noisy students staying at the inn for any relaxation there, so we spent nearly all of our time on the beach.

Tomboy that she was, Naomi cheered up as soon as she saw the ocean and forgot how dispirited she'd been on the train.

'I must learn how to swim this summer,' she said, clinging to my arm and splashing about wildly in the shallows. I held her with both hands and showed her how to float on her belly, taught her how to kick, as she grasped a post in the water, and let her go suddenly, so that she tasted the brine. When she tired of that, we practiced riding the waves, played with the sand as we lay on the beach, and in the evening rowed out toward the bay in a rented boat. With a big towel wrapped around her bathing suit, she'd sit on the stern or lie back against the gunwale, gaze at the blue sky, and sing the Neapolitan boat song 'Santa Lucia' – her favourite – in a shrill voice:

> 'Oh dolce Napoli
> O sol beato.'

As her soprano voice reverberated over the sea in the evening calm, I gently rowed the boat and listened, entranced. 'Farther farther,' she cried, as though she wanted to travel across the waves forever. Before we knew it, the sun had set and the stars were sparkling; as the darkness gathered around us, Naomi's form, wrapped in a white towel, blurred into indistinctness. But her bright voice continued. She sang 'Santa Lucia' over and over, then 'Lorelei', 'Zigeunerleben' and a melody from Mignon. Song followed song as the boat moved gently forward.

I suppose that everyone experiences something like this in his youth, but for me it was the first time. Being an electrical engineer, I knew less than others did about literature and art and hardly ever read novels, but that evening, I thought of Natsume Sōseki's *Pillow of Grass*, which I had read. The line 'As Venice sank, as Venice sank,' appears in that novel and somehow I was reminded of it as Naomi and I, rocked by the boat, gazed from the offing and through the veil of evening haze, toward the flickering lights on the shore. Moved to a tearful ecstasy, I wanted to drift away with Naomi to some uncharted faraway world. For a rustic like me to experience this sensation was enough by itself to make our short stay in Kamakura worthwhile.

**Iso Mutsu** from *Kamakura: Fact and Legend*

*Enoshima*

The little island of Enoshima – the sacred island dedicated to the sea goddess Benten, whose name is a talisman conjuring ineffaceable visions of beauty to the memory of the pilgrim – rises from the blue ocean some quarter of a mile from the mainland at Katase. This small town, although apparently of no great significance possesses more than one claim to distinction. Upon its shores the drama of the Mongolian ambassadors was enacted in 1275 and 1279 – the second party of envoys having been actually beheaded upon the beach; the nearby temple of Ryūkōji is immortalised and has even been the unceasing goal of the devout by its association with the saint Nichiren, who so barely escaped martyrdom by the intervention of the celestial thunderbolt within its precincts (1271); moreover, this delectable spot forms the mainland link, and principal approach to the 'mystic island, so full of strange gods and strange presences, so wrapped in the web of story and so little a part of the life of today that one almost expects to see it float out to sea and melt into cloud upon the horizon.'[14]

The best route for pilgrimage to the lovely islet is the main road from Kamakura, which leads through Gokurakuji across the 'velvety, soundless, brown stretch of sand known as Shichirigahama – Seven Ri beach, where a turn in the path suddenly reveals a panorama that is beyond description. Before one, glittering in the sunlight, lie the vast waters of Sagami Bay, whose western barrier of the Hakone peaks, culminating in the purple Amagi-san, is crowned by the snows of the Queen of Mountains high in the blue vaults of heaven forms the setting of the dusky embowered mass floating in haze and sunshine out at sea, the island of the tortoise, Enoshima.'[15]

Like Mont St. Michel in Normandy, and its namesake St Michael's Mount in Cornwall, Enoshima is only completely surrounded by the

14  Iso Mutsu is quoting Mary Crawford Fraser's book *A Diplomat's Wife in Japan*
15  Ditto

waves at high tide; when the waters abate, a stretch of sand is revealed, rendering it possible to cross to the island dry shod. However, as the pine-clad promontory of Katase is approached, it becomes apparent that a more permanent link with the mainland is informed by a long bridge of planks, swaying with the waves, and of such light construction that in the many tempests that attack this wild coast, it's a frequent occurrence that this frail causeway suffers damage and is washed away by the fury of the storm.

The march of progress, that is so fatal to Old World romance, scattering the fabled gods with the clang of its iron-shod feet, is already threatening the abode of Benten. Rumour whispers that the problem is afloat concerning the realising of a new approach, wrought of steel and concrete, permanent, storm defying and capable of hurling defiance at Neptune in his most ominous moods – and an electric car depositing the pilgrims at the very portals of the shrine of the sea goddess! Apropos of which, the number of visitors to Enoshima during the year 1920 amounted to the large figure of 400,000.

In bygone centuries Enoshima seems to have been completely isolated from the coast. According to an ancient record Azumakagami compiled (1180–1266) on the 15th day in the first month of Kenpo (1216), in accordance with a manifestation of the goddess, the ocean receded upon either side leaving a dry path from the island to the mainland and rendering it possible for worshippers to proceed on foot.

**Kaori Shoji** from *Shōnan Beach mystique evaporates upon arrival*

It's here: the season of *mizu nurumu* (water loosening) when one's thoughts turn to things ocean-like: surf and sand and this year's *ichiban kawaii mizugi* (the cutest bathing suit).

For those living in and around Tokyo, this often means piling into a car and driving down to the Shōnan area where lush green mountains offset the waves of the great *taiheiyō* (Pacific), fragrant bougainvillea trees sway in the breeze and local surfers cruise by on mountain bikes with boards tucked under their arms.

Ah, Shōnan. How wonderful the word sounds to ears that have listened to nothing but office and street noises for a whole miserable winter, how sunny and gloriously colorful are the images that persist at the back of one's otherwise tired brain? The truth is, though, that Shōnan, like a lot of other pleasurable things in the Kantō region, is largely a mirage glimpsed in the asphalt wasteland of dreary buildings. It's a fantasy product, a marketing concept. Or as my friend Gen-chan, a local Shōnan *saafaa* (surfer) likes to say: *Shōnan wa iku made ga tanoshii* (Shōnan is great until you get there).

Gen-chan has a point. But by the time one actually gets a full-length view of the sea and feels the sun pouring on one's upturned face and the breeze flapping through the front of one's T shirt - the three most palpable sensations of a Shōnan trip – well, the truth is that two-and-a-half hours or more have gone by, and the car is locked in Shōnan-bound traffic with millions of other Tokyo folks with the same idea, not to mention the same music on the *caasute*. And of course we all need to use the bathroom, but the chances of finding a legitimate parking space real soon are much slimmer than a *mizugi* (swimwear) model.

And later, when one finally plunks down on to the (nearly black) sand it's invariably next to a mound of tangled brown *kaiso* (seaweed) and an empty beer bottle. Gigantic and hostile crows circle overhead, ready to swoop down on anyone with less than a solid grip on their *onigiri* (rice balls). The great *taiheiyo* is that singular Shōnan shade of concrete gray.

So Shōnan is less a resort getaway than a state-of-mind. We all love to love it, but *Shōnan no genjitsu* (the reality of Shōnan) has never quite gelled with the *Shōnan no imeeji* (the image of Shōnan) we carry in our hearts.

Even the *jimo-pe* (locals) say living here has never been easy – Gen-chan talks of the high tax rate (Kamukura city has the highest in Japan); incredible damp and *kabi-kusasa* (mildew smells) that enshroud the whole area during the rainy season; the gridlock on the coastal freeways; the cacophony of the motorbike gangs that burn up and down the streets on weekday nights and the general lack of privacy that comes with living in a tourist hot spot. He also reports that the amount of trash left behind by tourists and *oka-safa* (weekend, or landlocked surfers) has doubled in the last ten years. The Shōnan portrayed by the media is a perfect collage of sunny skies and crowded but gentle beaches where families and couples toss frisbees and walk expensive pedigree dogs. Ancient Kamakura temples complement the beach and fishing culture, and classy cafés offer the sort of laidback atmosphere that's impossible to duplicate in Tokyo. Life is slow and beautiful. On summer nights one can imagine being a character from Haruki Murakami's earlier novels, and stroll over to the neighbourhood bar in shorts and flip-flops to cool one's tender *hiyake* (tan).

# 4

# The Izu Peninsula

'Trailing in the wind,
The smoke from Mount Fuji
Melts into the sky.
So too my thoughts –
unknown their resting-place.

SAIGYŌ

Izu is the lozenge-shaped peninsula that drops out into the Pacific
Ocean just south of the Kamakura peninsula. Formed out of the lava
flows from Mount Fuji, it has been dubbed 'the Japanese Riviera',
perhaps also because it is home to many spa towns, hot springs,
camellia forests, sacred mountains and even vineyards. It was a remote
place of exile for monks in the twelfth century, a major port during the
Edo period (1603–1867), when stone and timber was shipped down
river from the slopes of Mount Fuji at the top of the peninsula and
other major centres, then loaded up on boats to go to Edo for the
construction of the shogun's castle.

In 1853, Commodore Perry arrived at Edo bay from the USA in his
black ships, his *kurofune*, demanding open trade with Japan. His first
treaty, concluded a year later at Shimoda in Izu, opened up the ports
of Hakodate in Hokkaidō and Shimoda first of all. Around the port
now there are many monuments dedicated to the memory of Perry
and his successor, the American consul Townsend Harris who arrived
in 1856 to ratify the treaty, much to the disgust of his Japanese hosts
who wished the Americans had not returned.

Harris recorded his impressions of Shimoda in his diary:

It is situated on a plain at the opening of a fertile valley. Its name is

probably derived from its low position, Shimoda, meaning Low
Field. It is compactly built, and regularly laid out. The streets are
about twenty feet in width and are partly macadamized and partly
paved. A few of the houses of the better classes are of stone . . . But
whether of stone or of plaster on a wooden frame, the walls of most
buildings were covered by black tiles, more than a foot square laid
out diagonally and then framed in a heavy moulding of white
plaster. These handsome black-and-white walls pleased the people
of Shimoda, and moreover they were resistant to fire and tight
against the cold west wind of winter. *Namakokabe* is the name for
the tile and plaster walls of a Shimoda house.[16]

The seventeen-year-old girl Tojin Okichi abandoned her husband
Tsurumatsu in order to work for Harris. After Harris left, she tried to
return to Tsurumatsu but he divorced her, and she later drowned
herslf. The story was said to be the basis for *Madame Butterfly* by
Puccini.

Further up the coast is the town of Itō, where Will Adams or 'Anjin
Adams' (see Nagasaki chapter) built a shipyard and the first great sea-
going ships to cross the ocean, for Tokugawa Ieyasu, in 1605. Adams
himself went on diplomatic missions to the Philippines and to China,
was granted samurai status and a Japanese wife, as well as an estate.
Every August in Itō there is the *Anjin matsuri*.

Izu is a supremely volcanic area, with over 2,300 hot springs.
Shuzenji is the famous resort where Natsume Sōseki's anti-hero Ichirō
in the novel of the same name, comes to bathe. There is also a temple
which Kōbō Daishi founded in 807.

But Atami was always a place for pleasure-seekers including Mary
Crawford Fraser, a diplomat's wife who came here to get over her
rheumatism in 1889. Nowadays, thousands of *salariman* (or business-
men) come here to escape Tokyo to relax since it is just half an hour
from Tokyo's Shinagawa station. Although the town is now filled with

16 *The complete journal of Townsend Harris: first American consul and minister to
   Japan*/introduction and notes by Mario Emilio Consenza with a preface by
   Douglas Macarthur., C. E. Tuttle Co, 1959.

high-rises and the blaring sounds of karaoke, you can still see the forests of camphor and ferns that delighted Fraser.

The peninsula also gave its name to a prize-winning collection of short stories, *The Izu Dancer*, by Nobel Laureate Yasunari Kawabata, which won him critical acclaim in 1926. The title story is the romantic tale of a nineteen-year-old student from Tokyo, who meets a troop of Kabuki actors from Ohshima, an island off the coast, and they invite him to join them.

Mount Fuji lies at the head of the Izu peninsula. The poems in the *Man'y'oshu* or *Collection of Ten Thousand Leaves* (see Nara chapter), show how the mountain has been feted throughout history, and revered as 'this occultly dwelling god'. Shinto *torii* gates at the entrance to the mountain denote that you are in fact entering a vast natural temple. The mountain is still an active volcano and, after its eighteenth-century eruption is, according to seismologists, due for another explosion fairly soon. Lady Sarashina (the tenth-century traveller) saw fire at the summit. Although there are many great descriptions of the mountain by foreigners and Japanese alike, it was such a poetic cliché by the seventeenth century that Matsuo Bashō famously wrote a poem about not seeing the mountain.

**Oliver Statler** from *Shimoda Story*

*August 21, 1856*
From Shimoda town one cannot watch the sun rise out of the sea. Mountains rim the harbour and from Shimoda one looks out not to the open sea but across the harbour to the village of Kakisaki. The sun rises over the mountains behind Kakisaki and its glow hits first the mountains behind Shimoda. It touches the cone of Shimoda Fuji, local miniature of the great mountain. It caresses the rounded twin crowns Shimoda people call the Breasts. It slides down the ridges of the temples that stand along the lower slopes. At last it washes over the town, warming the houses and flooding into the streets.

By that hour, on a morning something more than a century ago, the town was stirring from a summer night's sleep. The night watch-

men had put away the clappers which had sounded reassurance
through the dark hours. Now and again the stillness was broken by the
racket of shutters being opened. A few breakfast fires had been lighted
and were sending tendrils of smoke into the pale sky. Crews of fishing
boats were gathering their gear to go after bonito fish. Stonecutters
were yawning and stretching. A farmer splashed cool water on his
face; in those days there were paddy fields and a farming village
between Shimoda and its row of temples.

But the centre of town, the area of shops and ships' inns, still seemed
drained of life. The shutters of the pharmacy Nagasakiya were closed;
above them sunlight slanted against the only Western letters to be seen
in Shimoda: a sign advertising a Dutch remedy of great repute. The
gate was barred to the house of Dr Asaoka Kyoan, the town's most
distinguished physician, who had studied not only Chinese but also
Western medicine. The sprawling establishment of Wataya Kichibei –
broker, shipowner, dealer in stone and charcoal – was quiet. No one
stirred around the town office, the harbour master's office, or the
Goyosho, the handsome new building from which this area was
administered. In the willow-tree pleasure quarter a solitary roisterer,
risen from a warm bed, moved unsteadily homeward past bars and
restaurants closed and withdrawn against the dawn. He paused at one
corner, braced himself against the cool stone wall of a shop and while
relieving himself, sang to the empty streets, only a little out of tune:

> 'A long stay at Shimoda of Izu –
> Oh, give it up!
> For your striped purse will soon be empty.'

It was an old song and well-worn, for of all Shimoda's products, its
most famous was feminine hospitality – more famous even than the
stone from its quarries, much of which had gone to the shogun's
capital at Edo to form the massive ramparts and foundations of his
great castle. Shimoda's hospitality was not for highway travellers: the
town was cut off from the heart of the country by almost the full
length of the long and mountainous Izu Peninsula. Shimoda's
hospitality was for those who travelled the sea, for the crews of the
hundreds of small unwieldy ships which kept the city folk of Edo –

today called Tokyo – supplied with rice to eat, sake to drink, and lumber to rebuild after their frequent fires.

Once Japanese ships had ranged the China Sea and Indian Ocean. Then came the edicts of the early seventeenth century, and isolation. Foreigners were forbidden to enter Japan, except that a few Chinese and fewer Dutch were permitted a trickle of trade at Nagasaki because it suited the government of Edo to have a source of information about what was going on in the world. And, by those same edicts Japanese were prohibited from going aboard. After that, the country had only coastal vessels. By dictate, they were built with a flat bottom, an open stern to accommodate a great retractable rudder, and but one sail, rigged so they could go only before the wind. In bad weather they had to seek refuge in some harbour.

On the long run between Ōsaka and Edo, Shimoda was the most famous port of refuge. Further, it once had been the checkpoint for all ships bound for Edo – a checkpoint, like the barrier gates astride the highways, to guard against contraband weapons being smuggled into the capital. There were stories of times when the little ships were so densely moored that a man could walk clear across the harbour on their decks, a full mile, all the way from Kakisaki to Shimoda. And each ship paid the town a harbour tax, and its sailors spent their money ashore. Establishment of that checkpoint in 1616 climaxed a series of events which brought Shimoda its era of greatest prosperity. A few years earlier the government had begun to exploit a nearby lode of gold: mines were dug, a boom town mushroomed and the gold had to be shipped out through Shimoda. Then came the decision to reconstruct Edo Castle on a scale hitherto undreamt of: Izu's quarries rang with the chisels of stonecutters struggling to keep up with the demand, while three thousand vessels bore huge blocks from Shimoda to Edo. In one feverish decade Shimoda burgeoned from a nondescript village to a bustling town.

Shimoda people preferred however not to think about a year one century later – the black year of 1720 when the checkpoint was shifted to Uraga, on the inner Bay of Edo and in truth a more logical location. Shimoda's prosperity went with it. Edo Castle was built, the quarries were no longer busy and the gold mines had played out.

The town drifted somnolent through the next century and more. It came alive only in winter when the rough seas and contrary winds around Izu might fill its harbour. Each ship had its designated inn. The ships of Awa Province had for generations called in at the Awaya, and ships from Ise, at the Iseya. Often it was the mistress and maids of the inn who rowed out to welcome the captain and the crew. Their greeting set the tone; sailors called Shimoda, 'the harbour of women', 'the harbour of song'. And with many masts in view, the town would become cheerful again. Night sounds of revelry would spill into the streets to mingle with the songs of strolling musicians and gray beards would compare that winter with legendary ones when a man could cross the harbour on the decks of ships.

**Mary Crawford Fraser** from *A Diplomat's Wife in Japan*

*Atami, August 1st, 1889*

The constant rain of the early summer gave me so much rheumatism that at last Doctor Baelz ordered me to boil it away in a course of hot baths. The heat in Tokyo has been rather wearing and although we had decided not to make a solemn *villeggiatura* this year, I was delighted to get away and to see something of the country, and as it was my first journey inland, everything was pleasantly fresh and interesting.

[...]

*Atami, August 5th, 1889*

The rooms are so full of flowers that I can hardly move. I come in from our expeditions with both hands full, and one of our servants (rather an idle boy) spends three or four hours every day out in the hillsides and brings me little forests of hydrangeas, white and blue and lilac with beautiful bright foliage, and lilies in hundreds, bursting from their stem like white fireworks, the blossoms nearly a foot in diameter, and growing high above my head. The blue hydrangea throws long branches of bloom down the clefts of the rocks, where they look like waterfalls reflecting the sky. The white one reaches farther but separates the clusters more; and they lie like forgotten snowballs dropped in the little angels' play for today is The Feast of Our Lady of the Snows, Sancta Maria ad Nives, and I am reminded of the old picture in Siena where all the court of heaven are standing round her throne with snowballs in their hand. How glad we should be to see a little cool whiteness here!

The heat is overpowering, and I have been seeking refreshment in the green wood of the old temple, behind the town. It stands between the hills and the plain, with the most lovely grove of trees around it that I have ever seen. They have long-pointed shining leaves of the most brilliant green and I think are entered on the civic lists of the forest as *Quercus Acuta*; but who cares about the name? You may be sure it is not the one they call themselves by in those long-whispered conversation that they carry on among the green arches far overhead. Their venerable feet are sunk in a cape of moss and ferns and translucent creepers with leaves like green stars and tendrils soft as a baby's fingers. That brooding peace I have spoke of the other day is in all the wood, and seems to have promised that the ruined temple shall not fall, but crumble dreamily in the sunshine unconscious of its own decay. Quite near it stands a colossal camphor tree (*Cinnamomum camphora*) so old that it has fallen apart with its own weight, and is like two trees in one, the two divisions measuring altogether over sixty feet round. In the odorous brown shadow inside is set a little shrine; but above, all is life and vigour. Every branch is smothered in fresh green foliage, the small pointed leaves shining like newly cut jade and giving out a fine aroma on the warm air. It is supposed to be the largest in Japan; and I think Sydney Lanier away in Baltimore must have seen its waving palace of verdure in his dreams […]

As I have mentioned the little town was crowded with holiday-makers in bright dresses. Among others, I noticed an Englishman, a tall, smart-looking man sitting in the native cotton dress on the step of the teahouse, laughing and chattering in fluent Japanese with a swarm of Atami girls, who all seemed very glad to see him. He looked at us as we passed, with an amused smile and his face seemed a familiar one though I could not put name to him. His dress was poor and common in the extreme. He was probably one of the harmless maniacs who travel everywhere without passports and try to see the country from the Japanese side of life. He must have seen a good deal of it.

**Yasunari Kawabata** from *The Izu Dancer*

With alarming speed, a shower swept toward me from the foot of the
mountain, touching the cedar forests white as the road began to wind
up into the pass. I was nineteen and travelling alone through the Izu
Peninsula. My clothes were of the sort that students wear, dark kimono,
high wooden sandals, a school cap, a book sack over my shoulder. I had
spent three nights at hot springs near the centre of the peninsula, and
now, my fourth day out of Tokyo, I was climbing toward Amagi Pass
and South Izu. The autumn scenery was pleasant enough, mountains
rising one upon another, open forests, deep valleys, but I was excited
less by the scenery than by a certain hope. Large drops of rain began to
fall. I ran on up the road, now steep and winding, and at the mouth of
the pass I came to a teahouse. I stopped short in the doorway. It was
almost too lucky: the dancers were resting inside.

The girl turned over the cushion she had been sitting on and
pushed it politely toward me.

'Yes,' I murmured stupidly as I sat down. Surprised and out of
breath. I found that simple word of thanks caught in my throat.

She sat near me, we were facing each other. I fumbled for tobacco
and she handed me the ashtray in front of one of the other women.
Still I said nothing.

She was perhaps sixteen. Her hair was swept up after an old style I
did not recognize. Her solemn oval face was dwarfed under it, and yet
the face and the hair went well together, rather as in the pictures one
sees of ancient beauties with their exaggerated rolls of hair. Two other
young women were with her, and a man in his mid-twenties, wearing
the livery of a Nagaoka inn. A woman in her forties presided over the
group.

[...]

A heavy rain began to fall from about sunset. The mountains, gray
and white, flattened and lost perspective, and the river grew yellower
and muddier and noisier by the minute. I felt sure that the dancers
would not be out on such a night, and yet I could not sit still. Two,
three times I went down to the bath. My room was dusky. A light hung

in a rectangular opening above the sliding doors separating my room from the next, to serve both rooms.

Then, distant in the rain, I heard the beating of a drum. I slid open the shutters, almost wrenching them from their grooves, and leaned out the window. The drum-beat seemed to be coming nearer. The rain, driven by a strong wind, lashed at my head. I closed my eyes and tried to concentrate on the drum, on where it might be, whether it would be coming this way. Presently I heard a *shamisen*, and now and then a woman's voice calling to someone, or a loud burst of laughter. The dancers had been called to a party in the restaurant across from their inn it seemed. I could distinguish two or three women's voices and three or four men's. Soon they will be finished there, I told myself, and they will come here. The party seemed to go beyond harmless merriment and to approach the rowdy. Now and again a shrill woman's voice came across the darkness like the crack of a whip. I sat rigid, more and more on edge, staring out through the open shutters. At each drum-beat I felt a surge of relief. 'Ah, she's still there. She's still there and playing the drum.' Each time the drumming stopped, the silence seemed intolerable. It was as though I were being driven under by the beating of the rain.

For a time there was a confusion of footsteps – were they playing tag, were they dancing? And then, complete silence. I glared into the darkness, trying to see what the silence might mean. What would she be doing, who would be sullying her through the rest of the night?

I closed the shutters and lay down. My chest was painfully tight. I went down to the bath again and splashed about violently. The rain stopped, the moon came out. The autumn sky, washed by the rain, shone crystalline in the distance. I thought for a moment of running out barefoot to look for her. It was after two.

**From** The Man'yōshū: Anonymous

*'Poem about Mount Fuji'*
Rising between the lands of Kai
And Suruga,
Where the waves draw near,
Is Fuji's lofty peak.
It thwarts the very clouds
From their path.
Even the birds
Cannot reach its summit
On their wings.
There, the snow drowns the flame
And the flame melts the snow.
I cannot speak of it,
I cannot name it,
This occultly dwelling god!
It envelops the waters
That we call a sea
The Sea of Seas.
The river called Fuji
That men must cross
Is but a stream of this mountain
God who dwells there,
Defender of the sun-source,
The land of Yamato,
Treasure of a mountain!
Though I gaze on Fuji's lofty peak
In Suruga
I never tire.

## Matsuo Bashō

> falling mist . . .
> the day when Mount Fuji is unseen,
> most fascinating![17]

## Engelbert Kaempfer from *Japan: Tokugawa Culture Observed*

### *From Hamamatsu to Edo: Suruga*

This town [Yoshiwara] is the closest we came on our journey to the said mountain Fuji: according to the compass, (which deviates five degrees to the East here), the distance in six Japanese miles in a straight line, but believed to be seven miles along the winding road to the foot of the mountain or the surrounding fields and a further six miles through the snow to the top. Similar to Mount Tenerife, it is of incredible height, so that in comparison the surrounding mountains look like low hills. Therefore the mountain served us for many miles as a point of reference, along the way and when plotting the map.

The mountain is conical in shape and so even and beautiful that one may easily call it the most beautiful mountain in the world, even though it is totally devoid of grasses and plants and the greater part of it is covered with a white mantle of snow most of the time. The snow disappears as the heat of the sun increases until it covers only the uppermost peak, but rarely disappears altogether. According to those who have climbed the mountain, there is a hollow, hilly area at the top, with a deep hole filled with water. Formerly flames and ashes surged forth from there and this finally produced this hill-like elevation. The snow always drifts up there from side to side as it is blown about by the wind, so that it looks as if it were smoke. Since the wind never stops at the top, but is constantly blowing, it is worshipped there, and the people climb the mountain to pay their respects to

---

17 *Records of a Weather-Exposed Skeleton*, 1684, translated by www.worldhaiku-review.org

Aeolo, the god of wind. The ascent takes three days, but the descent three hours, thanks to a reed or wicker basket, which is tied around the hips to slide down the sand in summer and the snow in winter. The *yamabushi*, or mountain priests, belong to the order of the wind god, and the formula they repeat when begging is the word Fuji *sama*. The poets and painters of this country never end praising and portraying the beauty of this mountain.

After we had our meal, we went on our way and after half a mile reached the miserable village of Moto Yoshiwara of about three hundred inhabited huts, scattered over half a mile along a stretch of sand road and fields. Here many village children came up to our horses and *kago*, asking for donations in return for their amusing antics, performing endless cartwheels and romping some twenty or thirty steps ahead of us. We threw plenty of money in their direction and watched with pleasure as they pushed each other over snatching the money from the sand. People generally get a string of *kansen* in Yoshiwara to give some pleasure to those poor village children, who often accompany the travellers for half a mile, or as long as coins are thrown. *Kansen* is a flat metal coin, the size of a three *groschen* piece, worth a penny. It has a hole in the middle, through which they thread a string so that they may take it along attached to their horse.

**Basil Hall Chamberlain** from *Things Japanese*

The following miscellaneous items will perhaps interest some readers: – The Japanese are fond of comparing Fuji to an inverted fan – Fuji is inhabited by a lovely goddess named *Ko-no-hana-saku-ya-hime*, which being interpreted, means 'The Princess who Makes the Blossoms of the Trees to Flower'. She is called Sengen or Asama, and numerous shrines are dedicated to her in many provinces – The peasants of the neighbouring countryside often speak of Fuji simply as O Yama, 'the honourable Mountain', or 'the mountain', instead of mentioning its proper name. One of Hokusai's best picture books is his *Fuji Hyakkei*, or *Hundred Views of Mount Fuji*, executed when he had reached the age of seventy-six. In it, the grand mountain stands depicted from every point of view and under every possible circumstance and a few impossible ones; for instance, the artist gives us Fuji in the process of being ascended by a dragon. Copies of this book are common, but good ones are rather scarce. According to a popular superstition, the ashes brought down during the day by the tread of pilgrims' feet reascend spontaneously at night . . . Steam sufficiently hot to cook an egg still issues from several spots on the crater lip – the Japanese have enriched their language by coining words for special aspects of their favourite mountain. Thus Kagami Fuji, literally 'mirror Fuji' means the reflection of Fuji in Lake Hakone. Kage Fuji or 'shadow Fuji' denotes a beautiful phenomenon – the gigantic shadow cast by the cone at sunrise on the sea of clouds and mist below. Hidari Fuji, 'left-handed Fuji', is the name given to the mountain at the village of Nango for the reason that that is the only place on the Tōkaidō where, owing to a sharp twist in the road, Fuji appears on the left hand of the traveller bound from Tokyo to Kyoto, instead of on his right.

# 5

# Chūbū

Near the old castle
A traveller grieves among white clouds.
Green chickweed hasn't sprung yet.
There's no young grass.
On the nearby hills a covering of silver:
The light snow is dissolving in the daylight.
Warmer brightness
No scents float from the fields.
A slight mist hangs over March.
A sparse hint of green shows new wheat.

SHIMAZAKI TŌSON

Chūbū is the mountainous region of central Honshū which incorporates the Japan Alps, stretching from Nagoya on the Pacific through Gifu to Fukui and Kanazawa on the Japan Sea. Nagano prefecture is also part of the Alps, made famous by its hosting of the 1998 Winter Olympics.

In October 1689, Bashō started a journey from Gifu through the mountains, which he recorded in his Sarashina diary. Gifu is an old castle town, most famous for *ukai* or cormorant fishing. After some emotional farewell drinks, Bashō set out on his way. The journey took him along the old Kiso road or Nakasendō, the inner road, which stretches along over five hundred kilometres of mountain country from Lake Biwa, through Nagoya and Gifu, Karuizawa and on to Tokyo. Bashō was journeying to Matsumoto, another *jōkōmachi* or castle town on the way north.

The Kiso valley passes through many dangerous places, 'one

terrifying and dreadful moment succeeded another, until finally I got off the horse and put the servant on instead,' writes Bashō. He passes through fantastically named gorges such as Nazame no Toko, 'The Rocks of Awakening' which are curiously shaped boulders rising from the Kiso river, so-called because the legendary fisherman Urashima Tarō was said to have woken from his long sleep here.[18] Kiso Valley is also famous for chestnuts.

Bashō takes a different route to Sarashina, writing, 'The moon of the sixteenth/And still in Sarashina Country/it would seem!' He stays for the moon-viewing and writes of the legendary Obasute ('Dump your Elderly'), mountain. In a legend dramatised by the father of Noh drama, Zeami (see Kyoto chapter), a man takes his decrepit old aunt up the mountain, with the intention of abandoning her at the back of the gorge. But when he sees how she has carefully arranged a trail for him to find his way back down, he decides against it and takes her back with him.

Lesley Downer describes the awesome procession of nineteenth century Edo period Princess, Princess Kazu, travelling through the Kiso valley to marry shogun Iemochi when she was only fifteen.

Magome, a *juku*, or post town, is further along the Kiso road on the way to the Shinshū mountains in present day Nagano-ken, the high Japan Alps. Magome was the home of Shimazaki Tōson (1872–1943) whose books, *Before Dawn* and *The Broken Commandment* are set around Nagano-ken. Tōson's father kept one of the *honjin* or stopping houses for travelling dignitaries. Accommodation in post-towns was strictly graded according to caste and travel was supposed to be restricted to officials or *daimyo* travelling because of *sankin kotai*, the law of alternate attendance in Edo. Tōson's poem about Komoro castle (above), another fifteenth-century castle in Nagano, also celebrates the new wheat that is used to make the famous *shinshu* soba, served cool in summer. Lesley Downer describes a great Edo-period *daimyo* procession along the Kiso road, one of the great spectacles of the period.

Nagano people are historically renowned for their devotion to

18 Urashima Tarō was lured down to the sea by Ōtohime, the Sea Princess, for decades of entertainment until, when he 'awoke' and returned to his home on land, his loved ones were all dead.

Pure Land Buddhism, also known as Jōdo or chanting Amida Buddha. There is a statue that stood in Zenkōji temple from King Paekche of Korea in the seventh century. Ushimatsu, the hero of *The Broken Commandment*, spends a lot of time at the local Jōdo Buddhist monastery.

**Bashō** 'The Journey to Sarashina' from *The Pleasures of Japanese Literature*

The insistent autumn moon kept stirring in my heart a longing to see the moon at Obasute Mountain in the village of Sarashina. My friend Etsujin[19] also urged me to share with him the pleasures of travel. The Kiso Road leads through remote mountains where the roads are steep, and *Kakei*,[20] fearing that the journey might prove too much for us, sent a servant along. These companions were determined to help me in any way they could, but having had no experience of travel, as it would seem, they were both quite helpless. Everything went topsy-turvy and utterly disorganized, but it all made for a delightful journey.

At a certain place we met a priest of about sixty years, a man with nothing of interest or humour about him. He was trudging along in grim silence, his body bent by the weight on his back. He was panting heavily, and his feet advanced in mincing little steps. My companions, moved to pity, bundled the things we were shouldering together with the priest's burden, piled them on a horse, and set me on top of the lot.

High mountains and curiously formed peaks hung in layers above our heads. In the valley a great river flowed; below us dropped an abyss that seemed a thousand fathoms deep. There was not a bare foot of level ground, and it was most alarming to be in the saddle. One terrifying and dreadful moment succeeded another, until finally I got off the horse and put the servant on instead.

We passed the hanging bridge over the gorge, the Rocks of Awakening and various other places. Next came the Monkey's

---

19  Etsujin (b. 1656) was a dyer in Nagoya. He accompanied Bashō on his trip to the village of Sarashina
20  Kakei (1648–1716) was a physician in Nagoya.

Racecourse and Tachi Pass, as we followed what they called the Forty-eight Turnings. The road twisted and turned so often that I felt as though we were winding our way up into the clouds. Even the two of us on foot felt so dizzy and frightened that our legs trembled under us, but the servant was calmly dozing on the back of the horse, absolutely untouched by fear. Very often he almost fell off, sending a chill of fear through me as I looked up at him from behind. The turbulent world must appear even so to the mind of the Buddha and when we reflect that change in its inexorable swiftness visits all men, we can see why 'the whirlpool of Awa is free of wind and waves'.

At night we found lodgings. I took out my brush and lay on the floor with my eyes shut underneath the lamp. I beat my head and moaned as I tried to get down on paper the sights of the day which I had thought of turning into verse, as well as various *hokku* on which I had not quite finished working. While I was so engaged the old priest, imagining that I was depressed by the journey or worried about something, attempted to comfort me. He told me all about the holy places he had visited as a pilgrim when he was young, and recounted the innumerable wonders of Amida. Then followed story on story about things which he considered to be remarkable. The result was that my poetic impulse was blocked, and it was quite impossible for me to compose a single verse.

The moonlight, from which I was distracted by his chatter, was streaming in from among the trees through a hole in the wall, and from here and there came the sound of scarecrow clappers and the voices of deer hunters. Autumn could not have been more melancholy.

'Well,' I cried, 'let's have something to drink at this feast of moon-light.' Wine cups were produced about twice the circumference of normal ones and of a coarse lacquer flecked with gold leaf. A Kyoto gentleman would have found such a cup in deplorable taste and refused even to touch it, but I felt surprisingly elated, as though I held a cup of chalcedony or of finest jade, no doubt because it suited the place [...]

> Inside your surface
> I'd like to sprinkle gold leaf
> Moon at the inn! [...]

I have at times been tempted on hearing of Shirara and Fukiage, and this year I kept thinking how I should like to see the moon at Obasute. I departed from the province of Mino on the eleventh day of the eighth month. The road was long and the days left before the full moon were few, so I had to set out by night and not sleep till evening, grass for my pillow. My plans did not go amiss: I arrived in the village of Sarashina on the night of the full moon. The mountains stretched in a South-westerly direction, about one *ri* South of the village of Yawata. It is not exceptionally tall, and has not even curiously formed boulders. But the mountain's appearance is filled with deep melancholy. I could understand why they said it is 'hard to be consoled' here. I felt vaguely depressed and, even as I wondered why anyone should have abandoned an old woman, my tears began to fall.

**Shimazaki Tōson** from *The Broken Commandment*

Ushimatsu would never forget the loneliness of that journey. Compared with the last time he had gone home, in the summer of the year before last, he felt himself to be utterly changed. Two years – not long, perhaps, but for Ushimatsu time enough for the great crisis of his life to have begun. Some, in different circumstances, go placidly through the world, changing but only subconsciously: for Ushimatsu the inner convulsion had been both violent and deeply felt. For the moment, at least, there was no need to be on his guard. Drinking freely of the crisp, dry air as he walked along the bank of the Chikuma River, he gave himself up to brooding on his uncertain destiny and wondering at the upheavals it had brought him so far. The waters of the Chikuma, a muddy yellowish green, flowing silently toward the distant sea; the squat willow trees, leafless now, cowering on its banks; river, trees, mountains, the unchanged landscape intensified his gloom still further. Sometimes he all but threw himself down by the roadside to weep in secret among the dead grasses, in the hope of lightening even a little his burden of near-despair. But he could not; his heart was too heavy, too tightly locked in darkness to be able to seek such easy relief.

Groups of travellers drifted past him, some with tear-stained faces, haunted by the memory of better days, haggard like starving dogs; some walking barefoot, in grimy *kimonos*, looking for work; a sunburnt father and son on a pilgrimage of penitence, chanting a sad hymn, the hardships of their journey transmuted into austerities of saving power; a company of strolling musicians in slatternly hats of straw, masquerading as innocent victims of the world, begging as they strummed a love song on their *samisen*. Ushimatsu watched them all, comparing their lot with his own: how wretched his life, how enviable their freedom!

Yet even for him, every step away from Iiyama seemed a step toward freedom. Gradually, as he tapped the grey earth of the Northern Highway in bright sunshine, now climbing gentle hills, now winding through fields of mulberry or straggling villages, sweating, his throat parched, socks and leggings white with dust, Ushimatsu began, paradoxically, to feel refreshed. Branches of persimmon trees by the roadside sagged under their load of ripening yellow globes; in one field, soy pods swelled; millet heads dropped, full-eared in another; in others, already harvested green shoots of wheat were sprouting. He heard farmers singing, birds chirruping – for the joy of 'little June', as the mountain dwellers call their Indian summer. Free of mist, that day even the high peaks of the Kosha massif revealed themselves in their splendour; from the valleys between them, blue smoke climbed into the sky from charcoal burners' fires.

Just past Kanizawa, a rickshaw with a fashionably dressed passenger overtook Ushimatsu. He recognized Takayanagi Risaburo, the politician who had made that speech at the Imperial birthday celebration the day before. This was the time of year, he recalled, when prospective Diet candidates began to work up publicity for themselves and their views; Takayanagi was no doubt off on a country tour to prepare the ground for the next election. Riding past with a pompous air, he gave Ushimatsu a supercilious glance but did not speak to him. Two or three hundred yards further on, he looked back again; but Ushimatsu took no particular notice.

As the sun climbed gradually higher, the plain of Minochi unfolded before Ushimatsu's eyes, spreading out on both sides of the Chikuma, its sandy topsoil, washed down from the upstream, testifying to the violence of the spring floods. Fields stretched away as far as he could see, interrupted here and there by clumps of zelkova trees. Plain and mountains seemed to be inhaling the deep blue November air, witnesses to nature's vitality even in the months of withering and decay. Ushimatsu hurried on, eager to make the best speed possible upstream to Chiisagata, to Nezu, drawn always by the blue skies that shone like a sea of light above his beloved home.

It was two o'clock in the afternoon when he reached Toyono, where he had to catch the train. Takayanagi, after arriving earlier by rickshaw, had apparently been waiting for the same train; a few minutes before it was due he came out of the tea house near the station. Where was he going, Ushimatsu wondered. Takayanagi looked at him, evidently asking himself the same question about Ushimatsu; yet he seemed to be taking care their eyes did not meet, as if he were somehow anxious to avoid him. At the ceremony the day before thay had only seen each other, had not been introduced, and neither made any move to speak now.

A warning bell rang; the waiting passengers pressed through the barrier. Belching black smoke, the train, which had come from Naoetsu down on the coast, drew into the little station. Takayanagi pushed through the crowd, opened a door and disappeared inside. Ushimatsu chose a compartment near the engine. Amazed, he recognized one of its occupants.

'Inoko sensei!' He took off his hat and bowed. Inoko too, looked overjoyed at this chance meeting.


**Lesley Downer** from *The Last Concubine*

*Kiso Valley 1861*

Genzaburo worked his way further along the branch, screwing up his eyes and peering into the distance.

'They're coming! They're coming!' he shouted.

In a minute everyone could see the first banners poking above the trees, red, purple and gold, fluttering like petals. Shards of light glanced off the steel tips of standards and lances. The children watched intently, their hearts thumping. They all knew exactly what 'Shita ni iyo!' meant. It was the first lesson they had ever learned. They had all felt their father's big rough hands on their heads, pushing them down on their knees until their faces were in the dirt, and could almost hear their father's voices barking, 'Get down, right now! You'll get yourself killed.'

No one had forgotten the dreadful fate of Sohei the drunkard. A few years earlier, after a few too many sakes he had gone staggering out into the path of a procession. Before anyone could pull him back, a couple of samurai whipped their swords out of their scabbards and cut him down, right there in the street. The villagers lugged his body out of the way in numb silence. It just went to show how cheap life was. The samurai were their masters; they had power of life or death over them. That was how it had always been and how it would always be.

But the banners were still far away. The children gazed and gazed, mesmerized by the thrill of doing something so forbidden and so dangerous.

In the distance tiny figures in blue and black were swarming out of the woods. Shading their eyes, the children made out battalions of soldiers tramping along in close formation, warriors on horseback with the horns on their helmets glinting and long lines of porters humping gleaming lacquered trunks. The figures grew larger as the column of marchers drew nearer. The jangle of the metal rings on the guards' staffs, the shuffle of feet, the crunch of hooves and the ominous chorus – 'Shita ni iyo! Shita ni iyo! Shita ni ... Shita ni ...' – grew louder and louder.

Suddenly the spell was broken. Grabbing each other's hands, tripping over in panic, the children turned and raced helter-skelter down the slope, the babies on the girls' backs bobbing and bouncing.

The mountain that shadowed the village was so high and steep that the first shafts of sunlight had only just begun to pierce the icy air, although it was the hour of the horse and the sun was almost at its height. As they reached the beginning of the street, the children paused for breath. They had never seen it so crowded with people. The rickety inns that lined each side seemed to teeter under the crush. The innkeepers had thrust the slatted doors right back and clouds of wood smoke swirled out of the cavernous interiors. Gangs of bow-legged porters in wadded cotton jackets and leggings hustled in and out, slurping bowls of barley gruel. Grooms grappled with bad-tempered horses no bigger than ponies, strapping saddles on to them and tying straw horseshoes on to their hooves. Other men bobbed through the throng in straw cloaks, like moving haystacks. Many just stood waiting, fondling their long-stemmed pipes. Some were from villages round about and always turned up when porters or grooms were needed, but most were strangers, gnarled men from villages deep in the hollows of the mountains, who had hiked for an entire day to get there.

Standing in the middle of the mob was a tall man with a broad, calm face and a thatch of thick hair tied back like a horse's tail. He was bellowing orders, waving his arms, sending people running here and there. Sachi and the others burrowed through the crowd, ducking under arms, and grabbed his sleeves.

'The princess is coming! The princess is coming!' they chorused.

He grinned down at them and slapped their heads approvingly.

'Good, good,' he barked. 'Now get back inside to your mothers, right now!'

## KANAZAWA

This is one of the major tourist destinations in Japan. It was the home of the Maeda, the lords of Kaga, one of Japan's wealthiest *tozama daimyo* (see Tokyo chapter). In the fifteenth century, there was a peasant uprising here and so the town was ruled for a while by peasant farmers. Gold was also found here, and was the source of the Maeda clan's ascendancy. The clan even illegally manufactured gunpowder, away from the watchful eyes of the shogunate. The town also escaped bombing during the Second World War and it has been promoted for its Edo style samurai houses, luxury goods, as well as artistic galleries and houses. The Kenrokuen, a great Edo period stroll garden, was developed in the 1670s and improved over several generations, including the installation of a special hydraulic system which also benefits the local town. The Kenrokuen, as Alan Booth points out, may be less desirable after the ravages of tourism. There is plenty more to see here including the myriad arts and crafts of Kanazawa: Kutani porcelain, lacquerware, gold leaf, metal leaf, Yuzen dying, Noh theatre, a Honda museum and even a Ninja temple.

**Alan Booth** from *The Roads to Sata: a 2000-mile walk through Japan*

The historic city of Kanazawa is well-used to visitors. It is one of the most frequented tourist centres on the Japan Sea side of the country. In Kanazawa you can see the ruined walls of a sixteenth-century castle, an ancient gateway, a university, temples, shrines, houses that once belonged to samurai, two Kentucky Fried Chicken outlets, and a shop that serves thirty-four varieties of doughnut. In the underground shopping arcades taped birds twitter and between the Mode Shop and the Mistress Shop, there is a small queue of people waiting patiently to use the *terefon kyapusuru* 'telephone capsule'. Street signs abound in English and Russian (Irkutsk is one of Kanazawa's six sister cities), and many of those street signs direct you toward this proud town's chief attraction: a landscape garden called Kenrokuen, which, the official guidebook notes, is 'one of the three most beautiful gardens in Japan'.

The name Kenrokuen means Park of the Six Virtues. These six virtues, the guidebook explains, are its size, its peace, its strength, its age, the impressive view one can obtain from it of the city, and its careful blending of natural objects such as ponds, trees, streams, and stones.

It is certainly large. When one thinks of Japanese landscape gardens, one tends to think of it in miniature – of the tiny rock or moss gardens that nest inside Kyoto temples. Kenrokuen is far larger than these, and while the temple gardens are meant strictly for contemplation, you can stroll along the pathways of Kenrokuen as you would through an English park. The garden is built on elevated ground, so the view it affords of the city is not a bad one. A European might not consider Kenrokuen old. It was laid out in 1822, and in Europe there are parks and gardens that predate it by several centuries. But here in Japan, where fires and earthquakes frequently ravish the cities, and where, consequently, many of the most famous landmarks have had to be rebuilt in modern times, anything that has stood for a hundred years can claim to be venerably 'old'.

You can experience a little of Kenrokuen's peace by looking at the photographs in the guidebook. The ponds are unruffled as they mirror the cherry blossoms from the deep blue irises that crowd the paths in early summer. Above the largest pond stands a little teahouse where Lord Maeda, the *daimyo* of Kanazawa, might have sat on an evening in late September improvising poems about the autumn moon. In a sense the guidebook is right about age, for here again, as in the gardens of Kakunodate, age is a matter of sensation, not of years. The stones, the moss, the dark rocks that look as if they have grown inch by slow inch in their places – these impart to the garden its feeling of timelessness, and this in turn inspires in the viewer a sense of peace.

## FUKUI

Further along the Sea of Japan coast lies Fukui, not a hotspot on the tourist trail, but interesting historically because this is where W. E. Griffis, once the standard interpreter of Japan to Americans, came to teach in the 1870s when the school was housed in the former castle. The subject he had been called to teach, chemistry, was hardly known in Japan at the time. Griffis was happy with his lot: 'I can study and be ordained, experience the grand opportunities of culture, travel and good climate, study on theology but collect materials to write a book. I can support my family, pay the rent and carpet the floors and send handsome sums home ... '

But if Griffis had illusions about the oriental glamour and opportunities for career advancement in Japan, working in Fukui quickly dashed them. He also realised that it was pointless to aspire to any great career as a foreigner in Japan: 'I quickly realised that the Japanese want helpers and advisers. They propose to keep the "bossing", officering and all the power in their own hands. All this "taking charge of", "being at the head of organizing etc", is sheer daydreaming. Nearly every appointee comes here "to revolutionize" his department, but the Japanese don't want that.' These days a tourist guide would send you out of Fukui central to learn Zazen meditation at Eihei-ji temple, the head of the Sōtō school of Zen Buddhism.

**W. E. Griffis** from *The Mikado's Empire*

*After describing the horses belonging to the grooms of the daimyo, Griffis quotes from the letter he receives from the chief of Fukui, Lord Matsudaira, Fukui Han Chi.*

I greatly rejoice and am obliged to you that you have arrived so promptly from so great a distance over seas and mountains, to teach the sciences to the youth of Fukui. Concerning matters connected with the school and students, the officers in charge of education will duly consult you.

As Fukui is a secluded place, you will be inconvenienced in many respects. Whenever you have need of any thing, please make your wants known without ceremony.

These words struck the key note of my whole reception in Fukui. During the entire year of my residence unceasing kindnesses were showered upon me. From the prince and officers to the students, citizens, and the children, who learned to know me and welcome me with smiles and bows and 'Good morning teacher', I have nothing to record but respect, consideration, sympathy and kindness. My eyes were opened. I needed no revolver, nor were guards necessary. I won the hearts of the people, and among the happiest memories were those of Fukui.

Among those whom I learned to love was the little son of the daimio, a sprightly, laughing little fellow, four or five years old, with snapping eyes, full of fun, and as lively as an American boy. Little Matsudaira wore a gold-hilted short sword in his girdle; while a lad of thirteen, his sword-bearer, attended him, to carry the longer badge of rank. His head was shaved, except a round space like a cap, from which a tiny cue protected. The photograph which his father gave me and the woodcut do but scant justice to the exquisitely delicate brown tint of his skin, flushed with health, his twinkling black eyes, his rosy cheeks, and his arch ways, that convinced his mother that he was the most beautiful child ever born of woman. I often met him in Fukui and later in Tokyo. He was to be educated in the United States.

All the excitement of travel was now over, and I was to see the actual Fukui. I rode around the castle circuit, and out into the city, and for a long distance through its streets. I was amazed at the utter poverty of the people, the contemptible houses, and the tumbledown look of the city as compared with the trim dwelling of an American town. I rode through many streets, expecting at last to emerge into some splendid avenue. I rode in vain; and as I rode, the scales fell from my eyes. There was no more excitement now to weave films of glamour before my vision. I saw through the achromatic glasses of actuality. I realized what a Japanese – an Asiatic city – was. All the houses of wood, the people poor, the streets muddy, few signs of wealth, no splendid shops. Talk of Oriental magnificence and luxury! What nonsense! I was disgusted. My heart sank. A desperate fit of the blues seized me. I returned home, to chew the cud of gloomy reflections.

On the next day my regular work was to begin. Horses were sent again, and I rode to the school, a building which was the citadel of the castle, and was once the residence of the old prince. I was met by the officers of the school in the room I was to occupy. On the table were sponge-cake, oranges, and plum-blossom bouquets, as usual, while the omnipresent tea was served and the tiny pipes were smoked. It was very evident that the men who had been desirous of a teacher of chemistry had very nebulous ideas about what that science was. However they were ready with money and patience, to furnish the necessary apparatus and lecture-room; and our preliminaries being agreed on, I was conducted through the other rooms to see the sights of the school.

I was surprised to find it so large and flourishing. There were in all about eight hundred students, comprised in the English, Chinese, Japanese, medical, and military departments. A few had been studying

English for two or three years, under native teachers who had been in Nagasaki. In the medical department I found a good collection of Dutch books, chiefly medical and scientific, and a fine pair of French dissection models, of both varieties of the human body. In the military school was a library of foreign works on military subjects, chiefly in English, several of which had been translated into Japanese. In one part of the yard young men, book, diagram, or trowel in hand, were constructing a miniature earthwork. The school library, of English and American books – among which were all of Kusakabe's – was quite respectable. In the Chinese school I found thousands of boxes, with sliding lids, filled with Chinese and Japanese books. Several hundred boys and young men were squatted on the floor, with their teachers, reading or committing lessons to memory, or writing the Chinese characters. Some had already cut off their top-knots.

At one end of the buildings were large open places, devoted to physical exercise. Several exhibitions of trial of skill in fencing and wrestling were then made for my benefit. Six of the students repaired to the armoury and put on the defensive mail, to shield themselves in the rough work before them – as Japanese swords are for use with both hands, having double-headed hilts without guards. The foils for fencing are made of round, split bamboo, and a good blow will make one smart, and bruise the flesh. So the fencing-master and students first donned a corselet, with shoulder plates of hardened hide padded within, and heavily padded gauntlets.

# KARUIZAWA

If you take the Hokuriku (Nagano) line from Tokyo, you pass Mount Asama, an active volcano 2,560 metres tall on the border of Gunma prefecture. Bashō also passed this way, and he wrote of the storms that regularly blow up around the mountain, 'A sudden storm/descends on Mount Asama/ Blowing stones all over me.' The mountain indeed erupted in 685, 1108 and in 1783 as well as in 1982, while lesser activity has since been recorded on many occasions and Tokyo University now has a volcanic observation point set up here.

At the foot of the mountain lies Karuizawa which has, since the nineteenth century, been the retreat for Tokyo's diplomatic elite, as it is within striking distance of Tokyo. Diplomatic staff, such as Mary Crawford Fraser, the wife of Hugh Fraser, frequently took up residence here in the mid-nineteenth century.

Karuizawa was one of the few summer resorts in Japan where foreigners and Japanese could mingle on an equal footing. It was also the spot where Crown Prince Akihito (now the Emperor) met his future wife Michiko on the tennis courts in the 1950s. She was a commoner, as opposed to an Imperial relation – just as Princess Chichibu (see Tokyo chapter) was before her. Elizabeth Gray Vining kept a diary of her time in Japan after 1946 as a tutor to Crown Prince Akihito. During this time she used to spend the summers in Karuizawa, which she describes in her 1952 memoir, *Windows for the Crown Prince*, offering a fascinating glimpse of the Japanese reaction to the modernisation of the Imperial family. In the old days, as she recounts, everyone would have turned up wearing black to see the Emperor pass, but now they can wave to him as they would to a normal human being. She also mentions visiting Shōji Hamada, the master potter and friend of British potter Bernard Leach, in his legendary *mingei-kan*, or folk art pottery at Machiko. This was where he built the *noburigama* or climbing kilns into the mountains.

**Mary Crawford Fraser** from *A Diplomat's Wife in Japan*

*Karuizawa, July 1890*

We left Ikao rather regretfully, and, mindful of past experiences, very early in the morning. The road, all shining in the early sunshine, did not seem to be the same one up which we had toiled in rain and darkness two weeks ago. The valleys were green and wet below us, and the hills beyond towered against a brilliantly blue sky just flecked with little clouds of dazzling white. The banks of the road were beautiful with blue lilies and the air was full of songbirds. The Japanese are early risers, and all the little cottage homes were open to the day; in almost all, the business of silk-spinning was going forward for this is the time when the cocoons are ripe, and the precious threads must be saved ere the moth feels his wings and bites his way through to freedom.

It is a pretty sight, when the little brown cottages are full of piles of the delicate cocoons, light as puff-balls and generally a snowy white, or soft flaxen colour, but mingled here and there with large cocoons of a paled yellowish green, the production of a silkworm who lives on a certain species of wild oak. As far as I could gather these cocoons are collected in the woods, and the worm, if reared in captivity, takes to mulberry leaves, and becomes tame like any other silkworm. But this may be only a peasant tradition. The silk reeled from these greenish cocoons is of a coarse and heavy kind, and cannot be used with other varieties. The work of reeling off the thread seems to be done in this part of the world by old people, who can no longer do rough work in the fields. I passed one cottage after another where an old man or woman, sometimes an aged couple, sat on the ground among piles of the soft white balls, reeling off the silk on the roughest kind of hand-wheel, to which it passes from a little trough filled with hot water, constantly renewed. The knotty old fingers manipulate the strands very delicately; but the reeled thread is full of knots and inequalities and could only, I should think, be used for inferior silks. Even in that form it is valuable and the old people's little crop will probably go far towards maintaining them for the rest of the year. [...]

From the top of the pass we descended quickly and easily for a little way, and then stood for a few minutes to gaze at Asama Yama, the great active volcano which dominates all this side of the hills, and has more than once filled the upland plain of Karuizawa with ashy desolation. It rises very grandly from beyond the green foothills, looking far nearer than it really is. Heavy clouds of smoke pour from the crater, which looks from Karuizawa towards the southwest and takes the form of a horizontal tunnel into the mountain as I am told. From that point on the pass there is a wonderful evening effect, as the sun sinks almost behind the peak and rims its heavy clouds of smoke with crimson and gold. We lost it as we plunged into the deep-cut paths below; and when at last we reached our own boundaries, the grey twilight calm was hushing the hills to rest.

And now I am writing in the most lovely study in the world. Over my head the pine branches meet in arches of kindly green; the pillars of my hall are warm brown trunks, roughened in mystic runes by the sun and the wind and full of sweet gums that catch and cling to my hand if I lay it against the bark; underfoot a hundred layers of pine needles have been weaving a carpet so elastic that the weariest foot must press it lightly; and, lest I should want for music, a stream deep running between hedges of wild clematis and white hydrangea and crowding wisteria tangle, sings a cool tune near by, while the hum of happy insects in the air sounds the high note of noon, the hot Eastern noon, when every bird is still.


**Elizabeth Gray Vining** from *Windows for the Crown Prince*

Each summer that I was in Japan the Imperial Household took a cottage for me in Karuizawa about ninety miles northwest of Tokyo, stood on a high plateau in the shadow of Mount Asama, an active volcano, and it is said to have been before the war the most popular summer resort in the Orient.

Our house was a comfortable, rambling one on a hill above the village, surrounded by huge, fragrant balsam trees, through which we got glimpses of distant mountains. Little orange and black and white birds flashed in and out of the balsams by the terrace and sometimes perched on our chairs and tables, cuckoos called in the early morning, and bush-warblers sang all day long. In an earlier house on the site of this one, Rabindranath Tagore had stayed when he visited Japan years ago; many of the poems in his volume, *Stray Birds*, were said to have been written there and are full of the atmosphere of that quiet, fragrant retreat. Esther Rhoads and the LARA staff [21] had a cottage nearby and together we had a house party for ten members of the little meditation group that had been meeting at my house two Sunday afternoons a month since January. I prepared for a strenuous program in the autumn. Near the end of August the princesses came. The three princesses and Miss Natori were spending the holidays at Nasu in the mountains about seventy-five miles to the east of Karuizawa. Because it was well understood that they would grow up to marry commoners and enter upon a life very different from that of the Imperial princesses of the past, Miss Natori was wisely preparing them for the change that lay ahead. This summer they were living not in the Imperial villa at Nasu but in a rented house behind the inn, helping with the housework and learning the ways of ordinary folk. One of the educational features of the summer was a visit of the two older girls to us in Karuizawa.

On Friday morning, we had a breakfast at six and started at seven for Nasu. So early a start was necessary because we were going to make a detour to Mashiko [in Kantō] to see the potteries there. Mr Shōji Hamada was a well known artist whose work had been widely exhibited in Japan about whom I had heard from connoisseurs in the United States; his house at Mashiko was a veritable folk art museum. Tané [22] and I had been there earlier, and our account of it had so interested members of the Imperial Family that it was decided that the princesses were to see it.

It was a beautiful morning after the rain and everything sparkled. We had no large cities to go through, just miles of peaceful farming country with thatch-roofed houses amid the rice fields and dramatic

21 Esther Rhoads was a fellow Quaker. LARA was Licensed Agencies for Relief in Asia
22 Tané Takahashi was Vining's secretary in Japan

mountains against the horizon. Every farmhouse was surrounded by trees and many of them had a crepe myrtle in full bloom.

At Mr Hamada's we ate our picnic lunch and saw the process of pottery making from the primitive wheel to the opening of the kiln. He talked with so much interest and authority about his own pottery and the other kilns in the village, whose smoke went up in several places, that we were late in getting under way again.

Each morning that they were at Nasu that summer of 1947, the Emperor and his two sons went riding before breakfast. A little after seven, Tané and I, in our second-storey front rooms at the inn heard the sound of horses' hooves and hurried out on the little balcony to look.

The inn stood on a hillside, and spread out before it was a vast plain, beyond which ranks of mountains loomed up through the morning mist. Down below our balcony, half hidden now and then by the twisted pines of the inn garden, came a little cavalcade: a groom first, then the Emperor on a white horse, followed by the Crown Prince on another white horse, Prince Masahito on a bay and several more grooms. It was a beautiful sight, the mounted figures against the vast panorama of plain and mountains. There is always something very appealing about the sight of a father riding with his sons, and this had drama besides. When they had passed, I turned to Tané and said, 'Well, now you have looked from above on your Emperor.'

She answered with her eyes shining: 'Mah! Things are different! This is real! This is nice! Before, when the Emperor went out, it was just as if the country was in mourning.'

# 6

# Kyoto

Once when I had gone to Kiyomizu Temple for a retreat
and was listening with deep emotion to the loud cry of the
cicadas, a special messenger brought me a note from Her
Majesty written on a sheet of red tinted Chinese paper:

> Count each echo of the temple bell
> As it tolls the vespers by the mountain's side
> Then you will know how many times
> My heart is beating out its love for you.
>
> *The Pillow Book of Sei Shōnagon*

## HEIAN PERIOD TO EDO PERIOD (794–1867)

No Western travellers had visited Miyako (present-day Kyoto) until
the sixteenth century, but many would have heard tell of it. The
ancient capital was written about by Marco Polo in the thirteenth
century. Writing from China, he said that in the land of Jipangu (*Jih-
pen-kwe* meaning 'land of the rising sun' in Chinese), 'the Emperor
had a golden palace'. Marco Polo didn't try to go to Japan, possibly
put off by the fact that the Mongols had tried to invade in 1274 and
1281. But one of the great motivations for later global explorers was to
discover the land that was home to the Golden Palace, where there
were infinite supplies of gold. It was even an incentive for Columbus
to sail west to the East Indies. Not one to leave a tale unembellished,
Marco Polo includes a passage of complete fabrication alleging that at
one point the Mongols laid seige to and posessed the Imperial city
itself and captured the 'pretty women' there.

Kyoto's one thousand years as capital city was remarkable in Japanese history since before 794, when it was established, no Japanese capital had lasted for more than 75 years. In 784, Nara was abandoned by Emperor Kammu who was escaping the influence of the big Buddhist monasteries greedy for power. A new palace was established at Nagaoka-kyo but it didn't work out, so the Emperor looked for the perfect place to build his new capital and found one at Heian Kyo, as Kyoto was then known. Here the land gently slopes towards Osaka and the sea, bordered north, east and west by mountains, forming a kind of protective bay. The Kamogawa rises north of Kyoto in Sajikigatake moutain and flows south through the city, eventually joining the Yodogawa in Osaka. Nearby Mount Hiei deflects evil forces according to Chinese geomancy or *feng shui*, a system of energy flows. Heian Kyo, the Capital of Peace, is modelled on the Chinese city of Chang-An (present-day Xi'an), a perfect rectangle two-and-a-half miles wide by three-and-a-half miles long around a central palace. From 794, for four centuries the Heian period flourished with unprecedented advances in culture and art.

This was the period of the great scholar sages such as Saichō (767–822), later known as Dengyō Daishi, founder of the Tendai sect of Buddhism which had its headquarters at Enryakuji on Hieizan, and his disciple Kūkai (also known as Kōbō Daishi 774–835), who travelled to China to bring back the Buddhist teachings or Sutras. The Emperor at this time favoured trade with T'ang China and Dengyō and Kūkai joined a trading mission there. During the eleventh century the life of the Heian court reached its peak, especially in literature written by women. The Imperial court was based in central Kyoto on Nijō Street, just near where the currently unoccupied palace stands. Two ladies at court, Sei Shōnagon and Lady Murasaki stand out as early literary geniuses. They were rivals, and although there is a gossipy tone to both women's work, the sense of an honest and respectful court life, based on equality between male and female courtiers is very evident. This was a highly sophisticated culture (learning Chinese was encouraged at court), based on the ideal of courtly love and a reverence for seasonal festivals – of which there are still five hundred celebrated every year in Kyoto.

*The Tale of Genji*, the first known novel in the world, written by Murasaki Shikibu herself, is also set in Heian Kyō – as Genji's love affairs in the first part of the novel, 'The house of the four seasons', are played out in different quarters of the city, according to the nature of each amorous liaison. After the intrigues at court, in which Genji sires a son by a liaison with the consort of his father, he finally leaves Kyoto to go to Lake Biwa. With distance, he sees the nature of the city:

The temple was fairly deep in the northern hills. Though the cherry blossoms had already fallen in the city, it being late in the Third Month, the mountain cherries were at their best [...] Genji climbed the hill behind the temple and looked off toward the city. The forests receded into a spring haze.

'Like a painting,' he said. 'People who live in such a place can hardly want to be anywhere else.'

There were heavy mists in the dawn sky, and bird songs came from Genji knew not where. Flowering trees and grasses which he could not identify spread like a tapestry before him. The deer that now paused to feed by the house and now wandered on were for him a strange and wonderful sight.[23]

Increasingly during the latter part of the Heian period, power was wrested into the hands of the Fujiwara family of ministers, which weakened the effectiveness of the Imperial House. After the end of the Heian court, and the removal of the capital to Kamakura, the military was in the ascendancy. Different clans were often at odds with one another. One of the most flamboyant emperors, Emperor Godaigo (ruled 1318–32), sired scores of children and desiring them to inherit the throne and move the centre of power back to Kyoto, waged a battle to overthrow the shogunate. Emperor Godaigo wrote about his scurrilous affairs in his book the *Diary of a Catamite*, which Yukio Mishima uses as a model for his own novel about homosexuality, *Forbidden Colours*. Ashikaga Takauji (1305–1358) helped to enthrone the Emperor and then turned against him and became shogun himself, ushering in two hundred years of conflict-riven Ashikaga rule.

23 *The Tale of Genji*, translated by Edward G. Seidensticker, Penguin, 1976

After this, the capital returned to Kyoto in the fourteenth century and remained here until 1615.

During the fourteenth century, Zen Buddhism reached its height in Kyoto, especially as Muso Sōseki, a Rinzai sect Zen priest (see Kamakura chapter) became the first abbot of the beautiful Nanzenji monastery, advising Emperor Godaigo on its building but then staying on at the temple to advise the man who defeated him, Ashikaga Takauji. Zen Buddhists then led the Ashikagas into further trade relations with the Chinese, ensuring their own wealth and power at court as well as enriching the art of Kyoto. During the following years Ashikaga Yoshimitsu (1358–1408) founded a shogunal palace (Nijō Castle) above the Imperial Palace (to the north) and encouraged the flourishing of art and theatre. The Kano school of painters flourished under the tutelage of Chinese masters influenced by Sung painting, and Yoshimitsu even founded an art school at Shōkokuji.

Yoshimitsu took Noh playwright Zeami as a lover, and Zeami's plays were imbued with *yūgen*, a mixture of mystery and spontaneity. The golden pavilion – Kinkakuji – was Yoshimitsu's retirement home where he watched Zeami perform on the Noh stage, before exiling him to Sado island (see Niigata and Sado chapter). Yukio Mishima dramatised the burning of the Kinkakuji temple centuries later in the 1950s, by a young Buddhist nationalist acolyte.

Yoshimitsu's grandson Yoshimasa (1436–90) built the silver pavillion – Ginkakuji. Yoshimasa wanted to create a second cultural renaissance and patronised a famous teamaster, Murata Shukō, but Yoshimasa proved to be an ineffectual leader and the Ashikaga shogunate disintegrated during the Ōnin wars (1467–77).

Daitokuji is a Zen temple which represents a different aspect of the Zen tradition. It did not have close ties with the Ashikaga shogunate and was destroyed during the Ōnin wars. The poet and Zen monk Ikkyū(1394–1481), who had also studied Chinese poetry, became the abbot and rebuilt the temple using funds from the wealthy merchants of Sakai and he mourned the way in which both monks and poets had fallen out with one another. Ikkyū found himself at the forefront of a general movement during the Muromachi period (1336–1573) which transmuted Zen into art and it was due to Ikkyū's creative influence that Daitokuji became the centre of innovation, so that later Zen masters like Sen no Rikyū established the tea ceremony here, along with others such as Furuta Oribe, Kobori Enshū and other leading teamen. Sen no Rikyū and Hideyoshi elevated the leisure activity of drinking tea to a kind of 'religious' ceremony. Unfortunately Rikyū himself, although he lived for a while in a tea arbour, constructed for him by Hideyoshi in the Juraku-tei, was later ordered to commit suicide by his warrior overlord.

During the sixteenth century, foreigners came to Kyoto from Nagasaki. Some, like St Francis Xavier (1534–82), were disappointed by finding the city at war and in ruins – he arrived during the Sengoku (country at war) period. But others, who came a little later, like Louis Frois, were truly amazed by the treasures of Kyoto. Frois visited the Sanjūsangendō, the temple of many Buddhas built for Emperor Go Shirakawa. At around this time, *daimyo* Oda Nobunaga (ruled 1568–82) marched into Kyoto in 1568 and five years later, the last Ashikaga shogun left Kyoto. Joao Rodrigues, a Jesuit, arrived in Japan when he was just sixteen in 1577, and became the official interpreter for Nobunaga's successor, *daimyo* Hideyoshi Toyotomi (ruled 1582–98) (who was bestowed the title *Kampaku*, or regent, by the Emperor). Rodrigues is really the first comprehensive interpreter of Japan. He was a gifted linguist and studied at the Jesuit mission in Hirado (see Kyūshū chapter). He took exams in theology, humanities and Japanese as part of his training to be a priest. Rodrigues also worked at the Jesuit mission in Kyoto and conducted many debates with Buddhist monks. His description shows how the city bore many of the traces of Heian Kyō – including poem-writing habits, silk-making, beautiful gardens and baths – were revived by Hideyoshi who was known for his extravagance in the arts. When, in 1587, Hideyoshi completed his Juraku-tei (or 'Pavilion of Accumulated Pleasures'), with doors of solid copper and luxurious gardens, Rodrigues arranged for the ambassadorial arrival of the Jesuit Visitor, Alessandro Valignano (see Nagasaki chapter). The whole city lined up to see the Southern Barbarians (as Europeans were known), process in 'barbarian' clothes and Valignano was honoured with a cup of *sakuzaki*, sake. Not all ambassadors were treated with such respect in the future (see Tokyo chapter), and it was no doubt due to the fine diplomacy of Rodrigues.

John Saris wrote the first account of Kyoto in English. He represented the East India Company, establishing the first trading post in Japan in 1613. Assisted by Will Adams, the shipbuilder to the shogun, he was able to meet with Ieyasu and his regent Hidetada. But he left Japan soon after, bringing back a suit of armour from the shogun to King James. At Miyako he reports on the Mimizuka, the mound of ears gathered from fallen Korean soldiers, a grisly memento of one of Hideyoshi's Korean campaigns (1592 and 1597) in which his main achievement was to capture Korean potters who introduced porecelain making to Kyoto.

**Marco Polo** from *The Travels of Marco Polo*

*Island of Zipangu, and Tartar Expedition thither*

This is a very large island, fifteen hundred miles from the continent. The people are fair, handsome, and of agreeable manners. They are idolaters, and live quite separate, entirely independent of all other nations. Gold is very abundant, and no man being allowed to export it, while no merchant goes thence to the mainland, the people accumulate a vast amount. But I will give you a wonderful account of a very large palace, all covered with that metal, as our churches are with lead. The pavement of the chamber, the halls, windows, and every other part, have it laid on two inches thick, so that the riches of this palace are incalculable. Here are also red pearls, large, and of equal value with the white, and many other precious stones. Kublai, on hearing of this amazing wealth desired to conquer the island, and sent two of his barons with a very large fleet containing warriors, both horsemen and on foot.

**Sei Shōnagon** from *The Pillow Book of Sei Shōnagon*

*Festivals*

There is nothing to equal the Festival of the Fifth Month, when the scents of the iris and the sage-brush mingle so charmingly. From the Ninefold Enclosure of the Imperial Palace down to the cottages of the common folk, there is not a place where people are not busy covering their roofs with leaves of iris and branches of sage-brush. Everyone wants his own house to be decorated most luxuriantly. All this is a splendid thing which never occurs on any other occasion.

On the actual day of the festival the sky is usually cloudy. Herbal balls, decorated with braided strings of many colours, have been brought to the Empress's palace by the Bureau of the Wardrobe, and they are now attached to the pillars on both sides of the main hall in which stands Her Majesty's curtain-dais. They replace the chrysanthemums that have been hanging there ever since the ninth day of the Ninth Month, wrapped in their plain cases of raw silk. The herbal balls are supposed to remain on the pillars until the next Chrysanthemum Festival; but, whenever people need a string, they tear a piece off the herbal balls, so that before long nothing is left.

During the course of this festival day, gifts are exchanged, and young people decorate their *hari* with iris; they attach taboo tags to their clothes, and adorn their coats and Chinese jackets with long iris roots or sprigs of azaleas and other attractive plants, which they secure to their sleeves with plaited cords dyed in uneven shadings. Though there is nothing new about any of this, it is very charming. After all, do people tire of the cherry trees because they blossom every spring?

The little girls who trip along the streets are also decorated with iris, but the flowers they wear are smaller than those worn by the grown-ups. The children are proud of themselves and keep looking at the flowers on their sleeves, comparing them with those of their companions. This is all delightful as are the little pages who play with the girls and snatch away their iris, making them burst into tears.

I also like to see camelia flowers wrapped in purple paper; thinly rolled iris leaves done up in green paper and attached to people's clothing and iris roots tied to white paper. Some very elegant men enclose long iris roots to their letters and it is a pleasure to watch the women who have received the contents discussing them with their companions and showing each other their replies. People who have chosen this day to send letters to a wellborn girl or to a high ranking gentleman at court exude a particular grace. Indeed the Iris Festival is nothing but a delight until the *hototogisu* (cuckoo) brings the day to an end by announcing its name.

**Murasaki Shikibu** from *The Diary of Murasaki Shikibu*

For seven nights every ceremony was performed cloudlessly. Before the Queen in white, the styles and colours of other people's dresses appeared in sharp contrast. I felt much dazzled and abashed and did not present myself in the daytime, so I passed my days in tranquillity and watched persons go up from the eastern side-building across the bridge. Those who were permitted to wear the honourable colours put on brocaded *karaginu*, and also brocaded *uchinigi* (a long flowing robe put over a dress). This was the conventionally beautiful dress, not showing individual taste. The elderly ladies who could not wear the honourable colours avoided anything dazzling, but took only exquisite *uchigi* trimmed with three or five folds, and for *karaginu* brocade either of one colour or of a simple design. For their inner kimonos they used figured stuffs or gauzes. Their fans, though not at first glance brilliant or attractive, had some written phrases or sentiments in good taste, but almost exactly alike, as if they had compared notes beforehand. In point of fact the resemblance came from their similarity of age, and they were individual efforts. Even in those fans were revealed their minds which are in jealous rivalry. The younger ladies wore much-embroidered clothes; even their sleeve openings were embroidered. The pleats of their trains were ornamented with thick silver thread and they put gold foil on the brocaded figures of the silk. Their fans were like a snow-covered mountain in bright moonlight; they sparkled and could not be looked at steadily. They were like hanging mirrors.

On the third night, Her Majesty's major domo gave an entertainment. He served the Queen himself. The dining table of aloe wood, the silver dishes, and other things I saw hurriedly. Minamoto Chunagon and Saisho presented the Queen with some baby clothes and diapers, a stand for a clothes chest, and cloth for wrapping up clothes and furniture. They were white in colour, and all of the same shape, yet they were carefully chosen, showing the artist mind. The Governor of Omi Province was busy with the general management of the banquet. On the western balcony of the East building there sat court nobles in two rows, the north being the more honourable place. On the southern balcony were court officials, the west being the most honourable seat. Outside the doors of the principal building (where the Queen was) white figured-silk screens were put.

On the fifth night the Lord Prime Minister celebrated the birth. The full moon on the fifteenth day was clear and beautiful. Torches were lighted under the trees and tables were put there with rice-balls on them. Even the uncouth humble servants who were walking about chattering seemed to enjoy the joyful scene. All minor officials were there burning torches, making it as bright as day. Even the attendants of the nobles, who gathered behind the rocks and under the trees, talked of nothing but the new light that had come into the world, and were smiling and seemed happy as if their own private wishes had been fulfilled. Happier still seemed those in the audience chamber, from the highest nobles even to men of the fifth rank, who, scarcely to be counted among the nobility, met the joyful time going about idly, and bending their bodies obsequiously.

## Ikkyū

> Daito's descendants destroyed his remaining light.
> Hard to melt the heart in song on an icy night.
> For fifty years, a wanderer with a straw raincoat and hat,
> Shameful today, a purple robed monk
> To hear a sound and awaken to the way.
> Striking Bamboo one morning he forgot all he knew.

Hearing the bell at fifth watch, his many doubts vanished.
The ancients all became Buddhas right where they stood.
T'ao Yuan ming alone just knit his brows.

\*       \*       \*

Many are the men who enter Daito's gate.
Therein who rejects the veneration of the master role?
Thin rice gruel, coarse tea, I have few guests;
Singing drunkenly, all alone, I tip up a cask of muddy *sake*.

**Louis Frois** from *They Came to Japan*

*Letter*

As Brother Luis Almeida was on his way back to Bungo in Kyūshū, he and I went sight-seeing in this city of Miyako, the second week after Easter, because there are many things to see and it is the custom of the Japanese to enjoy themselves by going to see the temples and ancient monuments of this part of the country. People are always coming from other kingdoms in order to see the sights, but as it is not possible to describe them all, I will only mention in this letter the ones that I still remember.

First of all we went with a party of about thirty Christians to see the palace of Kubo Sama,[24] the lord of all Japan. Through the good offices of one of his Christian servants, we were granted admittance and saw some chambers which are set apart for his recreation. They are certainly the cleanest, pleasantest and most splendid apartments that I have ever seen in my born days. In front of the windows of this suite was a garden with delightful and strange trees – cedars, cypresses, pines, orange trees, as well as other varieties unknown in Europe – all of which were cultivated artificially, so that some are shaped like bells, others like towers, others like domes and so on. There are so many lilies, roses, violets and other flowers with such diverse colours and scents (for much care is lavished upon them for his enjoyment) that they cause much admiration among those who

24  The shogun

continually see them and even more so among people like ourselves
for whom they are so novel.

They took us thence to see another garden within the same palace
and this seemed to us to be even better than the first one. The stables
are a building made of cedar, in which they could well entertain great
nobles. The floor is covered all over with fine matting and each of the
horses is kept in its separate compartment with wooden floors and
walls. And all these parts are matted so that the men who look after
these horses may rest themselves there.

On leaving by another gate we came out on to a street which I
suppose would be six or seven times as broad as the Rua Nova in
Lisbon and twice as long. All along this street there were delightful
trees on both sides. The street comes to an end at the palace of the
Dairi,[25] who is the lord to whom most honour is due in all Japan; in
ancient times he was the Emperor, but now he is obeyed no longer.
We saw his palace and one of its gardens from the outside only,
because nobody enters within save those who wait on him. From
whichever part you may leave the city, the outskirts are very lovely
and the countryside is the most luxuriant and agreeable of all Japan,
for there is no better place in the whole of this island than the site of
this Miyako.

From there we went along some long streets, very straight and
level, all of which are closed by gates at night; and the distance we
walked along those streets would be as from the cathedral of Lisbon to
Nossa Senhora da Esperança de Boa Vista. All of these streets are
occupied by merchants and craftsmen who weave and embroider
damask and other silks, and make golden fans and all the other things
used in this country. In the middle of these streets is a temple of Amida
which is the most frequented in all the city. An enormous crowd of
people comes to give alms and pray to the idol all day long, but
especially in the afternoon when the shops have been closed and the
people are free. The Christian gentlemen who were accompanying us
then led us from this temple to the palace which belongs to the
governor of all this kingdom. There are many things I could write

25  The Emperor

about this, but I will only describe to you one of its gardens. In addition to the great variety of trees (just like the ones in the gardens of the Kubo Sama) which we saw there, in the middle of the garden there is a pond of special water which is brought at great cost from two or three leagues away and runs into the pond through a large rock, which, although artificially wrought, looks like a work of nature. In the middle of this pond there are many kinds of islands linked by lovely wooden and stone bridges, and all this is shaded by beautiful trees. Without any doubt at all it is impossible to give an adequate description of this garden.

**Joao Rodrigues** from *Historia do Japao*

It is situated in the middle of spacious plains surrounded on three sides by high mountains, which, however, are not close enough to cast their shadow on it. Mount Higashi to the east, Hiei-no-yama (or Hiei-zan) to the north east, Kitayama and Kurama to the north, Nishiyama and Atagosan to the west, while the whole of the southern side remains open. All of these mountains are adorned with various monasteries and gardens. As these mountains are covered with snow in the winter, they make the city a very cold place. The actual site of the city is not quite flat but slopes almost imperceptibly from south to north. It is a very pleasant spot and its many abundant springs provide excellent water, and the streams which run down the hills irrigate the region and make it cool in summer; whence on summer mornings there is a lot of mist until the heat of the sun disperses it […]

The city was built on this site about the year of the Lord 800 when the king transferred it from the court of Nara, where it had been situated, to this place near the university of Hie-no-yama, the foot of which is about three short leagues from the city. This university had been founded shortly before with three thousand monasteries of priests who worshipped the idols of the Tendai.

Taiko, or Kampaku,[26] succeeded Nobunaga, and he ennobled and

26  Daimyo Hideyoshi

enlarged the city, for he first of all made much of the king[27] and the
*kuge*, he built the king a famous palace which was gilded both inside
and out like the ancient palaces and was set in a square compound with
lovely gates on the four sides. He donated the revenues from around
Miyako for the upkeep of the royal person and family, the staff and the
guards both inside and outside the palace. He ordered palaces to be
built for the *kuge* (Emperor) around the Dairi with sufficient revenue
for the upkeep of each one. He thus relieved them from the former
wretchedness in which they lived, and each one enjoyed the rank and
office which he possessed inside the palace of the royal household.
The royal palace was situated in the eastern part of Kamigyo, and in
front of it to the west he built a very large fortress with walls of stone
and a broad moat; inside this he constructed such a beautiful palace
that, it was said, there had never been anything so splendid in Japan
in the past nor would there be in the future, as indeed so far there has
not. He called it Juraku,[28] meaning the assembly of delights, or
paradise. He ordered all the lords of Japan to build their palaces next
to Juraku and they did this to the best of their ability.

The city of Miyako is extremely clean, and in each of its broad
streets is to be found water from excellent springs and streams which
flow along the middle. The streets are swept and sprinkled with water
twice a day and are thus kept very clean and fresh, for every man looks
after the part in front of his own house. As the ground slopes there
is no mud, and when it rains the water dries up in no time. The
inhabitants' houses lining the streets are usually offices, shops and
workshops of many crafts, and the people have their living quarters
and guest rooms inside. Some streets are very long and wide, and and
on either side they have arcades under which people walk to avoid the
rain or the sun or to look in the shops. In those streets they sell only
bolts of silk and silk articles, supplying the entire kingdom. These
arcades have curtains hanging up in front to protect the shops from
dust and to keep them clean and to provide light. Each house has a
curtain hanging up in front of the door in the arcade and it bears a

27  The Emperor
28  The juraku-tei

painted device of an animal, tree, plant, flower, bird, mathematical figures, numbers and a thousand and one other things which serve as a nickname or emblem of the family and house.

Even though they may live in another street or place, all the members of such a family display the same device, as if we were to speak of the house of the tiger, the crane, the pine, the circle, the square and so on. In Miyako there is a register of more than five thousand looms which weave various lengths of silk and almost all are to be found in one ward (Nishijin). Women usually serve in the shops and sell cloth and other wares, while their menfolk go out either on business or to amuse themselves in various places. They say that this custom is designed to keep the peace and avoid brawls in the shops for the men are very high-spirited and the women, being women, take care to disregard what they say.

The people and residents of Miyako are very even-tempered, courteous and very hospitable; they are well-dressed, exuberant and are much given to continual recreation, amusements and pastimes, such as going on picnics in the countryside to enjoy the sights of flowers and gardens. They entertain each other to banquets, comedies, plays, farces and various other shows which are performed according to their fashion. They often go on pilgrimages and show great devotion towards their temples; there are usually so many men and women going to pray there and hear sermons that it seems like a jubilee. Their speech is the best and most eloquent of the whole kingdom because of the presence there of the court and *kuge*, among whom the language is best preserved.

On going out of the city at any point, you find the loveliest and most delightful countryside of all Japan, and there are refreshing woods and groves round about. Every day crowds of people from the city enjoy themselves there with banquets in a kind of tent which they put up to obtain some privacy. The people of the city are very fond of the poetry of this nation, for in its own way, it is very excellent and subtle. In these parts there are also many great monasteries with beautiful and refreshing gardens. They highly esteem flowers and cultivate them in this region, and when these flowers are in bloom a person will send a branch of them to the tent of another person even though they may not be acquainted. This is an even more common practice among acquaintances, who will send a poem about a flower and place written on a long narrow piece of paper, excellently decorated with gold, silver and various flowers, hanging from the branch rather like a flag and made for the purpose. The people in the other tent reply with another poem about the same subject.

At certain places on the roads at the entrances to the city there are gated wooden enclosures in which are held continuous performances of comedies, farces and other plays which recount ancient legends to a certain singing and tone, accompanied by musical instruments, and these provide much recreation for the Japanese. The gates are always kept closed and the people who enter each pay a certain sum, and the actors earn their living with the money thus collected because a goodly number of people attend each performance. When the play is over, they leave and others enter, and there begins another play or drama, in which the actors wear rich silk costumes suited to each character. At the end of every play they put on an amusing farce at which their actors are extremely skilful.

The city is provided with abundant provisions, such as a great deal of game, wild birds, many varied kinds of excellent fresh fish from the rivers and lakes, as well as sea fish, especially in the winter when it is brought from the sea in the north, about nine leagues away, and from the sea in the south, some dozen leagues distant. There are many different kinds of vegetables and fruit according to season; these are brought at dawn from nearby places and farms in caravans of two hundred or more carriers. In addition to the markets where every kind of food is sold, men walk through the streets selling their wares and crying out in a loud voice to buy such and such a thing. There are also all over the city a great number of inns and taverns which provide food for travellers, and there are public baths where a man blows a horn and invites people to the baths, for the Japanese are much given to this. There are many other trades and it would take too long to describe them; anybody who has seen the city will know that our description has indeed been very brief.

It is possible to navigate in boats along a big river from the coastal city of Ōsaka right up to the vicinity of Miyako; there are many of these boats, and they are very smart and they carry provisions and every other kind of goods. There is also a service of pack horses (instead of mules) and many carts drawn by oxen as well.

**John Saris** from *They Came to Japan*

Miyako is the greatest Citie of Japan, consisting most upon merchandizing. There is an Idoll, by the natives called Amida, made of Copper, much resembling that of Daibutsu formerly spoken of, but is much higher for it reacheth up to the very Arch. This Hotoke was begun to be built by Hideyoshi in his life time and since his sonne has proceeded to the finishing thereof, which was newly made an end of when we were there. Within the inclosure of the walles of this Hotoke there are buried (by the report of the inhabitants) the Eares and Noses of three thousand Coreans, which were massacred at one time: Upon their grave is a mount raised, with a Pyramid on the toppe thereof; which mount is greene, and very neatly kept. The horse that Hideyoshi last rode on, is kept neare unto this Hotoke, having never been ridden since, his hoofs being extraordinarily grown with his age, and still standing there. The Hotoke standeth upon the top of a high hill, and on either side, as yee mount up to it hath fiftie pillars of free stone, distant ten paces one from the other, and on every pillar a Lanterne, wherein every night lights are maintained of Lamp oyle. In this city of Miyako the Portugall Jesuits have a very stately Colledge, wherein likewise were divers Jesuits, Natural Japonians, which preach and have the New Testament printed in the Japan language. In this Colledge are many Japonian children trayned up, and instructed in the rudiments of Christian religion, according to the Romish Church: There are not lesse than five or six thousand Japonians in this Citie of Miyako professing Christ. Besides the Hotoke before described, there are many other Hotoke in this Citie. The Tradesmen and Artificers are distributed by themselves, every Occupation and Trade in their severall streets and not mingled together, as heer with us.

# MEIJI PERIOD TO TODAY (1868–)

The maples carried but a touch of new green, and over the bamboo drain a single bud of Indian quince was opening. In the stillness, one seemed to know the very heart of the nunnery. Delighted with the mountain water, Sumiko and her husband drank glass after glass. They walked the mile or so back down the mountain while it was still daylight . . . and shortly after five they left Kyoto Station with regrets for the mountains and valleys to the North and East and West that they had to leave unvisited.

JUNICHIRŌ TANIZAKI

During the Tokugawa period (1600–1868), Kyoto became a backwater town of artisans, while the Emperor was secluded in his palace. The city of artisans survived until it found new export markets once the country opened up to foreign trade again during the Meiji period. Suddenly the artefacts of Japan were all the rage throughout Europe and the traditions which had been preserved for centuries by the artists were in high demand. The ubiquitous Rudyard Kipling came to Japan as a young man for six months in 1889. Travelling at the height of the British Imperial experiment Kipling finds the Japanese to be a 'near perfect' race and Japan an 'empire of artists'. He manages to be at the opening of the Tōkaidō railway built by a British engineer (see Yokohama chapter) as well as the mustering of Japanese army troops of about 170,000. But in Kyoto he simply he enjoys 'happy lazy sumptuous Kyoto' and attempts to capture the meticulousness, patience and sheer artistry of Japanese *cloisonné* craftsmen, and also the Kano school of painters who decorated Nijo castle during the Tokugawa period. He also joined in the cherry blossom festival at Chion-in, the temple which houses the great bell of Kyoto, which sounds every New Year. This was where the monk Hōnen (1133–1212) preached his Pure Land (also known as Jōdo) Buddhism with twenty-four-hour cycles of prayer to Amida Buddha in the twelfth century.

Kipling stays at Arashiyama, in the hills to the west of Kyoto, which aristocrats, poets and writers had been visiting for centuries. Arashiyama is rich in literary history which Kipling would not have known. Emperor Saga of the nineth century transplanted cherries from nearby Yoshino to here, while in later years Musō Soseki, a Zen Buddhist monk, advised Ashikaga Takauji to build Tenryūji to placate the angry spirit of Emperor Godaigo. Rakushisha is a hermitage where Bashō spent a summer at the home of his disciple Mukai Kyorai (1651–1704) and wrote the Saga diary (1691). Prince Genji also comes here in the Tale of Genji.

Although it may be less easy to find artisan merchants at work nowadays, there are a few around Raku-chu, the busiest, most densely populated area of Kyoto that runs from Kita-oji street in the north to Kyoto station and Nishi-oji in the west to the Kanogawa River. It is the ancient heart of the capital as designed by Kammu in 794. It also includes both the geisha (also called *geiko*) quarter called Pontochō and the old Nishiki, the market street. Behind the *noren* curtains, people still dye clothes for indigo, make traditional sweets, noodles and *yuba tofu* and of course there are some latterday painters of *nishiharu, ukiyo-e* woodblock prints.

Zen has intrigued the West since the Americans 'discovered' it in the peace-seeking 1960s. The Swiss writer Nicolas Bouvier, unlike many of his contemporaries went as a traveller in the true sense of the word, and lived in the temples and the old fashioned mansions around Kyoto. *The Japanese Chronicles* is his perceptive account of a group of Americans misunderstanding the Zen garden at Ryōanji, with its garden of fifteen rocks placed on a rectangle of fine white gravel.

Pico Iyer, another Japanese manqué came to Japan in the 1980s to study in Kyoto. His mission was to experience the simple life of solitude, like Bashō, Emerson or Thoreau, remembering Thoreau's famous claim that no one can know the pleasures of loneliness and Bashō's that 'my solitude shall be my company, my poverty, my wealth' (*Narrow Road to the Deep North*). He seems to have been exceptionally fortunate in his stay in Japan, as he met a wonderful Japanese lady (who he later married) with whom he could engage in some profound cultural dialogues. The shock was to come when he tried to actually become a

Zen monk at Tōfukuji temple, a temple founded in 1236 by Fujiwara no Michiie taking the characters of *tō* from the Tōdaiji temple and *kō* from the Kōfukuji temple in Nara.

But it was the merchants rather than the monks who kept Kyoto going during tough times. They were the people who suffered most during the Ōnin wars, which reached their height in the fifteenth century (1467–77). Every time a temple was destroyed, it had to be rebuilt and frequently the merchants had to pay for it. They also gained most by playing the Emperor and shogun off against each other. The area around Gion, north of Shijo-dori, is full of the *machiya* houses, the famous 'eel-like' houses that are peculiar to Kyoto. Film maker Yasujirō Ozu celebrates them in his film *End of Summer* – they are long, thin wooden houses, built in groups of forty in the *chō* or district, for a specific craft (such as dyers, weavers, lacquerers). Each craft was distinguished from the next by distinctive features on the gables, or on the tiles. Alex Kerr is invited to visit these old townsmen's houses on a more recent trip to the Gion festival, the townsmen's float festival held every July around the Yasaka jinja shrine.

## Rudyard Kipling from *Sea to Sea*

How I got to the tea-house I cannot tell. Perhaps a pretty girl waved a bough of cherry-blossom at me, and I followed the invitation. I know that I sprawled upon the mats and watched the clouds scudding across the hills and the logs flying down the rapids, and smelt the smell of the raw-peeled timber, and listened to the grunts of the boatmen as they wrestled with that and the rush of the river, and was altogether happier than it is lawful for a man to be.

The lady of the tea-house insisted upon screening us off from the other pleasure-parties who were tiffining in the same verandah. She brought beautiful blue screens with storks on them and slid them into grooves. I stood it as long as I could. There were peels of laughter in the next compartment, the pattering of soft feet, the clinking of little dishes, and at the chinks of the screens the twinkle of diamond eyes. A whole family had come in from Kioto for the day's pleasuring. Mamma looked after grandmamma, and the young aunt looked after a guitar, and the two girls of fourteen and fifteen looked after a merry little tomboy of eight, who, when she thought of it, looked after the baby who had the air of looking after the whole party. Grandmamma was dressed in dark blue, mamma in blue and grey, the girls had gorgeous dresses of lilac, fawn, and primrose crêpe with silk sashes, the colour of apple-blossom and the inside of a newly-cut melon; the tomboy was in old gold and russet brown; but the baby tumbled his fat little body across the floor among the dishes in the colours of the Japanese rainbow, which owns no crude tints. They were all pretty, all except grandmamma, who was merely good-humoured and very bald, and when they had finished their dainty dinner, and the brown lacquer stands, the blue-and-white crockery, and the jadegreen drinking-cups had been taken away, the aunt played a little piece on the *samisen*, and the girls played blindman's-buff all around the tiny room.

Flesh and blood could not have stayed on the other side of the screens. I wanted to play too, but I was too big and too rough, and so could only sit in the verandah, watching these dainty bits of Dresden at their game. They shrieked and giggled and chattered and sat down on the floor with the innocent abandon of maidenhood, and broke off to pet the baby when he showed signs of being overlooked. They played puss-in-the-corner, their feet tied with blue and white handkerchiefs because the room did not allow unfettered freedom of limb, and when they could play no more for laughing, they fanned themselves as they lay propped up against the blue screens – each girl a picture no painter could reproduce – and I shrieked with the best of them till I rolled off the verandah and nearly dropped into the laughing street. Was I a fool? Then I fooled in good company; for an austere man from India – a person who puts his faith in race-horses and believes nothing except the Civil Code – was also at Arashima that day. I met him flushed and excited.

'Had a lively time,' he panted, with a hundred children at his heels. 'There's a sort of roulette-table here where you can gamble for cakes. I bought the owner's stock-in-trade for three dollars and ran the Monte Carlo for the benefit of the kids – about five thousand of 'em. Never had such fun in my life. It beats the Simla lotteries hollow. They were perfectly orderly till they had cleared the tables of everything except a big sugar-tortoise. Then they rushed the bank, and I ran away.'

And he was a hard man who had not played with anything so innocent as sweetmeats for many years!

When we were all weak with laughing, and the Professor's camera was mixed up in a tangle of laughing maidens to the confusion of his pictures, we too ran away from the tea-house and wandered down the river bank till we found a boat of sewn planks which poled us across the swollen river, and landed us on a little rocky path overhanging the water where the iris and the violet ran riot together and jubilant waterfalls raced through the undergrowth of pine and maple. We were at the foot of the Arashima rapids, and all the pretty girls of Kioto were with us looking at the view. Up-stream a lonely black pine stood out from all its fellows to peer up the bend where the racing water ran deep in oily swirls. Downstream the river threshed across the rocks and troubled the fields of fresh logs on its bosom, while men in blue drove silver-white boats gunwale-deep into the foam of its onset and hooked the logs away. Underfoot the rich earth of the hillside sent up the breath of the turn of the year to the maples that had already caught the message from the fire-winds of April. Oh! it was good to be alive, to trample the stalks of the iris, to drag down the cherry-bloom spray in a wash of dew across the face, and to gather the violets for the mere pleasure of heaving them into the torrent and reaching out for fairer flowers.

I have seen one sort of work among the Japanese, but it was not the kind that makes crops. It was purely artistic. A ward of the city of Kioto is devoted to manufactures. A manufacturer in this part of the world does not hang out a sign. He may be known in Paris and New York: that is the concern of the two cities. The Englishman who wishes to find his establishment in Kioto has to hunt for him up and down slums with the aid of a guide. I have seen three manufactories. The first was of porcelain-ware, the second of *cloisonnée*, and the third of lacquer, inlay, and bronzes. The first was behind black wooden palings, and for external appearance might just as well have been a tripe-shop. Inside sat the manager opposite a tiny garden, four-feet square, in which a papery-looking palm grew out of a coarse stoneware pot and overshadowed a dwarfed pine. The rest of the room was filled with pottery waiting to be packed – modern Satsuma for the most part, the sort of thing you buy at an auction.

'This made send Europe – India – America,' said the manager calmly. 'You come to see?'

He took us along a verandah of polished wood to the kilns, to the clay vats, and the yards where the tiny 'saggers' were awaiting their complement of pottery. There are differences many and technical between Japanese and Burslem pottery in the making, but these are of no consequence. In the moulding house, where they were making the bodies of Satsuma vases, the wheels, all worked by hand, ran true as a hair. The potter sat on a clean mat with his tea-things at his side. When he had turned out a vase-body he saw that it was good, nodded appreciatively to himself, and poured out some tea ere starting the next one. The potters lived close to the kilns and had nothing pretty to look at. It was different in the painting rooms. Here in a cabinet-like house sat the men, women, and boys who painted the designs on the vases after the first firing. That all their arrangements were scrupulously neat is only saying that they were Japanese; that their surroundings were fair and proper is only saying that they were artists. A sprig of a cherry-blossom stood out defiantly against the black of the garden paling; a gnarled pine cut the blue of the sky with its spiky splinters as it lifted itself above the paling, and in a little pond the iris and the horsetail nodded to the wind. The workers when at fault had only to lift their eyes, and Nature herself would graciously supply the missing link of a design. Somewhere in dirty England men dream of craftsmen working under conditions which shall help and not stifle the half-formed thought. They even form guilds and write semi-rhythmical prayers to Time and Chance and all the other gods that they worship, to bring about the desired end. Would they have their dream realised, let them see how they make pottery in Japan, each man sitting on a snowy mat with loveliness of line and colour within arm's length of him, while with downcast eyes he splashes in the conventional diaper of a Satsuma vase as fast as he can! The Barbarians want Satsuma and they shall have it, if it has to be made in Kioto one piece per twenty minutes. So much for the baser forms of the craft.

The owner of the second establishment lived in a blackwood cabinet – it was profanation to call it a house – alone with a bronze of priceless workmanship, a set of blackwood furniture, and all the medals that his work had won for him in England, France, Germany, and America. He was a very quiet and cat-like man, and spoke almost in a whisper. Would we be pleased to inspect the manufactory?

He led us through a garden – it was nothing in his eyes, but we stopped to admire long. Stone lanterns, green with moss, peeped through clumps of papery bamboos where bronze storks were pretending to feed. A dwarfed pine, its foliage trimmed to dish-like plaques, threw its arms far across a fairy pond where the fat, lazy carp grubbed and rooted, and a couple of eared grebes squawked at us from the protection of the water-butt. So perfect was the silence of the place that we heard the cherry-blossoms falling into the water and the lisping of the fish against the stores. We were in the very heart of the Willow-Pattern Plate and loath to move for fear of breaking it. The Japanese are born bower-birds. They collect water-worn stones, quaintly-shaped rocks, and veined pebbles for the ornamentation of their homes. When they shift house they lift the garden away with them – pine trees and all – and the incoming tenant has a free hand.

Half a dozen steps took us over the path of mossy stones to a house where the whole manufactory was at work. One room held the enamel powders all neatly arranged in jars of scrupulous cleanliness, a few blank copper vases ready to be operated on, an invisible bird who whistled and whooped in his cage, and a case of gaily painted butter-flies ready for reference when patterns were wanted. In the next room sat the manufactory – three men, five women, and two boys – all as silent as sleep. It is one thing to read of *cloisonné* making, but quite another to watch it being made.

I began to understand the cost of the ware when I saw a man working out a pattern of sprigs and butterflies on a plate about ten inches in diameter. With finest silver ribbon wire, set on edge, less than the sixteenth of an inch high, he followed the curves of the drawing at his side, pinching the wire into tendrils and the serrated outlines of leaves with infinite patience. A rough touch on the raw copper-plate would have sent the pattern flying into a thousand disconnected threads. When all was put down on the copper, the plate would be warmed just sufficiently to allow the wires to stick firmly to the copper, the pattern then showing in raised lines. Followed the colouring, which was done by little boys in spectacles. With a pair of tiniest steel chopsticks they filled from bowls at their sides each compartment of the pattern with its proper hue of paste. There is not much room allowed for error in filling the spots on a butterfly's wing with avanturine enamel when the said wings are less than an inch across.

I watched the delicate play of wrist and hand till I was wearied, and the manager showed me his patterns – terrible dragons, clustered chrysanthemums, butterflies, and diapers as fine as frost on a window-pane – all drawn in unerring line. 'Those things are our subjects. I compile from them, and when I want some new colours I go and look at those dead butterflies,' said he. After the enamel has been filled in, the pot or plate goes to be fired, and the enamel bubbles all over the boundary lines of wires, and the whole comes from the furnace looking like delicate majolica. It may take a month to put a pattern on the plate in outline, another month to fill in the enamel, but the real expenditure of time does not commence till the polishing.

A man sits down with the rough article, all his tea-things, a tub of water, a flannel, and two or three saucers full of assorted pebbles from the brook. He does not get a wheel with tripoli, or emery, or buff. He sits down and rubs. He rubs for a month, three months, or a year. He rubs lovingly, with his soul in his finger-ends, and little by little the efflorescence of the fired enamel gives way, and he comes down to the lines of silver, and the pattern in all its glory is there waiting for him. I saw a man who had only been a month over the polishing of one little vase five inches high. He would go on for two months. When I am in America he will be rubbing still, and the ruby-coloured dragon that romped on a field of lazuli, each tiny scale and whisker a separate compartment of enamel, will be growing more lovely.

'There is also cheap *cloisonné* to be bought,' said the manager, with a smile. 'We cannot make that. The vase will be seventy dollars.'

I respected him for saying 'cannot' instead of 'do not'. There spoke the artist.

**Nicolas Bouvier** from *The Japanese Chronicles*

*Kyoto: Temple of the Ryōan-ji, 1964*

Three portly American ladies, solidly encased in hats and corsets and wielding cameras – the type that can digest a few dozen temples, along with a couple of Imperial residences, in a single day without even getting a bellyful – go to see the famous Garden of Stones, firmly resolved to gulp it down in one mouthful. The April sun, pale and sly. And the garden (one of the most perfect manifestations of the Zen aesthetic), a few tortured rocks chosen with zealous care by 'specialists' some five hundred years ago and marvellously arranged on a dazzling backdrop of white sand. That and no more. Each element of this microcosm has its traditional significance – the sea of clouds, the rocks representing the crane (felicity) and the tortoise (longevity) etc. – as a young official of the Japan Travel Bureau tells the ladies. Explained in a meek voice by this person in a guide's cap, these allegories seem a bit veneered and silly. Faced with her clients' perplexity, she adds that one must not attach too much importance to this symbolism – that the garden is a masterpiece of pure abstraction, an instrument of meditation that allows each viewer to let her spirit float freely.

'Cute little garden,' say the three ladies, and the boldest adds in a stentorian voice, 'As I look at these rock patterns, I can't help thinking of . . . Jesus Christ.'

I truly fear, like Kipling, that this West and this East will never meet.

Looking at the way the Japanese visit their own temples, I sometimes wonder if the Japan of today has any better chance of meeting the Japan of the past. Every half hour at the Silver Pavilion (Ginkakuji), entire villages and whole schools press themselves into the bamboo doorway, I tell myself that I have chosen a poor day and should return: ten minutes later, I am alone. Remarkably that is all it takes to be rid of them [...]

'Step in a little closer,' (and everyone hurries over). 'Built by the order of Lord Yoshimasa, such and such epoch, the two cups of sand on your right represent the repose of the spirit, move along please, we will meet at the number 4 bus stop in ten minutes . . . '

They take off again in tight groups aiming their cameras, but many of the photos will be blurred (*Osanai de kudasi* – do not push please!); because the ones in the back can't help pushing. Later today, in the lobby of the Kyoto Hotel, I met some other foreigners, these are French. They were cold on the island of Sado. Moreover, after two weeks of cultural circuits and surfeits, they suspect their guides of not having delivered the 'soul of Japan'.

There are some things you don't say even to the woman you love, or to a beloved brother. And these women, who are not stupid, these women in knit gloves, who in Paris would hesitate to change their butchers (it's a risk you never know who you'll be doing business with, the lamb won't be as tender), demand that before they leave, someone should wrap up the 'soul of Japan' for them. What do they want? Watch this! Suddenly through a simple mental process, their ignorance should be transformed into knowledge, clear cut and precise please, so that they can discuss it when they get home. I judge them, but I too would sometimes like to find my meal set in front of me and fast. We come to this thin and frugal country with our greedy metabolisms: the whole West is that way. The golden dishes, the maharajahs, the rubies as big as duck eggs – that is what struck our first explorers, that is what they wanted to see, not the frugality that is truly one of the marks of Asia. Here, anyone who doesn't serve an apprenticeship to frugality is definitely wasting his time.

**Pico Iyer** from *The Lady and the Monk: Four Seasons in Kyoto*

*Tōfukuji*

One day on a clear spring morning, I decided it was time at last to go and stay in a Japanese monastery – not a temple like the one where I had lived on first arriving, but a training centre where I could briefly sample the rigours of the monastic life. The natural choice seemed Tōfukuji where first I had tried *zazen* and where first I had met Sachiko. The largest Rinzai sect monastery in Japan, Tōfukuji was also well known for its cosmopolitan *roshi*, one of the few Zen masters in Japan willing to take in Western students, even women, and concerned about the state of Zen around the world.

When I arrived at the temple gates, I was met by a young fifth-year monk from California. In the heavy silence of the entrance hall, a would-be monk was kneeling on the polished wooden stairs, head bowed in supplication, maintaining a motionless position that he would have to keep up for two days or more while his petition to enter the temple was ritually refused. Nearby in a tiny antechamber, another aspirant – at the next stage of the process – was seated alone, in silence, in a position he would have to keep up for five more days before being admitted to the temple. Once inside, each of them would have to spend three years or more in a regimen unswerving as the temple's cedar pillars.

Greeting me in the silence and with a bow, the monk led me along the narrow polished corridors of the monastery, a few busy figures robed in black gliding past us. As we went, he explained, in a whisper, all the disciplines that I would have to observe: how I must walk, hands folded across my chest, and how I must bow each time I entered and left the *zendō*; how I must step across the threshold with my left foot first, and how I must line up my sandals, in a perfect row, at the base of the meditation platform. How I must sit, how I must breathe: how I must learn to live deliberately.

He led me to a tiny guest room and asked me to take off my watch. Then, serving tea, he told me a little about his life. At times when he talked of LA and his family, he sounded like a kid again, the twenty-two-year-old college boy he had left behind, at other times when he talked of Zen, he acquired a sonorous gravitas that made him indisputably my elder. It was like being with Sachiko again: when the monk asked about where he could find the best pizza in town – on his one day off each month – he seemed a guileless teenager; when he showed me how he wanted me to live, I could see he was the *rōshi*'s prize student.

Then the training began in earnest. In silence we went into a simple medieval chamber and in silence we ate a dinner of vegetables, served from wooden buckets, if I wanted more, my guide had explained, I would have to tap my bowl; and after I was finished, I would have to rinse out the bowl with my finger and hot tea, ensuring that not a speck of rice was left. Then I would have to wrap the bowl up in the *furoshiki* that was almost the monk's only possession. They were allowed no books, no keepsakes, no reminders of their lives outside; nothing but their robes, their bowls, and the body length mats on which they slept face-up.

Our dinner finished, we walked across, in the chill of the darkening afternoon, to the wooden shack where the monks were allowed, once every five days, to take baths. The man preparing the bath today, a bespectacled man in his fifties with a look of frightened bewilderment, was rushing around in panic while the younger monks shouted orders at him. Only a week before, I learned, this man had been a regular salary man living with his family at home; then, however, he had learned that he would have to take over his family temple and had been obliged to join a monastery. Now, as the junior monk in the place, he was the one the others were obliged to toughen up.

Scrubbed and rinsed clean in the scalding water of the tub, we proceeded to the ancient meditation hall. As the last light of day seeped in through the pulled back screens I sat with the monks, erect on the wooden platform, in silence. Occasionally, a monk, standing silent sentry by the door strode forward and whacked with his long wooden stick anyone whose form was slipping – usually the terrified looking newcomer in spectacles. The other seven sat in motionless *zazen*. Now and then in the bird-scattered quiet of dusk, the mournful melody of the garbage collector's truck floated up from a nearby street. Occasionally there was a swish of black robes, a flash of motion, as a monk headed away for *dokusan*, his daily private conference with the *rōshi*.

I too, once, at school, had gone off on evenings such as this for private meetings, and alone with my thoughts – too new to be above this – I thought back in the dark to school in England, so similar to this: the cold showers at dawn, the ascetic bare rooms, the beatings, the daily prayers in five-hundred-year-old chambers. The sense of hierarchy, the all-male rites, the chores, the fears, the longings, all seemed eerily the same. But that kind of school had been preparing its students to take over the world, while this one taught them to renounce it; ruling ourselves, at school we were made to feel we could rule everything; while here, ruling the self, one was trained to need nothing from the world.

My legs by now were aching, my body was stiff: I waited and waited for the session to end. Finally with relief, I heard a monk stir and draw back the screens against the night. In a flash, with movement as quick and precise as in some army drill, the monks whipped out their bedrolls and stood at attention; the poor businessman wrestling unhappily with his lot and unable to get it all done in five seconds earned more sharp shouts and rebukes. Then, single file, we walked off to the temple garden, silver in the moonlight.

Nine figures, eerie in black robes, shaven heads shining in the silent dark, sat perfectly erect in the cool night air. When at last I left to sleep, all eight were sitting there, ready to continue through the night. By three o'clock the next morning, my guide was rustling me awake. Bare feet cold on the wooden planks, we shuffled back into the meditation hall.

There, still groggy, I followed the monks to another room, where gongs sounded and sutras were chanted, broken by the ringing of a bell. Then we returned to the hall for more zazen, screen doors open to the chilling dark as, very slowly, the light began to seep in and the birds to sing.

**Alex Kerr** from *Lost Japan*

*Kyoto hates Kyoto*

It was only after I had lived on the outskirts of Kyoto for eighteen years that I managed to enter the home of one of its great old families. Kyoto is that kind of city. Restaurants and geisha houses routinely refuse entrance to the *ichigen* 'first look'; that is a customer who has not been introduced. A foreign acquaintance once made the mistake of trying to make a booking at Doi, a lavish restaurant in the eastern hills. When he called, the owner asked, 'Do you know anyone who eats here?' 'No.' 'In that case,' she murmured in her soft Kyoto dialect, 'I must respectfully advise you to "forget it" in English.'

Kyoto is unfriendly, and it is unfriendly for a reason; it is an endangered species. A way of life was built up in Kyoto which has miraculously survived all the changes of the nineteenth and twentieth centuries to make it into our time. It had relatively little to do with the city's famous monuments, such as the Gold Pavilion, the Silver Pavilion, Nijō Castle and the Hall of the Thousand and One Buddhas, crowded though they are with tourists. The monuments stand un-changed form the past, but the Kyoto way of life is nearing its last gasp as modern development sweeps over it, and so the guardians of Kyoto culture are nervous. Their way of life is fragile, like a dying person who mustn't be allowed too many visitors lest he becomes overexcited. Only the few who really loved him can understand the world of significance in each feeble gesture and whisper.

The day I first visit that great house was in summer, during the Gion Matsuri – a festival which takes place in the old neighbourhoods in the heart of the city, bounded by Gojo, Oike, Kawamachi and Karasuma streets. Over the course of the year, prominent houses in this district store wooden frameworks and decorations which are brought out into the streets for the festival and assembled into floats. The decorations, some of which are centuries old, included metal work, lacquer, woodcarving, brocades and rugs. During the week of Gion Matsuri hundreds of thousands of people, many dressed in summer kimono, mill through the streets, looking into the open windows of shops and houses decorated with folding screens and artworks. In the evening, children striking chimes sit in the upper balconies of their floats, beating out the slow hypnotic rhythm of the Gion music. On the final day, the floats parade through the city.

My guide was flower master Kawase Toshiro, who grew up next door to Rokkakudo, the temple where *ikebana* was born, and is a Kyotoite down to his fingertips. Kawase is mostly active in Tokyo these days, so he was seeing the Gion festival for the first time in years. I had not attended in maybe ten years. How the city had changed! Where there were once rows of wooden houses, each hung with lanterns, most had been replaced with shop fronts of glass and aluminium. The narrow backstreets were impossibly crowded because little *yomise* (stalls) selling food, souvenirs and goldfish for children stood in front of most of the buildings. '*Yomise* are fun enough, I suppose,' said Kawase. 'They are what you see everywhere throughout Japan during the summer. But his is Kyoto! When I was a child, the main attraction was looking at the neighbours artworks and then playing in the streets with fireworks. We didn't need *yomise*.'

Kawase took me and a couple of friends to two houses. The first was an old Kyoto *machiya*, a town house. Taxes used to be levied according to frontage, so the old houses of Kyoto tended to have narrow street entrances, and stretch far back into the interior of the block. The building's paper and wood sliding doors had been removed for summer, and replace with doors made of reeds, *sudare* (bamboo blinds) and gauze hanging – all more or less transparent. As we walked through the house, the blinds and hangings revealed ever-changing vistas, with room after room, separated by gardens, disappearing into the distance. On the floor were blue Nabeshima rugs, each the size of one tatami mat.

Tradition in Japan demands a sweep of empty tatami mats, against a row of stark pillars made of white wood and that is mostly what we see in modern versions of old architecture. But the residents of Kyoto overlaid the mats with coverings of blue and brown and hung the pillars with bamboo blinds and gauze. Of course, being Kyoto, where only the suggestion of a decoration counts as true decoration, they did these things in moderation. They did not cover the whole floor with rugs; instead, they put Nabeshima on only a few mats where guests would sit. Most of the blinds and hangings were rolled up, allowing freedom to move around.

As we filed through the house, Kawase said, 'This house is old of course, but it has been largely redone in the last few years. They Japanized it. They did an excellent job, and I'm glad it's here. But now let me show you the real thing.'

We pushed our way through the crowds again, at last arriving at a complex of buildings and *kura*, surrounded by a long wall extending back a full block. This house, Kawase told us, was the last great house of inner Kyoto. The owners had almost lost the land a few years ago, and there was a plan to tear the house down and turn it into an apartment block. But a group of Kyotoites joined forces with the owner and saved it.

It was one of the houses which store the Gion float decorations and the gateway was thronged with people coming to view the metalwork and brocades on public display inside. Just beyond the gateway was a walkway, with a bamboo barrier at one end. Kawase pushed the barrier aside and motioned for us to step into the entranceway. The elder daughter of the house, dressed in a yellow kimono, bowed at the edge of the steps and invited us in.

The din of the crowds outside faded away. Ahead of us was the foyer, decorated with long leaves of *susuki* grass in a vase. The *sudare* blinds were rolled up and secured with dangling ribbons of purple silk. Beyond the foyer was a small room looking out onto a garden of moss, one of the Kyoto *tsubo-niwa* (gardens in a bottle) encased by a high wall. You could see bits and pieces of the garden through oddly placed Mondrianesque openings, a square window at ground level covered with a bamboo lattice or an open wall hung with *sudare* bamboo blinds from China covered with pictures of birds and flowers created by winding silk threads over each thin slat of bamboo.

From there, we entered another room and then another, each separated by different types of doors or gauze hangings. There were a variety of floor coverings: blue and pale orange *nabeshima* or a three mat expanse of shiny brown paper dyed with persimmon juice, giving the room a crisp cool feeling. I noticed a stone at the entrance to one of the inner gardens, with two straw sandals set neatly beside it. Beyond the stone was an inviting path leading through to another part of the complex. As I was about to step into the sandals, Kawase stopped me. The sandals are arranged to the side of the stone, not on top of it. 'That means, "Don't go here."' He was alerting me to the subtle sign language of Kyoto life.

# 7

# Nara

Would I could obtain
a dragon steed right now,
so I could fly
to the capital at Nara,
beautiful in blue earth.

ŌTOMO NO OABITO

Founded in 710, Nara is the first great capital of Japan, built on Yamato, the rich and fertile plain stretching between the foot of the mountains and the sea. But the origins of the city go much further back. Great palaces were established at Ōtsu and Asuka to begin with, but Nara was finally chosen, perhaps because of its proximity to the Temple at Hōryūji. Also, for the new capital, it was necessary to find a place that satisfied the *feng shui* elements of air and water. The building of an administrative home and centre for the arts was an important and unprecedented development in Japan.

In the seventh century, Japan was involved in the politics of Korea and sent an army there to counter Chinese pressure on the Kingdom of Paekche. But, when challenged by the T''ang empire, Japan withdrew and instead sought friendly relations with China. Between 630 and 665, four missions were sent to China and Chinese culture and administration were adopted at court. The Japanese Emperor Tenji (reigned 661–672) was a scholar of Chinese culture and a patron of the arts. He spawned the first flowering of literary and artistic culture in Japan. China had a huge impact on Japan at the time and many visitors to China, whether students, traders, scholars or official, wrote detailed accounts of the country.

Asuka and Ōtsu are best remembered in verse; the spirit of the early

Japanese court is one in which the poet was allowed free expression, and the mythology of the gods and heroes of Japan were knitted into the Yamato landscape. The *Man'yoshu* (*Collection of Ten Thousand Leaves*) contains 31-syllable *waka* poems and *choka* or longer poems composed as public poetry. As distinct from the Chinese-style historical myths of the *Kojiki*, or *Record of Ancient Matters*, the *Man'yoshu* were written in Japanese for the first time.

As Geoffrey Bownas points out, 'the spirit and the culture of the Nara period, its art and its architecture, and its sculpture as well as its poetry is summed up by the Japanese by the word *makoto* or sincerity. Most of the better known poets such as Tabito, Okura and Yakamochi served the state and many of these have recourse to using other social classes as their mouthpiece, so Okura speaks through the mouth of fishermen and Yakamochi speaks for the departing frontier guard off to Dazaifu in Kyūshū, with the charge of coastal defence. Nature, love, partings and time were the subjects that engaged the Manyo poet most. The contrast of past with present and the preoccupation with change occur constantly and there are the first hints of the influence of Buddhism.' [29]

This was also a time when poetry by women flourished. Princess Nukuda's seventh-century poem comparing spring and autumn seems very relevant to the Japanese sensibility. Her contemporary Kakino moto no Hitomaro who was active as a court poet, died before the capital was established at Nara. His poems are lyric chronicles of the loves and wars, deaths and births of the Imperial drama of the seventh century, as his life spanned several battles of succession. Hitomaro is sometimes dubbed a saint of poetry since his own poem on his wife's death is among the most beautiful in the Japanese tradition. He wrote poetry that was rich with associative expressions for the landscape and wordplay, sometimes known as *makura kotoba* or 'pillow words'.

Emperor Tenji was patron of continental Chinese and Korean culture and fostered indigenous Japanese verse to match it in *The Man'yōshū*. The mountains and landscape of the area around Nara take on a mythic reality, from the 'age of the gods'. But, as Japanese

29 Introduction to *The Penguin Book of Japanese Book of Verse*, pp. lviii and lix

culture flowered, with the birth of Japanese art as is revealed in the sixth-century Buddhist art and architecture (often built by Korean workmen), it was appropriate that Japan should have its own capital, adapted from Chinese classical design. The description of the move from the Fujiwara palace at Asuka to the new capital at Nara is recorded beautifully by an anonymous poet in *The Man'yōshū*. Book Five is written during the Nara period when the Emperor established a garrison at Dazaifu on the island of Kyūshū to protect the embassies he sent to China. Some of the most beautiful poetry is written by Ōtomo Tabito (see above), one of the garrison generals, longing for life back in Nara. Book Five of *The Man'yōshū* also includes letters rich with Chinese-style rhetorical phrases.

Emperor Mommu set in motion plans for the new Imperial capital for Japan at Nara just before his early death at the age of twenty-six in 707. His father-in-law, a Fujiwara, became the first ruler of Heijo-kyō (Citadel of Peace) as Nara was known. The city was perfectly laid out according to the laws of Chinese geomancy. There is a symmetrical grid plan of streets in Nara just as in Ch'ang an, the great Tang dynasty capital in China, and as there would be in the future, in Kyoto. In Nara, there were mountains at the back and to either side as well as two rivers coursing across its level plain from the north-east (the Saho river) and the north-west (the Akishino river). These combined to flow into the open valley to the south and on to Naniwa (Ōsaka) and to the Inland Sea. The grid-like pattern of streets and temples with temple parks and enclosures (like a miniature version of the plan for Kyoto) makes this a beautiful, walkable city.

It was Fujiwara-no-Fuhito's grandson, the pious Emperor Shōmu, who endowed Nara with splendid temples. Shōmu had been a devotee of pleasure, until, in 737, smallpox arrived from China and swept through Japan. He became a pious Buddhist and a dedicated religious ruler, decreeing that a Buddhist temple and Buddhist sutras be established in the heart of each Japanese capital. His consort, Empress Kōmyō, was supposedly the reincarnation of Kannon, the Bodhisattva of mercy. They both did countless good works and she established orphanages, centres of medical care for the poor, as well as houses of refuge for the sick and the elderly.

Emperor Shōmu started Tōdai-ji, the Great Eastern Temple, the largest wooden building in the world. The Buddha, or *Daibutsu*, there was dedicated in 752 before gold leaf had been applied after the Emperor's death. Shōmu also endowed the five-storey pagoda built in 730 at the request of Kōmyō, which burned down on five occasions. It is a well-documented literary pastime to gaze at the pagoda reflected in the Sarusawa pond in the moonlight or to read the signs posted there by trickster monks as in Ryūnosuke Akutagawa's story *Dragon: The Old Potter's Tale*.

The Hokkeji temple in the northern part of the city was created from the mansion of Fujiwara-no-Fuhito and, during the time of the Emperor Shōmu (ruled 724–48) and the Empress Kōmyō, it became the head convent in Yamato, providing equality of status for women within the Buddhist faith.

In the Hondō, or main hall, of the Hokkeji temple there is a Juichimen Kannon (goddess of mercy) carved from a single block of camphor wood in a lacquered cabinet from India. Legend has it that an Indian king dreamed he would find a living Bodhisattva in Japan, who was the Empress Kōmyō. Within the nunnery grounds and gardens is a tea house and beyond a bathhouse. It recalls the legend that when the magnificent Tōdaiji Daibutsuden was completed, the Empress vowed to wash one thousand indigent or aged persons in gratitude to the Buddha.

After the death of this line of Buddhist emperors, the priest Ganjin (688–763) abandoned Tōdai-ji to create his own temple with his own Chinese priests prevailing upon Shōmu and Kōmyō's child, the Empress Kōken, to create Toshodaiji in the south-west of Nara in 759. During Kōken's reign, some of the leading Buddhist clergy became more interested in political power than Buddhism.

Not far to the east of Nara was the Futaiji, also known as Kaya palace, associated with the Emperor Heizei (774–824). The retired Emperor Heizei lived in the Kaya palace from 810–24, and at one point he was embroiled in a failed attempt to regain the throne, with his wife and brother-in-law. But in doing so, he lost his wife, who drank poison, and her brother, who was executed. The ex-Emperor Heizei and his oldest sons had to become monks. The mansion passed

to Heizei's son Abe Shino and then to his grandson Ariwara no
Narihira (823–80). Narihira was renowned as a poet and as a rake. 'It
is a general rule in this world that some men love some women but not
others. Narihira did not make such distinctions', says the tradition.
The ghosts of the past which haunt ancient Nara, are well described
by photographer and travel writer Herbert Ponting who visited in the
early 1900s and was later to show slides of the visit to the explorers on
Scott's expedition to the Antarctic.

## HŌRYŪJI

While there were many earlier sites for the capital including Ōtsu
and Asuka, few deny the importance of Prince Shōtoku (572–622)
who built a temple at Hōryūji, eight miles from present day Nara.
He inherited the role of regent from his aunt, Empress Suiko (592–
628), when he was just twenty-one and it was he who was responsible
for establishing Buddhism in Japan. He learnt Chinese and sent an
embassy to China so that Japan could learn from the more advanced
culture. By promoting the Confucian Constitution of seventeen
Articles, he steered the Japanese government towards becoming an
organised state. He retired to Hōryūji in later years to study the
Buddhist sutras.

Hōryūji is one of the most beautiful wooden temple complexes
in the world, built by workmen from Paekche, Korea, who were
experienced in fine temple construction. The buildings were arranged
in a north-south direction and aligned with the North Star. The
temple pagoda and the *kondō*, main hall, are the oldest wooden
buildings in Japan. The treasure hall is a double-roofed building from
the Asuka period (552–645) architectural style, while the pagoda is
five stories tall with a tapered roof, so that the pagoda looks taller than
it is. In the four corners of the base of the pagoda, there are four
grotto-like areas with scenes illustrating events around the life of
Sakyamuni, the historical Buddha, including the grieving disciples
standing around his tomb.

**Princess Nukuda** from *Women Poets of Japan*

*When the Emperor Tenji ordered Fujiwara Kamatari to judge between the beauty of cherry blossoms and the red autumn leaves on the hills, Princess Nukuda gave judgment with this poem.*

When spring escapes
freed from being huddled in winter's sleep,
the birds that had been stilled
burst into song.
The buds that had been hidden
burst into flower.
The mountains are so thickly forested
that we cannot reach the flowers
and the flowers are so tangled with vines
that we cannot pick them.
When the maple leaves turn scarlet
on the autumn hills,
it is easy to gather them
and enjoy them.
We sigh over the green leaves
but leave them as they are.
That is my only regret –
So I prefer the autumn hills.

**Hitomaro** – *Written to Emperor Temmu, Tenji's younger brother following the Jinshin war of succession in 671*

> Our Emperor,
> a very god,
> has turned the fields
> where red steeds wandered
> into his capital city.
>
> Our Lord,
> a very god,
> has turned the marshes
> where nested flocks of waterfowl
> into his Imperial city.

**Anon** – *On the move from Asuka to Nara* from *The Man'yōshū*

> In awe of our Emperor's command,
> We left our homes,
> and our soft living,
> and set our ships afloat
> down Hatsuse River,
> down that hidden land.
> Not one of its eighty bends
> did we sail by,
> without looking back
> ten thousand times.
> We trod till dusk
> came over our path,
> straight as a spear of jade
> and reached the Saho River
> by the capital at Nara,
> beautiful in blue earth.
> As we perceived the morning moon

crystalline above our sleeping clothes
we saw, where evening frost had fallen
white as brilliant mulberry cloth,
the river frozen
like a bed of stone.
Come, O Lord, into the house
that we have toiled,
back and forth
in that chill night,
unresting
for a thousand generations
and I too shall go
back and forth
there, to serve you.

**Prince Shōtoku**

If he were home
he would be pillowed
in his wife's arms,
but here on the journey
he lies with grass for pillow –
traveller, alas!

**Masaoka Shiki**

I was eating a persimmon.
Then, the bell of Hōryūji temple
echoed far and wide.

**Herbert Ponting** from *In Lotus Land Japan*

*Nara – the heart of old Japan*

A Japanese proverb says, 'Never use the word "magnificent" till you have seen Nikkō.' They should have added, 'Nor the word "peaceful" till you have been to Nara.'

Nara is the very heart of old Japan. The capital, which in ancient times was removed to a new site on the death of each Mikado – but was always situated somewhere in the provinces of Yamato, Yamashiro or Settsu – came to its first permanent stop at Nara in AD 709. At that time, we are told, the city was ten times larger than at present. But though it is nearly twelve hundred years since Nara's glory departed, the passing centuries have been pitiful and gentle. They have cherished the city's environs and the monuments embosomed in them, instead of harming them, and have clothed them with the sweet, serene beauty of honourable old age. For miles around, Nara is beset with the ghosts of a thousand years ago – ghosts as thickly cloaked with history as they are overgrown with moss and lichens.

As one leaves the railway station (the very name of such a thing sounds almost like sacrilege here) the eye is arrested by a beautiful pagoda standing on an eminence in the grounds of Kōfūkuji temple. It completely dominates the landscape with its tiers of dark-grey roofs standing out in contrast to the cedar-clad mountains beyond it.

The pagoda overlooks a pond called Sarusawa no ike, about which, there is, of course, a legend. There was once a beauteous maiden, who, though beloved by all the gentlemen of the Court, rejected all their offers, as she had eyes for the Mikado alone. For a time she found favour in his sight, but 'the heart of man is fickle as the April weather', as the Japanese say, and the Mikado's heart was after all but a mortal one, though it pulsed with the blood of gods. He neglected his beautiful plaything, until she, unable to endure his indifference any longer, stole out of the palace one night and drowned herself in the garden lake. Her spirit still haunts its shores on dark nights, and you can hear her sighs as the breezes play softly in the trembling osiers round her grave.

The atmosphere of peace and restfulness that encompasses Nara comes to a focus at the temple of Kasuga. It is the peace of many centuries. In AD767, the temple was founded and dedicated to the ancestor of the Fujiwara family, which rose to be the most illustrious in Japan. The picturesqueness of the temple buildings themselves and the beauty of their surroundings, make a deeper, more touching appeal, however, than their mere association with this great name. The lofty cryptomerias rear their heads highest here, and among the brown shades of their mossy, gravelled aisles, great splashes of white and vivid colour are painted into the picture with grand effect. These are the gateways and pavilions of the temple, finished in snowy white and vermillion.

Massive rooves of thatch, a yard thick, cover all the buildings, and every colonnade, gallery and courtyard is kept as fresh and clean as ever it was a thousand years ago.

Giant wisteria vines have crept to the very utmost branches of the trees, and in May the tall cedars themselves seem to burst forth into clusters of drooping purple blooms. Through many an opening in the glorious arches overhead, the sun throws long shafts of light, which touch the pendent blossoms, and then, glancing downwards, melt moss and gravel into golden pools, or, searching out some spot on the brilliant lacquer, make it glow with ruddy fire as the great orb himself glows at daybreak.

The deer roam undisturbed about the mossy, lanterned avenues of this fairyland, and form lovely pictures as they stand framed in the burning lines of some vermillion gateway. Fearing no rebuffs, they even wander into the temple courtyards to be petted by the little daughters of the priests, whose duty it is to go through the stately measures of the ancient religious dance *kagura*, whenever called upon. The priests are born, live out their lives, die and are buried in the heavily scented shade of the towering cryptomeria trees, and their children succeed them to live and die here also.

Kasuga's numerous galleries and colonnades are hung with innumerable lanterns of carved and fretted brass and bronze. There are at least as many round its courtyards as there are *ishi doro* in the gravelled avenues, and every gentle zephyr sets them swinging. When these are all alight the gaily coloured temple must be a very fairy palace of beauty.

Pilgrims are ever haunting the temple precincts. With slow step, and eyes bright with happiness, they softly tread the avenues, kneel before every shrine, and rest at every stall to feed the deer that nose around them. With staff, broad brimmed hat, and tinkling bell, they come to Nara from the uttermost parts of Japan, just as they flock to Fuji and every place of holy fame throughout the land.

# 8

# Ise

Oh how steadily I love you –
You who awe me
Like the thunderous waves
That lash the seacoast of Ise!

LADY KASA

Ise jingū, also known as the grand shrine of Ise, has great significance
as a popular place of pilgrimage as well as as a tourist attraction. The
*naiku* (inner shrine) holds the sacred mirror of Amaterasu Omikami,
the sun goddess. Her great grandson was said to be Emperor Jimmu,
the first Japanese emperor. In ancient times an unmarried princess
was chosen as the high priestess of the shrine. She guarded the sacred
mirror and was written about by the poet Ariwara no Narihara, who
drew on established myths and emphasised the fact that she could not
show her face.

'The outer shrine, or *geku*, was founded in the fifth century and is
dedicated to Toyouke O'kami, the goddess of agriculture and food.
The shrine is built of *hikoki* wood and is surrounded by dense forests of
the same; *muchikake*, rows of slender pegs, jut out from the gable ends.
Both shrines have been rebuilt every twenty-one years since 690.

The cult of Ise has always been linked to the state of Japan – and the
Emperor still performs rites for a good rice harvest here behind the
towering cryptomerias that keep the shrine secret. And Ise is the site
of thousands of annual festivals, in order to raise funds for the shrine.
During the Edo period (1603–1867), ambassadors were sent out to
popularise Ise, setting up regional associations to support the shrine.
*O-Ise mairi*, the once-in-a-lifetime pilgrimage, became a national
craze, since the Japanese were not really allowed to travel otherwise.

Millions came with only the clothes on their backs, dancing, singing and pilfering their way to Ise. There was a busy pleasure quarter around the shrine and sometimes spontaneous Ise fever swept the country. Admiral Togo (1848–1934) came here to thank the gods for victory during the Russo-Japanese war in 1904–5, a tradition continued to this day by Japanese prime ministers and officials who visit the outer and inner shrines. Yukio Mishima evokes the spirit of old Japan, the *yamato daimashi*, in the figure of an Ise fisherman in *The Sound of Waves*. A new tourist attraction is a visit to Toba, the home of Miki-moto Pearl Island where Kokichi Mikimoto (1858–1954) created the world's first cultured pearl. You can also see *Ama* (female divers) picking up pearls from the seabed and admire the statue of the Pearl King standing over the shore.

**Ariwara no Narihira** from *The Tales of Ise*

Once a man went to the province of Ise as an Imperial Huntsman. The Ise Virgin's mother had sent word that he was to be treated better than the ordinary run of Imperial representatives, and the Virgin accordingly looked after his needs with great solicitude, seeing him off to hunt in the morning and allowing him to come to her own residence when he returned in the evening.

On the night of the second day of this hospitable treatment, the man suggested that they might become better acquainted. The Virgin was not unwilling, but with so many people about, it was impossible to arrange a meeting in private.

However, since the man was in charge of the hunting party, he had not been relegated to some distant quarter, but had been lodged rather close to the Virgin's own sleeping chamber and so the Virgin went to his room around eleven o'clock that night, after the household had quieted down. He was lying on his bed wide awake, staring out into the night. When he saw her by the faint light of the moon, standing with a little girl in front of her, he led her joyfully into the bedchamber; but though she stayed from eleven o'clock until two-thirty, she took her leave without exchanging vows with him.

The man, bitterly disappointed, spent a sleepless night. The next morning, despite his impatience, he could not very well send a message, and was obliged to wait anxiously for a word from the Virgin. Soon after dawn she sent this poem without an accompanying letter.

> Did you, I wonder, come here,
> Or might I have gone there?
> I scarcely know.
> Was it dream or reality –
> Did I sleep or wake?

Shedding tears of distress, he sent her this:

> I too have groped
> In utter darkness.
> Can you not determine tonight
> Which it might have been –
> Whether dream or reality.

Then he went off on a hunting excursion. As he galloped over the plain, his thoughts strayed to the coming night. Might he not hope to meet the Virgin as soon as the others had gone to bed? But word of his presence had reached the governor of the province, who was also in charge of the Virgin's affairs, and that official proceeded to entertain him at a drinking party that lasted all night. It was impossible to see the Virgin, and since he was to leave at dawn for Owari Province, there could be no further opportunity, even though he was quite frantic with longing, as indeed was the Virgin.

As dawn approached, the Virgin sent him a farewell cup of wine with a poem inscribed on the saucer. He picked up the vessel and examined it.

> Since ours was a relationship no
> Deeper
> Than a creek too shallow
> To wet a foot-traveller's garb . . .

The last two lines were missing. He took a bit of charcoal from a pine torch and supplied them:

> I shall surely again cross
> Ōsaka Barrier.

At daybreak he set out toward the province of Owari.

**Arthur Lloyd** from *Every Day Japan*

When Admiral Togo at the conclusion of the Russo-Japanese war was returning to Tokyo with his ships to be present at the great naval review and to receive the ovations of the citizens and the thanks of his Sovereign, he landed first in the peninsula of Ise and there offered his thanks at the shrine which all Japan reveres as the most holy place in the whole country. The gods, to whom this service of thanksgiving was offered, are popularly esteemed to be the divine ancestors of the present reigning sovereign, and victory against Russia is considered by the pious sentiment of the country to have been due, not only to the valour of the Japanese rank and file and the prudence of the Japanese generals, not only to the many virtues of the reigning sovereign whose faithfulness to duty has given and sustained the impulse to reform, but also and mainly to the invisible aid of the divine Ancestors of the imperial house. To the long line of sovereigns who ruled once as gods on the plains of heaven, who descended upon Japan in the person of Jimmu Tennō the first earthly Emperor (660–585BC) from when all the other Emperors are descended in a long and unbroken line, each at his decease returning to the plains of heaven, to join the venerable company of divine ancestors whose privilege it is to receive the adoration and worship of the Japanese people, and to watch perpetually with paternal care over the destinies of the beloved land. As a corollary to this conception the actual occupant of the throne for the time being is often looked upon as the intermediary between the nation and the gods. On solemn occasions of worship it is he that presents the adoration and prayer as representative and mouth-piece of his subjects; conversely, the wisdom of the divine ancestors descends upon him for the guidance and governance of his people.

**Yukio Mishima** from *The Sound of Waves*

Returning from fishing the next day, Shinji set out for the lighthouse carrying two scorpion-fish, each about five or six inches long, strung by the gills on a straw rope. He had already climbed to the rear of Yashiro Shrine when he remembered that he had not yet offered a prayer of thanks to the god for having showered him with blessings so quickly. He went back to the front of the shrine and prayed devoutly.

His prayer finished, Shinji gazed out over the Gulf of Ise, already shining in the moonlight, and breathed deeply. Clouds were floating above the horizon, looking like ancient gods. The boy felt a consummate accord between himself and this opulence of nature that surrounded him. He inhaled deeply and it was as though a part of the unseen something that constitutes nature had permeated the core of his being. He heard the sound of the waves striking the shore, and it was as though the surging of his young blood was keeping time with the movement of the sea's great tides. It was doubtless because nature itself satisfied his need that Shinji felt no particular lack of music in his everyday life.

Shinji lifted the scorpion-fish to the level of his eyes and stuck out his tongue at their ugly, thorny faces. The fish were definitely alive, but they made not the slightest movement. So Shinji poked one in the jaw and watched it flop about in the air. Thus the boy was loitering along the way, loath to have the happy meeting take place too quickly.

**Tobias Hill** 'On the Island of Pearls'
(In memory of Kokichi Mikimoto, inventor of the cultured pearl)

> From *Year of the Dog*
>
> Along the jetty, sparrows nag
> at the green shells of plum blossom
> still clenched, and the sea-sky
> luminous as the nape of an abalone.
>
> Something was invented here.
> We tour boutiques and show-rooms, where
> days are measured out in strands,
> their length, lustre. Weeks in the sphere
> of one perfect pearl. An organic jewel
> that comes in all the colours of the skin.
>
> Something was invented. So many kinds
> of failure: the Odd, the Butterfly, the Twin,
> which grows into an hourglass.
> The Lobe and Tongue, grotesqueries,
> worthless. Pain embalming itself like wax
> dropped down the candle's shank.
> The pearl is a function of pain.
>
> In the next room, a young woman
> sits between baroque sculptures;
> an ocean shrine, a sea-god's crown
> nacred. She bows and demonstrates
> the method of insertion,
> the oyster's poached skin
> slit like the white of an egg. Somewhere
> outer doors open, her words
> drowned in the sea's yawn and boom.

The jetty smells of white salt, sunshine, plum.
We rest under the massive bronze
of the Pearl King. He stands like one, eyes
setting his lands in order
through cataracts of verdigris.
Still looking for the hearts, to find
always inside the immaculate pearl

dirt. The lustre of mud.
We buy rice-cakes, walk among
the blossom trees to the arcades,
hoardings on old nails screeching
in the load of the wind. The sound
sweet as bird-song.

# 9

# Ōsaka

The breezes of love are all-pervasive
by Shijimi River, where love-drowned guests
like empty shells, bereft of their senses,
wander the dark waves of love
lit each night by burning lanterns,
fireflies that glow in the four seasons,
stars that shine on rainy nights
by plum bridge, blossoms show even in summer.
Rustics on a visit, city connoisseurs,
all journey the varied roads of love,
what a lively place this New Quarter is!

CHIKAMATSU MONZAEMON

Ōsaka built itself up as a port and a stepping-off point for Chinese trade and travel through the Inland Sea. Known as Naniwa in ancient times, this was the place where Emperor Jimmu (660–585BC) was said to land when he arrived in Yamato (present day Kinki) from Kyūshū. In the grounds of Ōsaka castle lie the remains of the first political centre for Japan, Naniwa palace, founded by Emperor Temmu in around AD680. The earliest Buddhist temple, founded by Prince Shōtoku (AD572–621), was at Shitennoji. Later on Pure Land Buddhists built a temple here too.

Hideyoshi (1536–98) organised goods to be delivered to Ōsaka and then shipped throughout the nation through a system of canals which he created in the city. By 1700 there were about ninety-five *daimyo* warehouses in Ōsaka, which became the centre of the rice exchange. Merchants of Ōsaka prided themselves on their taste and indulged their appetites for cloth, ceramics, lacquerware and gold. Ōsaka was often compared to Renaissance Venice by foreigners with as many as eight hundred and eight bridges and canals. But it could equally be compared to Venice for its less restricted fiscal laws.

Ōsaka was pivotal to the rise and fall of the Tokugawa shoguns. After laying siege to Ōsaka castle in 1615, Tokugawa Ieyasu secured absolute power in Japan, throwing his predecessor's heir – Hideyori – out of the castle with false promises of a truce. But the siege of Ōsaka-jō left the Tokugawa shogunate in debt to the city of Ōsaka, whose favour they urgently needed to secure the so-called Great Peace. They therefore kept a hands-off approach to the city – offering a remission of taxes and little military enforcement, unlike almost every other city in Japan. The merchant class gained clout during the Tokugawa period when a rice economy (the measurement of a samurai's wealth was in *tsubo* or rice) was traded through the merchants for coins. Powerful moneylenders included the Mitsui family (see Tokyo chapter).

Shogun Tsunayoshi ruled in a more relaxed way during the Genroku (1680–1709) era, and the spirit of liberty and convivial living was best expressed in Osaka resident Chikamatsu Monzaemon's plays (1653–1725). Monzaemon's *Love Suicides of Amijima* was a *bunraku* puppet play (the playwright turned to puppet plays after 1705, to avoid censorship), written in response to a report that a man and a woman committed *shinjū*, or double suicide, together on an island in Ōsaka Bay. The married man and courtesan speak of how they had to cross many bridges, both literal and metaphorical, to get to where they were going.

But Ōsaka-jō was also the site of the fall of the shogunate in 1867, when the last shogun, Yoshinobu, resigned the shogun's power following the arrival of the American Black Ships ten years earlier. These stormy times, when Japan was both amazed and terrifed by the arrival of foreigners on their streets and when European ambassadors vied to give advice about the imminent collapse of the stage, are all described by Ernest Satow, the official interpreter to Sir Harry Parkes, the British Ambassador.

Pat Barr's book *The Coming of the Barbarians* covers the reception of the foreign delegation to Ōsaka and follows the diaries of Sir

Rutherford Alcock (1809–1897), the British envoy during a trip through Japan in 1860–61. A. B. Mitford's description of the last stand of the shogun is included here as well.

But although Ōsaka's wealth declined after the fall of the shoguns, and the return of the Emperor to the capital (for a story of the decline of the merchant class, see *The Makioka Sisters* by Junichirō Tanizaki) – it did not lose its inclination towards entertainment, pleasure and comedy. Oda Sakunosuke (1913–47) is the writer who best chronicled the twenties and thirties in Ōsaka. In his stories he conjures the greatness of the city – the food, the seedy entertainment and the sea. Sakunosuke belonged to the *burai ha*, or hooligan group, of writers and prided himself on his rebellious spirit:

> I thought of all the writers of *gesaku* (playful) fiction in the Edo period who ended up in prison because of their writings and I felt a kind of perverse delight in what I was doing . . . Like a little boy who, when told he's being naughty, acts even naughtier, the least I could do to maintain my self-respect was to show I could thumb my nose at the world.

It is lucky that Sakunosuke did describe the world of Ōsaka in such detail because the whole city was firebombed in the Second World War. But in the 1990s, Ōsaka bounced back, becoming a showcase for Japan's bold new architecture and other ventures. Several of the old sites such as the old rice exchange, the Nakanoshima, were renewed as well as the new technology sites like Panasonic Square.

In addition there is the Umeda sky building (Umeda is the name for the 'plum bridge' described in *The Love Suicides of Sonezaki*) designed by Hara Hiroshi as well as the WTC building, part of a programme by Junichi Seki, the governor of Ōsaka, to attract foreign investors to the city. At Shinsaibashi there is a gathering of foreign residents as well as hip young Japanese, but Alex Kerr goes further in, to Shinsekai and Tobita, downtown areas of the city.

**Chikamatsu Monzaemon** from *The Love Suicides of Amijima*

JIHEI   Although I am born a parishioner of such an exalted deified man,[30] I shall kill you and die myself. This is because I do not have enough discretion to fill one of those tiny shells of the Shijimi River. The Shijimi Bridge is short. Things that are short are our stay in this life and an autumn day. We are tired of living. Although we are only nineteen and twenty-eight, this very night is the end, the moment to throw away our two lives. We vowed to live devotedly together until our end as an aged man and woman, but before we have had three full years of intimacy, we have met with calamity. Look there. We have come past the Naniwa Small bridge to the bank by Funairi Bridge. We've come this far, and the farther we go, the closer we get to the road to Hades.

*[He laments and she clings to him.*

KOHARU   Is this already Hades?

*[And they look at each other, but their tears are falling*
*so fast they can hardly see each other's faces, and they*
*seem to flood the bridges over the Horikawa.*

JIHEI   If I should walk toward the north, I could have another glimpse of my home but I do not look that way. I suppress in my breast thoughts of my children's future and my wife's pitiable lot. Toward the south stretches the bridge which we cross with its innumerable piles. The other shore has houses, so why should it be named 'Eight Houses'? We must hurry along the road before the boat from Fushimi lands there. I wonder who are sleeping together on it. To us, who are abandoning this world, it is frightening even to hear of the demon.[31] The two rivers, the Yodo and the Yamato, flow into one stream, the Ōkawa. The water and fish go along together inseparably, just as the two, Koharu and I go

30   Michizane
31   of Temma Bridge

together and cross the River Styx by the blade of one sword. I should like to receive this river water as an offering of water from the living.

KOHARU  What is there to lament? Although indeed, we cannot go together through this life, in the future one, needless to say, and in the next and next, and through all future worlds, we shall be man and wife. As a request that we be reborn on one lotus calyx, I have performed the summer writing of one copy each summer of the most merciful, most compassionate *Fumombon* of the Lotus Sutra. When we cross Kyō Bridge, we reach the other bank – Nirvana. We will mount the lotus calyx, attain the Law, and achieve the form of Buddha. If I may save mankind as I wish, I should like to protect prostitutes so that hereafter they will never commit love suicides.

> [*This unattainable wish is a worldly complaint. It makes us sympathise with her and pity her. In the inlet toward Noda, the mist rises from the water, and beyond one sees, faint and white, the edge of the hills.*]

JIHEI  There the bells of the temples are sounding. We cannot remain like this. We cannot live out our lives, so let us hurry to our end. Come this way.

**Algernon Bertram Mitford** from *Mitford's Japan*

*Civil War*

On 30 November 1867 – at daylight – Satow and I, in our usual characters as diplomatic stormy petrels, said that Ōsaka should make all the preparations for the opening of that city and Hyōgō on the first day of that new year which was to come big with the birth of new power and fraught with events as momentous, perhaps, as any that the history of the world has seen. We reached Ōsaka on 3 December and were at once plunged in the political whirlpool. Besides that we had to prepare quarters for the Minister and his staff and the mounted escort, with fifty men of the 9th regiment. Much building of palisades, bonded warehouses, custom houses, etc, was going on at what was to be the future foreign settlement. This was going a little too fast, and we had to put a stop to any further work until the Ministers should arrive. They might have a good deal to say upon the subject, especially as to the pallisades, which were not a very encouraging indication of the intentions of the Government to promote intercourse between East and West.

On 7 December we had an interview with members of the Tycoon's Council of State who were on their way to Edo, and whom he had ordered to see us. We did not get much information out of them except that the Tycoon's resignation was merely the carrying out of an intention formed long ago. We were not convinced, nor were we shaken in our beliefs that he had been driven to it by the persistent attitude of the clans.

On 12 December, we had to leave for Hyōgō in order to see what preparations were being made there for the great event. We found that the people were in high spirits at the prospect of the opening of the port. In Kōbe, where the foreign settlement was to be, there had been seven days of feasting and merrymaking, and there had been processions of people dressed in red crepe with carts which were supposed to carry earth for the site of the new settlement. Similar feats were in prospect in the town of Hyōgō. The people obviously saw the foreign trade would spell prosperity for them.

*W. G. Aston, who was later to become one of the best Japanese scholars, had reported to Mitford that the preparations for the opening of Hyōgō, i.e. Kōbe, were well advanced. The levelling and clearing of the site were finished; the sea wall was almost complete and workmen were busily engaged on the dock. The custom house and bonded warehouses together with temporary accommodation for foreign merchants were expected to be ready by 1st January 1868.*

When we got back to Ōsaka on 13 December we found the city in an uproar of joy and excitement. It appeared that all this was in honour of a miraculous shower which had recently taken place of slips of paper bearing the titles of the Gods of Ise – the ancestral shrine of Old Japan and the chief place of the Shinto cult. Thousands and thousands of happy fanatics were dancing along the streets dressed in holiday garb of red and blue crepe and carrying red lanterns on their heads, shouting till they must have been hoarse, '*Iija nai ka, iija nai kai!*' (How delightful, how delightful!). The houses were decorated with many coloured cakes, oranges, silken bags, emblematic ropes of straw such as are hung before the Shinto shrines, and a profusion of flowers.

It was a weird and wonderful sight, such as, maybe, will never be seen again; and yet folklore and old reverences die hard. Even though all this should be *mukashi* as much so as the mysteries of Stonehenge are to us, one may hope that it may yet have some life in it. *Le respect du passé est la piété filiale des peuples*, was a fine saying of the Duc de Broglie; one which, in these degenerate days, I never weary of quoting, and we foreigners must not forget what the Japanese owe to the Yamato Damashii, the spirit of old Japan. It is upon the legends of the Shinto that it is founded.

No sooner were we back in Ōsaka than the old political conversations began again. Satsuma, Chōshū, Tosa, Uwajima and Geishu were solid for a change; other daiimyo inclined to join but were vacillating. One thing we were clearly given to understand; if the intrigues now going on at Kyoto failed, the *Daimyo* would revert to the old game of murderous attacks upon foreigners, not from any dislike of foreign intercourse, of which they were indeed in favour, but simple in order to embroil the Tycoon [32] with the Treaty Powers. The obvious answer to this was that whatever might happen in that way, the Tycoon could not be held responsible for the action of persons over whom he, as they admitted, had not control!

The arrival of leading men in Ōsaka, so near Kyoto, at this time was very significant. Saigo Takamori, the famous Satsuma general, who died years afterwards by *harakiri* in the rebellion of his Satsuma clan, and Goto Shojiro, were very conspicuous figures. The latter talked a great deal about the scheme to murder Satow and myself at Ōtsu in August and gave us many particulars. It was a merciful escape.

*As the shogun's troops attempted to make a last ditch stand against the Emperor – the year of unrest continued with plots and counterplots, conspiracies and intrigues, and finally a showdown with the Tokugawa and Imperial troops, which A. B. Mitford observed:*

32 shogun

A more extravagantly weird picture it would be difficult to imagine. There were some infantry armed with European rifles, but there were also warriors clad in the old armour of the country carrying spears, bows and arrows, falchions, curiously shaped, with sword and dirk, who looked as if they had stepped out of some old picture of the Gempei wars in the Middle Ages. Their *jimbarois*, not unlike heralds' tabards, were as many coloured as Joseph's coat. Hideous masks of lacquer and iron, fringed with portentous whiskers and moustachios, crested helmets with wigs from which long streamers of horsehair floated to their waists, might strike terror into any enemy. They looked like the hobgoblins of a nightmare. Soon a troop of horsemen appeared. The Japanese all prostrated themselves and bent their heads in reverent awe. In the midst of the troop was the fallen Prince, accompanied by his faithful adherents, Aizu and Kuwana. The Prince himself seemed worn and dejected, looking neither to the right nor to the left, his head wrapped in a black cloth, taking notice of nothing. Some of those with him recognized us and returned our salutes. It was a wild and wonderful sight and one of the saddest that I have ever beheld. At the gate, all dismounted, according to custom – save only the Warlord himself – he rode in, a solitary horseman. It was the last entry of a shogun into the grand old castle which had come into the heritage of the Tokugawa by one tragedy and was to pass out of their possession by another. In each case fire, 'the calamity of the dancing horse,'[33] played its cruel part.

---

33  A term borrowed from the Chinese classics. In the days of the Sung dynasty in China a tower called the 'Tower of the Dancing Horse' was burnt down, since which time a great fire is called after it.

**Pat Barr** from *The Coming of the Barbarians*

They did [the party of foreigners] at any rate explore Ōsaka fairly thoroughly – a mediaeval township peopled with craftsmen, merchants, and hired hands and dominated by the grim, grey, castle of the shogun. The whole population spilled out to see the hairy barbarians ride by and their escort had to clear a passage through the quiet, curious throng by banging citizens over the head with weighty fans. For part of one day the Westerners were punted in small open boats along the city's bustling, fetid canals which were darkened by the shadows of overhanging balconies and edged by the granite outer walls of merchants' residences and warehouses. The canals were spanned by wooden bridges which vibrated under the constant pad of coolies' feet and whose rails, that day, were knobbed with rows of watchful heads as the foreigners passed beneath. Ōsaka, decided Alcock – who was adept at coining the cliché which bevies of subsequent globe-trotters would find useful for their journals – Ōsaka, said Sir Rutherford, 'is the Venice of Japan'.

The party also visited Kabuki and saw the theatre in its original, pre-westernised form in which the whole of the auditorium was divided into separate wooden compartments. A family would hire one of these for the day and, squatting comfortably on the *tatami*, father, mother, children of all ages and grandparents would alternately watch the action, smoke, sleep through the dull bits and chat among themselves. During the leisurely intervals, lacquer lunch-boxes were opened, servants arrived bearing more food and the floor of the little compartments became a glorious messy heap of fish-bones, chopsticks, thimble-sized sake cups, beans, bowls and teapots as the family feasted – feasts which often continued long after the actors had returned to rant up and down and kill each other all over the stage. Sir Rutherford enjoyed the audience immensely, but found the drama so indelicate that, after making all possible allowances for different cultural tastes, he still could not 'conceive how anything of purity or sanctity could enter into the lives of the young girls and respectable matrons who find their recreation in witnessing such plays'.

When Alcock wrote about his visit to Kabuki several months later, he found that one particular scene was fixed indelibly in his mind, more because of what had ensued in the intervening period than because of its intrinsic merit. The scene showed a large dark house surrounded by a wall. Over the wall silently appeared several muffled figures, who crept menacingly towards the house, swords glinting in their hands. The house and its occupants were asleep, cradled in the light of a full moon. Cat-like men leap on to a low balcony, slide slim shutters, raise their bright weapons. There is a scream, noise of a scuffle . . . it was an unpleasant thought.

The next day the party left Ōsaka for Yedo and were at first annoyed by groups of peasant boys who popped from around corners and behind trees bawling something that sounded like 'Tojin Baba' at them from a wary distance. It was not, apparently a compliment, as 'Tojin' meant Chinese and 'Baba' meant an old woman or a wily merchant – or both. After a time, however, they outpaced their detractors and fell into an easy loiter through a sweet countryside which dozed and buzzed in the summer sun. Occasionally they passed primitive refreshment stalls and on the counters of these, displayed among the sticky yellow buns and pink bean curd pastries were light wooden frameworks from which hung rows of tiny tortoises, suspended by their hapless middles in midair. These desperate little creatures turned their scaly heads and constantly pawed at space in a vain endeavour to make some progress toward the earth below them. The plight of these tortoises worried Alcock considerably, not only because of its essential discomfort, but because it aroused in him a strong sense of fellow feeling, for, he writes, 'I was struck with the analogy to my own position as diplomatic Agent in Japan. Doomed, like them, to unceasing effort, without any very sensible progress.' Poor Alcock, he could rarely escape from the impression that he was being put upon and that the world, on both its oriental and occidental sphere, was against him.

**Oda Sakunosuke** from *Stories of Ōsaka Life*

*City of Trees*

People say Ōsaka is a city with no trees, but when I think back to my childhood I find I have a remarkable number of memories that involve trees. There were the big old camphor trees in the grounds of the Ikutama Shrine, that were supposed to have snakes living in them and that I consequently was afraid to go near. Or the gingko trees in the grounds of the Kitamuki Hachiman Shrine where I hung out my clothes to dry after I accidentally fell into the lotus pond there. And the old pines in the temple compounds in Nakadera-machi that were the same colour as the cicadas that hid their branches, or the rest that spread their green shade over the steep lanes of Gensho-ji Slope or Kuchinawa Slope. No, I wouldn't say I grew up in a city without trees. As far as I am concerned, Ōsaka has lots of trees.

Try going up in one of the tall buildings in the Sennichi-mae area. If you look east toward the Kozu bluff on the north and the Ikutama and Yuhigaoka bluffs that flank it on the south, you will see that, beyond the smoke and dust that smudge the air, there is still a mass of luxuriant green there, its depths peaceful and silent as they have been for countless centuries.

That is the area of Ōsaka popularly referred to as *uemachi*, the High City. We who were born and raised in the High City, always spoke of 'going down below' when we went to the Semba, Shima-no-uchi or Sennichi-mae areas. But we did not think of the High City as being in contrast to the Shitamachi or Low City. The High City in Ōsaka is called that because it is situated on the bluffs, but the bluff area has none of the associations of elegance or elitism that go with the Yamanote or hilly region of Tokyo. The communities on the Ōsaka bluffs grew up around the temples and shrines there, or on what was said to be the site of the Takatsu palace, where Emperor Nintoku in ancient times wrote the poem that begins:

> Ascending my high hall
> I see the smoke rising –

> The kitchens of my people
> Are bustling indeed![34]

Such communities prided themselves on the degree to which they preserved the quiet dignity associated with these traditions of the past, and indeed something of that atmosphere did cling to the areas. But there were other areas such as the main street in front of the Kozu Shrine, the Babasaki area around Ikutama Shrine or the *gataro* alley district in Nakadera-machi that as early as the Genroku era in the seventeenth century had become thoroughly imbued with that air of freedom and liveliness characteristic of the Ōsaka Low City. So, even those of us who were born in the High City in a sense grew up as Low City children.

The High City had a lot of little alleys – which is to say there were a lot of poor people living there. At the same time there were lots of slopes and rises, which is natural enough since the area was situated on the bluff. When we spoke of 'going down below' we meant going west down these slopes. Jizo Slope, Shogen-ji Slope, Aizen Slope, Kuchinawa Slope – just saying the names over brings back happy memories. Kuchinawa in particular has fond associations for me.

In Ōsaka dialect Kuchinawa is another name for snake, and as one may have guessed, Kuchinawa Slope was so-called because of the way the old flight of stone steps that went up the slope wriggled up and down like a snake as it threaded among the trees. If you had come right out and called it Snake Slope, the whole effect would have been ruined, but by calling it Kuchinawa Slope you give it a feeling of quaintness and humour, and for that reason when I think of the slopes in Ōsaka, Kuchinawa is the first name that comes to mind.

When I was a boy, however, I took no interest in what kind of atmosphere was suggested by the name Kuchinawa Slope. Rather it was the name associated with the area at the top of the slope,

---

34  A poem in the *Shinkokinshū* – attributed to Emperor Nintoku (313–99). The exact site of Takatsu Palace has never been determined, though several areas in the hilly section of Ōsaka lay claim to it.

Yuhigaoka or Evening Sun Hill that attracted me and roused my curiosity. The name Yuhigaoka I'm sure dates back a long way. In the old times if you looked West from the bluff here you could no doubt have gotten a good view of the sun as it went down in Naniwa Bay. I think it was Fujiwara no Ietaka who wrote the poem that goes:

> Bound by karma,
> I've come to make my home
> in Naniwa village
> and to gaze in reverence
> at the setting sun on the waves.[35]

Because he was living on the bluff at the time he wrote the poem, I guess it was inevitable that the place should come to be called Evening Sun Hill.

**Alex Kerr** from *Lost Japan*

*Bumpers and Runners*

Welcome to Ōsaka. Few major cities of the developed world could match Ōsaka for the overall unattractiveness of its cityscape, which consists mostly of a jumble of cube-like buildings and a web of expressways and cement-walled canals. There are few skyscrapers, even fewer museums and other than Ōsaka Castle, almost no historical sites. Yet Ōsaka is my favourite city in Japan, it is where the fun is: it has the best entertainment districts in Japan, the most lively youth neighbourhood, the most charismatic geisha madams and the most colourful gangsters. It also has a monopoly on humour, to the extent that in order to succeed as a popular comedian it is almost obligatory to study in Ōsaka and speak the Ōsaka dialect.

A few blocks away from the neighbourhood of Shinsekai is Tobita,

---

35  The famous courtier and poet Fujiwara no Ietaka (1158–1237) retired from public life in Kyoto and came to live in Naniwa shortly before his death. A stone that is said to mark his grave is still to be seen near the top of Kuchinawa Slope.

Japan's last *kuruwa*. In Edo days, prostitution was strictly regulated and the courtesans lived in small walled towns within the cities, which had gates and closing times. These cities-within-the city were known as *kuruwa* (enclosures). In Kyoto the old gate to the *kuruwa* of Shimabara still stands, although Shimabara itself is defunct. The largest *kuruwa* was Yoshiwara. Within the walls of Yoshiwara, there was a lattice of streets lined with pleasure houses, a scene familiar in the Kabuki theatre, where such streets form the backdrop of many love plays. The entrance to each pleasure house featured a banner with the name of the house on it; inside, women wearing gorgeous kimonos were on display. Today, Yoshiwara is still in business, but the boundaries, the street grid, the houses and the banners have been replaced by a jumble of streets sprinkled with love hotels and saunas, with the result that it looks not much different from most of the other places in Tokyo. If you can't read the signs, you might not realize the nature of the neighbourhood. Tobita, however, survives almost completely intact. There are no walls, but there is a precise gridwork of streets lined with low tile-roofed houses. In front of each house is a banner and inside the entrance a young woman and the madam sit side by side next to a brazier. This is as close to Kabuki in the modern age as you can get.

A word of caution: it is best not to stroll around Shinsekai or Tobita without a Japanese friend if you are a foreigner, as you might be accosted by a gangster or an unfriendly drunk. I usually go there in the company of an Ōsaka friend, Satoshi; he looks so tough that once, when he was on his way to a wedding dressed in a black suit and sunglasses, the police picked him up on suspicion of being a gangster. Many Japanese are afraid to enter the downtown neighbourhoods of Ōsaka. There is one area in particular that taxi drivers will not go into at all because of the *atariya* – bumpers – who make a living from bumping into your car and then screaming that you have run over them. The whole neighbourhood rushes out to support the *atariya* threatening to act as witnesses in a lawsuit against you until you pay up. Even so, this pales in comparison to what can happen in New York and many of Europe's largest cities. The gangsters of Ōsaka and Kōbe, known as Japan's most vicious, keep largely out of sight, and in general, violent crime is rare. One of Japan's greatest achievements is its relative lack of crime, and this is one of the invisible factors which make life here very comfortable. The low crime rate is the result of those smoothly running social systems and is the envy of many a nation – this is the good side of having trained the populations to be bland and obedient. The difference in Ōsaka is only one of degree. The streets are still basically safe. What you see in Shinsekai is more a form of misbehaviour rather than serious crime. People do not act decorously: they shout, cry, scream and jostle one another; in well-behaved modern Japan this is shocking.

Ōsaka does not merely preserve old styles of entertainment, it constantly dreams up new ones. For example, Ōsaka premiered the 'no panties coffee shops', with pantyless waitresses that later swept Japan. In other places, the boom remained limited to coffee shops, but in Ōsaka they now have '*no panties okonomiyaki*' *(omelette)*, '*do it yourself pizza*' and '*no panties gyudon*', beef and rice bowls. The latest, I hear, is a breast rub coffee where a topless waitress on delivering coffee to the table rubs her customer's face in the way the name would suggest.

The entertainment is by no means limited to the sex business. Ōsaka pioneered a new type of drive-in public bath in Goshikiyu near the Toyonaka interchange on the expressway. In general, public baths are slowly dying out in Japan as the number of homes with their own bath and shower increases. However, an Ōsaka bathhouse proprietor with an entrepreneurial bent promoted the idea that an evening out at a public bath was the perfect family entertainment. He built a multi-storey bathhouse with a large parking lot to service Japan's new car-centred lifestyle. Inside he installed restaurants, saunas and several floors of baths with every type of tub, hot, cold or tepid with Jacuzzi shower or waterfall. On a Saturday night you can hardly get into Goshikiyu's parking lot. The place is jammed with families with small children.

[...]

Donald Richie, dean of the Japanologists in Tokyo once made this observation to me: 'The people of Iya were not the only people who escaped regimentation during the military period. There was one other group: people living in the downtowns of big cities like Edo and Ōsaka.

The merchants in these cities were a different breed from the farmers, with their need to cooperate in rice growing, and the samurai, with their code of loyalty and propriety. The samurai despised the merchants as belonging to the bottom of the social totem pole, but at the same time, the merchants had the freedom to enjoy themselves. The brilliant realm of the 'floating world' Kabuki, the pleasure quarters, colourful kimonos, woodblock prints, novels, dance, belonged to the old downtowns. Even today, people from these neighbourhoods were different from ordinary Japanese. This is especially true of Ōsaka. The downtown neighbourhoods of Tokyo, while they still exist, have largely lost their identity, but Ōsaka maintains a spirit of fierce independence which goes back a long way. Originally Ōsaka was a fishing village on the Inland Sea called Naniwa. The writer Shiba Ryotaro maintains that the colourful language and brutal honesty of Ōsaka people can be traced to Naniwa's seaport past.

Ōsaka dialect is certainly colourful. Standard Japanese has an almost complete lack of dirty words. The very meanest thing you can shout at somebody is *Ishisunma*, which means literally, 'honourable you'. But Ōsaka people say such vividly imaginative things that you want to sit back and take notes. Most are unprintable, but here is one classic Ōsaka epithet: 'I'm going to slash your skull in half, stir up your brains and drink them out with a straw.'

The fishwife invective and the desire to shock produced the playful language that is the hallmark of Ōsaka dialect. When Satoshi describes a visit to the bank, it's funnier than the routines of most professional comics. It begins with the bank and ends with the dice tattooed on his aunt's left shoulder. Free association of the sort he employs is called *manzai* in the blood. That's why comedians have to come here to study.

During the early Nara period, Naniwa was Japan's window to the world, serving as the main port of call for embassies from China and Korea. Ōsaka was so important as the seat of diplomacy that the capital was based there several times in the seventh century before finally being moved to Nara. In the process, numerous families from China and Korea emigrated to the Naniwa region, and Heian period censuses show that its population was heavily of continental origin. In the late sixteenth century, Ōsaka's harbour shifted from Naniwa to

Sakai, a few kilometres south. As Chinese silk and Southeast Asian ceramics flooded into Japan, the Ōsaka merchants grew rich; among them was Sen no Rikyū, founder of the tea ceremony (see Kyoto chapter). For several decades Ōsaka was again Japan's window to the world and outshone Kyoto as the source of new cultural developments. During the Edo period, the shogunate closed the ports and three hundred years of isolation set in. But Ōsaka continued to thrive, its merchants establishing themselves as wholesale rice brokers and moneylenders. Certain unique occupations grew up, such as 'runners' who still exist even today; their job is to visit one wholesaling street and jot down prices, then dash over to the next street to report them to competitors and then do the same thing in reverse.

The mercantile ethos in Ōsaka resulted in many of Japan's largest business being based there, such as Sumitomo and the trading house C Itoh, which did more volume of business in 1995 than any other company in the world. Ōsaka's good fortune lay in the fact that the government left the city mostly totally free of control. In Tokyo there was the shogun, in Kyoto there was the Emperor but in Ōsaka there was nobody on top, except a skeleton staff of the shogun's officials holed up in Ōsaka Castle, pitifully unprepared to join in a battle of wits with wily Ōsaka merchants. The ratio of samurai to population was so low that people could go their whole lives without meeting one. In Edo, the shogunate built bridges; in Ōsaka, private business-men built them. In other words, in Ōsaka, the people ran their own lives.

In recent years the fact that certain areas like Shinsekai have become slums has acted as protection, scaring away the developers and investors who raised land prices and transformed the face of Tokyo. Ōsaka preserved its identity, which goes right back to the old seaport of Naniwa, so when friends asked me to show them the 'true Japan of ancient tradition' I don't take them to Kyoto, I take them to Ōsaka.

# 10

# Hiroshima and Chūgoku

'A film about Peace. What else do you expect them to make
in Hiroshima except a picture about Peace?'

*Hiroshima Mon Amour*

Hiroshima is the 'broad island' at the mouth of the River Ota; beyond
it, just out to sea, lies the island of Miyajima, settled by no less a
general than Taira no Kiyomori in the twelfth century. When Kiyomori became governor of Aki in 1146 – the province facing the Seto
Naikai, the Inland Sea – he wanted to profit from trade with China, so
he dredged the channels of the river and built a sanctuary on nearby
Miyajima. The bright red lacquered *torii* on Miyajima, surrounded
by maple and acer trees, dates from the Heian period (794–1185).
Hideyoshi (see Kyoto chapter) added the Itsukushima *jinja* with
red columns and lantern-filled corridors as well as a *senjokaku*, a
thousand-tatami-mat pavilion. The island was considered so sacred
that ordinary people were originally not allowed to approach. Many
deer, so-called messengers of the *kami* (gods), were also kept here,
and sailors sought protection at the Miyajima shrine.

During the Edo period (1603–1867), Hiroshima expanded into
a bustling sea-faring community that was controlled by a succession
of different clans. It suffered few military disturbances until the
surrounding coast was bombarded from the sea by Choshu and
Satsuma forces during the so-called Summer War of 1866. At that
time, Ujina harbour was dredged to accommodate ships and a railway
line, which ran from Kyoto to Kyushu, was built through the city.
Hiroshima became a commercial centre during the Sino-Japanese
war of 1894 and, during the Russo-Japanese war of 1904, a staging
post for troops going to the mainland front.

During the Pacific War in the early 1940s, the Japanese sought to expand the boundaries of their empire, leaving the *hinomaru* flag flying over the Philippines, the China coast and much of Southeast Asia. As a result of early Japanese successes, in 1942 the army headquarters at Ujina was reorganised to include the marine headquarters. When a series of Allied operations pushed the Japanese back from the south Pacific, the government had to recruit thousands of extra servicemen who swelled Hiroshima's population. The authorities also became concerned about Allied firebombing, as most houses in Hiroshima were made of wood. In the spring of 1945, elementary-age school-children were evacuated and firebreaks constructed to criss-cross the city and prevent total conflagration. Although the city was on the alert for attack, it was still believed that continuous efforts by the Japanese people could bring about ultimate victory, and the planes dropping leaflets warning of impending doom were dismissed as propaganda.

When the atomic bomb was dropped on August 6th, 1945, it killed upwards of 100,000 in a flash. The one building to survive was the Old Industry Promotion Hall, and its iron girders have become a symbol for the survival of the city. The Genbaku Dōmu (the atomic bomb dome) is preserved in the Peace Park and stands opposite Kenzō Tange's design of the Heiwa Kinen Shiryōkan, the peace museum.

Kenzaburo Ōe visited Hiroshima several times to talk to victims and wrote his reflections on the peace movement and the experience of atomic bomb victims in his book, *Hiroshima Notes*. As Lisa Yoneyama has pointed out in her penetrating study, *Hiroshima Traces*, there has recently been a memory boom, with both eye-witness and other accounts, as well as more memorials including one to the Korean atomic bomb victims. This details about 25,000 Korean forced labourers who were at work in Hiroshima when the bomb fell. Alan Booth's *A Thousand Cranes, A Thousand Suns* goes some way to describing the unresolved feelings relating to the war that still exist beneath the surface of Japanese society.

# CHŪGOKU

Hiroshima lies in an area known as Chūgoku, or the middle country. This is the part of Japan that, along with Shikoku and the Inland Sea, were the setting for the twelfth century battles between the Taira and the Genji clans. Shimonoseki, on the southern tip of Honshū, was the site of the battle of Dan no ura, the decisive clash between the Taira and Minamoto clans fought in 1185. The Akama *jingū* there is dedicated to the defeated Taira. The historian and contemporary of those times, Kamo no Chōmei (1155–1216), wrote the history of the warring clans.

The Taira's claim to supremacy was through Taira no Kiyomori's grandson, Emperor Antoku, who was next in line to the throne. But in the 1180s the Genji, the Northern tribe, under Minamoto no Yoritomo, marched on the capital, taking advantage of Kiyomori's indisposition with a raging fever in 1181. For two long years the Genji and the Taira fought in central Japan, while the Emperor Go Shira-kawa slipped out of Kyoto to the more peaceful Mount Hiei, tacitly supporting the Yoritomo Genji cause, while the Taira retreated with the would-be child Emperor Antoku to Western Honshū.

Then, in 1185, Yoshitsune, the younger brother of Yoritomo of the Genji, forced the Taira clan to put out to sea and sail West to Itsukushima and then to Shimonoseki at the western limit of the Inland Sea. This is where Kiyomori's father had been governor. But at Dan no ura on April 25, 1185 the navies, each with about four to five hundred ships, clashed in the straits with the tide favouring the Taira. At the crucial moment, the tide turned and betrayed the Taira, taking the Emperor with it. The mother of the emperor, Nii Dono, famously sang a last lament.

Other towns in Chūgoku distinguish themselves for their fierce warlike pasts. Tsuwano's castle was built to protect Japan against the Mongols in 1295 by *daimyo* Yoshimi Yoriyuki and the castle town still has many samurai houses or *tonomachi* as well as a museum to the novelist Mori Ōgai (1862–1922). The Yoshimi followed their allies to Hagi after they fought on the losing side of the battle of Sekigahara.

Hagi is the home of samurai Yoshida Shōin, whose aim was to displace the Tokugawa government and to '*sanno joi*' or 'revere the Emperor and expel the barbarian'. However, he was executed for his pains in 1860 aged only twenty-nine. Yamaguchi became famous to foreigners because St Francis Xavier preached on its streets in 1549, licensed by the *daimyo* of the tolerant ruling family, Ouchi Hiroyo.

But the highlight of any trip to Western Honshū must be to see Matsue, where Lafcadio Hearn, one of the first professional Western 'Japanologists' lived. Hearn was extraordinary among foreigners at the time, as he was adopted by Japanese society. The town is dominated by the seventeenth century samurai castle, the Oshiroyama. Arriving in Matsue from Yokohama in 1890 in order to teach English, Lafcadio quickly married a local, Setsuko Koizumi, and was adopted into her family as Yakumo Koizumi. He also stayed in the nearby seaside resort of Izumo, where the Izumo Taisha (shrine) is the site of many festivals to the sun goddess, which enchanted Hearn when he first arrived in Japan.

Setsuko was the daughter of an impoverished samurai family, her father Minato Koizumi's mansion was located in a quiet residential quarter overlooking the castle. Here is the Yakumo Kin'en Kan, the Hearn museum, built in 1936 by his Japanese fans. After a lifetime of globetrotting, Hearn found that he had never been happier than in Matsue and the letters written to his half-sister in England are ecstatic. He fell in love with the simple pleasures and kindness of the people. But in the end he decided to leave Chūgoku because, as he wrote to his mentor and fellow Japan expert, Basil Hall Chamberlain, 'I fear a few more winters of this kind will put me underground.'

**Kenzaburo Ōe** from *Hiroshima Notes*

Perhaps it is improper to begin a book with reference to one's personal experience. But for myself and Mr. Ryosuke Yasue, an editor, fellow worker, and companion, all the essays about Hiroshima in this book touch the innermost depths of each of our hearts. Hence, our personal experiences when we first went to Hiroshima in the summer of 1963 are pertinent. For myself, there was no hope of recovery for my son, who was on the verge of death and lying in an incubator. Mr Yasue had just lost his first daughter. A mutual friend had hung himself in Paris, overwhelmed by the spectre of a final world war and of impending nuclear doom – an image that daily flooded his consciousness. We were utterly crushed. Even so, we set out for Hiroshima in midsummer. At no other time have I experienced so exhausting, depressing, and suffocating a journey.

In Hiroshima, the Ninth World Conference against Atomic and Hydrogen Bombs – which would last several days and further deepen our gloom – was beset with much difficulty and bitterness. At first it was doubtful if the conference would be held at all: and when finally convened, it was rent by factions. Swathed with sweat and dust, first sighing and then falling into dark and dreary silence, we merely moved about aimlessly among the crowds of earnest people who had come to the conference.

By the time we were ready to leave Hiroshima a week later, we had found a clue as to how we might extricate ourselves from the deep gloom into which we we had fallen. That clue came from the truly human character of the people of Hiroshima . . .

As I arrive in Hiroshima in the summer of 1963, day has just dawned. No local citizens have appeared on the streets yet; only travellers stand here and there near the railroad station. On this same morning in the summer of 1945, many travellers had probably just come to Hiroshima. People who had departed from Hiroshima eighteen years ago today or tomorrow would survive; but those who had not left Hiroshima by the day after tomorrow in August 1945 would experience the most merciless human doom of the twentieth century. Some of them would have vanished in an instant, vapourized by the heat and blast of the atomic bomb, while others would live out their cruel destinies, always afraid to have their leukocytes counted.

The morning air is already dry, with a hot white sheen to it. After an hour, the citizens begin to stir. Although it is still early morning, the sun is as bright as it will be at high noon; and it will remain so till evening. Hiroshima no longer looks like a ghost town at dawn; it is now an active city, with the largest number of bars in Japan. Many travellers, including some whites and blacks, mingle among the local citizens. Most of the Japanese travellers are young. The visitors are walking toward the Peace Memorial Park – Heiwa Kinen Koen, bearing flags and singing songs. By the day after tomorrow, over twenty thousand visitors will have come to Hiroshima.

At nine in the morning I am standing in the Hiroshima Peace Memorial Hall, at the main entrance to the Peace Park. After going up and down stairs and walking back and forth through the corridors, I am finally at a loss about what to do; so I sit on a bench with other people who, like me, are not sure what is going on. A journalist friend has been coming here for several days and, also uncertain, just sits. The air is full of anxiety: is the Ninth World Conference against Atomic and Hydrogen Bombs really going to be held? Various meetings to prepare for the conference are being held in this Memorial Hall, but almost all are secret meetings. Even though I wear a journalist's badge on my shirt collar, I am shut out of all the meetings. The shut-out jounalists and the conference participants who arrived too early – 'too early'? – thousands of people are due to arrive in Hioshima for the Peace March this afternoon, and there is to be a reception for them this evening, and even the regular members of the board of directors of the Japan Council against Atomic and Hydrogen Bombs are all at their wits' end. They slump down on benches, sighing and grumbling 'any country' as if it were a greeting. Initially there was a consensus. 'We oppose nuclear testing done by any country'. But now everyone murmurs 'any country' and sighs gloomily. 'Any country?' What country is meant? The country of the dead? Someone else's country? I recall my first impression of this desolate no-man's-land and of the shivering travellers at dawn.

**Alan Booth** from *The Roads to Sata: a 2000-mile-walk through Japan*

*A Thousand Cranes, A Thousand Suns*

At the point where the atomic bomb was dropped on Hiroshima, there is a Peace Park, and in the Peace Park there is a museum. I visited the museum with no illusions that I would be able to write about what I saw and little real hope that I would comprehend it. The three hours that I spent there, forcing myself to look at every item, reading each caption in English and then again in Japanese, brought me no closer to an understanding but they knocked a gaping hole in my spirit.

It is not the vastness of the destruction that moves you so much as the relics of individual suffering. These speak with the most eloquence, a melted desktop Buddha, a burned watch, the scorched blazer of a thirteen-year-old schoolboy, one of more than six thousand who had been led out to participate in an air-raid defence programme and so were on the unprotected streets when the bomb fell. There are the photographs of a little girl, her will snapped, refusing the cup of water that might have made her death easier; of a young soldier bleeding obscenely from the pores, who died two hours after his picture was taken; of keloid formation on the face and body of a teenage boy, bald as an egg; of a young housewife who had put on, in these last breathless days of the war, a bright, cheerfully patterned summer kimono and the dye of the cloth had burned lines and squares into her back and arms and neck so that she looked, in her death agony, like a plaid doll.

There is a display in which two or three department store mannequins have been dressed in rags and smeared with rubber latex to represent the peeling of their skin. They slouch through a yellow cardboard inferno, so gross, so like a comic strip that I could not bear to look at it. For the three hours I was in the museum my eyes kept drifting to the windows and through them, into an impossibly remote world where fountains played in the sunlight of the park.

I was staggered to see so many schoolchildren being shepherded around the exhibits by their teachers. They were very young and very quiet, shuffling along wide-eyed in their little yellow hats, some holding each other's hands, some pointing and asking their teachers questions that were answered in an almost inaudible drone. I did not see a single child smile, and the seriousness of their faces made them appear very much older and wiser than they were. Many stared as they passed me, and I could feel the bewilderment and tension in their little bodies. One boy turned round from an exhibit to find me standing close behind him and threw up an arm as though to protect his face from a slap. None of the little children laughed at me or shouted greetings, but several whispered to each other, quietly and seriously: 'Look, it's a foreigner. Look, it's a foreigner.' Slowly I shuffled past the exhibits toward the exit with my sunglasses on my foreigner's face, breathing easier because I was almost out of the museum, and quite unprepared for what happened next.

I was looking at one of the last of the displays – a shelf of melted roof tiles and bottles that had fused together in the twelve-thousand-degree heat of the bomb – a heat sufficient to melt human bones. I felt a nudge at my elbow and looked round to find a man in his early thirties – too young, I think to have remembered much about the bombing – standing beside me wearing workman's clothes and smelling (or perhaps I imagined this) – of sake.

He said, 'Your country did this.'

My eyes must have altered behind my sunglasses. I slid away from him and stopped in front of a large photograph of a junior high-school girl with half her face missing. I felt the same nudge and now the man was grinning.

'Do you like this picture?' he asked. 'Do you find it interesting at all? Does it amuse you? Do you find it amusing?'

And suddenly the part of the museum where we were standing was very still because, suddenly, it contained no other people, only a young man with a camera – a student, I think – who came up and slipped quietly between us and said to the workman: 'Stop it, please. Please stop it. Please, leave him alone. He's not an American. Please, stop it.'

But the workman would not be stopped now, and his voice had begun to rise.

'He was rude to me,' he said. 'He turned his back when I spoke to him. He mustn't do that to me. I'm Japanese.'

I drifted on toward the exit, past another group of staring children whose teachers had stopped answering their questions and were looking vacantly at the windows or at the walls. I could hear the workman and the student still arguing and I managed to pause at the souvenir stand long enough to buy some books I wanted – one that contained poems by survivors of the bombing, one with the photograph of the school girl who had no face. When these were wrapped and paid for, I turned round to find the workman waiting for me in the doorway.

At first I pretended I hadn't seen him and tried to walk past him, through the pool of space that other visitors had left around him, out into the impossible world where the fountains played. But it was a narrow doorway, and as I stepped through it, he prodded me, and I took a deep breath and swung round and looked him in the face.

'I'm very sorry,' he said.

'It's all right,' I said. 'I'm sorry I was rude.'

'I'm sorry I was rude,' he said.

'No,' I said, babbling like an idiot. 'I'm sorry, I'm sorry. This is the Peace Park.'

'I'm sorry,' he said.

'No, I'm sorry too,' I said.

I left him in the doorway and went and sat on a bench with my books still wrapped in their paper bag and watched the autumn sun light the leaves of Hiroshima trees.

It was from a cloudless sky like this that the bomb dropped – 'brighter' say the people who saw it, 'than a thousand suns'. Later in the North and East of the city, the sky turned dark and a 'black rain' fell. As painful as the deaths and the lingering disease was surely the bewilderment of the stunned survivors: no such suns, no such rain had ever before intruded into mankind's history.

From my seat under the trees in the Peace Park I watched an old man sweep coloured garbage into a heap that he arranged very carefully beside one of the park's stone monuments. When I passed it on my way to the gate, I saw that it was not a heap of garbage, but thousands upon thousands of tiny folded paper cranes.

There is a story about a little girl, Sadako, who fell desperately ill some two or three months after the bombing. For a long time, the exact nature of A-bomb sickness was dimly understood, and treatment was haphazard and ineffectual. This fact, combined with the soaring black-market prices of foreign medicines in post-war Japan, condemned most of those who contracted radiation-induced diseases to agonizing death. But the girl's mother was stubborn and resourceful and hung on to her wits far longer than most mothers would have. Patiently she persuaded her little daughter that if she could fold one thousand paper cranes and string them together like a rosary she would recover. Millions of these tiny cranes – the work of well-wishers and pilgrims – hang today in coloured festoons from the stone monuments in the park, and it was these that the old man was arranging in heaps. The little girl began to make her cranes, but daily her fingers lost their strength and eventually the sheer effort of folding them was a torture both to her and to her mother. Still her mother – by now, and of necessity, a believer in the myth she had concocted – stubbornly urged her daughter to fold another crane and then another, and painfully the little girl folded her cranes and one by one the number grew. She died after making nine hundred and sixty four cranes.

Some 200,000 people are thought to have died as a result of the world's first atomic holocaust, and their names are contained in a stone chest that is one of the park's simplest and most eloquent memorials. But looking at the words carved on the chest, I couldn't help wondering whether the passing of time had not transformed their ringing promise into a strangled wholly incredible prayer:

> Sleep in peace.
> The mistake will not be repeated.

## Kamo no Chōmei from *Tales of Heike*

### *The Drowning of the Emperor*

Both sides set their faces against each other and fought grimly without a thought for their lives, neither giving way an inch. But as the Heike had on their side an Emperor endowed with the ten virtues and the Three Sacred Treasures of the Realm, things went hard with the Genji and their hearts were beginning to fail them, when suddenly something that they at first took for a white cloud but which soon appeared to be a white banner floating in the breeze, came drifting over the two fleets from the upper air and finally settled on the stern of the Genji ships hanging on by a rope.

When he saw this, Yoshitsune, regarding it as a sign from Hachiman Dai Bosatsu, removed his helmet, and after washing his hands, did obeisance; his men all following his example. Moreover a shoal of some thousands of dolphins also made its appearance from the offing and made straight for the ships of the Heike. Then Munemori called the diviner Ko-hakase Harunobu and said: 'There are always many dolphins about here, but I have never seen so many as these before: what may it portend?'

'If they turn back,' replied Harunobu, 'the Genji will be destroyed; but if they go on then our own side will be in danger.'

No sooner had he finished speaking than the dolphins dived under the Heike ships and passed on.

Then, as things had come to this pass, Awa-no-Mimbu Shigeyoshi, who for three years had been a loyal supporter of the Heike, now that his son Dennai Saemon Noriyoshi had been captured, made up his mind that all was lost, and suddenly forsook his allegiance and deserted to the enemy. Great was the regret of Tomomori that he had not cut off the head of 'that villain Shigeyoshi', but now it was unavailing.

Now the strategy of the Heike had been to put the stoutest warriors on board the ordinary fighting ships and the inferior soldiers on the big ships of Chinese build, so that the Genji should be induced to attack the big ships, thinking that the commanders were on board them, when they would be able to surround and destroy them. But

when Shigeyoshi went over and joined Genji, he revealed this plan to
them, and with the result that they immediately left the big ships alone
and concentrated their attack on the smaller ones on which were the
Heike champions.

Later on the men of Shikoku and Kyūshū all left the Heike in a
body and went over to the Genji. Those who had so far been their
faithful retainers now turned their bows against their lords and drew
their sword against their own masters. On one shore the heavy seas
beat on the cliff so as to forbid any landing, while on the other stood
the serried ranks of the enemy waiting with levelled arrows to receive
them. And so, on this day, the struggle for supremacy between the
houses of Gen and Hei was at last decided.

Meanwhile the Genji warriors sprang from one Heike vessel to the
other, shooting and cutting down the sailors and helmsmen, so that
they flung themselves into a panic to the bottom of the ships unable to
navigate them any longer. Then Shin Chūnagon Tomomori rowed
in a small boat to the Imperial Vessel and cried out: 'You see what
affairs have come to! Clean up the ship, and throw everything unsightly
into the sea!'

And he ran about the ship from bow to stern sweeping and cleaning
and gathering up the dust with his own hands. 'But how goes the
battle, Chūnagon Dono?' asked the Court Ladies.

'Oh, you'll soon see some rare gallants from the East,' he replied,
bursting into loud laughter.

'What? Is this a time for joking?' they answered and they lifted up
their voices and wept aloud.

Then the Nii Dono, who had already resolved what she would do,
donning a double outer dress of dark gray mourning colour and
tucking up the long skirts of her glossy silk *hakama* put the Sacred
Jewel under her arm, and the Sacred Sword in her girdle, and taking
the Emperor in her arms, spoke thus: 'Though I am but a woman
I will not fall into the hands of the foe, but will accompany our
Sovereign Lord. Let those of you who will, follow me.' And she glided
softly to the gunwale of the vessel.

The Emperor was eight years old that year, but looked much older
than his age, and his appearance was so lovely that he shed as it were a

brilliant radiance about him, and his long black hair hung loose far down his back. With a look of surprise and anxiety on his face, he inquired of the Nii Dono: 'Where is it you are going to take me?'

Turning to her youthful sovereign with tears streaming down her cheeks, she answered,

'Perchance our Lord does not know that, though through the merit of the Ten Virtues, practised in former lives you have been reborn to the Imperial Throne in this world, yet by the power of some evil karma destiny now claims you. So now turn to the east and bid farewell to the deity of the Great Shrine of Ise, and then to the west and say the Nembutsu that Amida Buddha and the Holy ones may come to welcome you to the Pure Western Land. This land is called small as a grain of millet, but yet is it now but a vale of misery. There is a Pure Land of happiness beneath the waves, another Capital where no sorrow is. Thither it is that I am taking our Lord.'

And thus comforting him, she bound his long hair up in his dove-coloured robe and blinded with tears, the child Sovereign put his beautiful little hands together and turned first to the east to say farewell to the deity of Ise and to Sho Hachimangū and then to the west and repeated the Nembutsu after which the Nii Dono, holding him tightly in her arms and saying consolingly: 'In the depths of the Ocean we have a Capital.' She sank with him at last beneath the waves.

Ah the pity of it! That the gust of the spring wind of Impermanence should so suddenly sweep away his flower form. That the cruel billows should thus engulf his Jewel person. Since his Palace was called the Palace of Longevity, he should have passed a long life therein. Its gate was called the Gate of Eternal Youth, the barrier that old age should not pass; and yet, ere he had reached the age of ten years, he had become like the refuse that sinks to the bottom of the sea.

How vain it was to proclaim him as one who sat on the Throne as the reward of the Ten Virtues! It was like the Dragon that rides on the clouds descending to become a fish at the bottom of the ocean. He who abode in a Palace fair as the terraced pavilions of the highest heaven of Brahma, or the paradise where Sakyamuni dwells, among his ministers and nobles of the Nine families who did him humble obeisance, thus came to a miserable end beneath the ocean waves.

**Lafcadio Hearn** from *The Chief City of the Province of the Gods*

XVI

The city, Matsue, can be definitely divided into three architectural quarters: the district of the merchants and shopkeepers, forming the heart of the settlement, where all the houses are two stories high; the district of the temples, including nearly the whole Southeastern part of the town; and the district or districts of the *shizoku* (formerly called samurai), comprising a vast number of large, roomy, garden-girt, one-storey dwellings. From these elegant homes, in feudal days, could be summoned at a moment's notice five thousand 'two-sworded men' with their armed retainers, making a fighting total for the city alone of probably not less than thirteen thousand warriors. More than one third of all the city buildings were then samurai homes; for Matsue was the military centre of the most ancient province of Japan.

At both ends of the town, which curves in a crescent along the lake shore, were the two main settlements of samurai; but just as some of the most important temples are situated outside of the temple district, so were many of the finest homesteads of this knightly caste situated in other quarters. They mustered most thickly, however, about the castle, which stands today on the summit of its citadel hill – the Oshiroyama – solid as when first built long centuries ago, a vast and sinister shape, all iron-grey, rising against the sky from a cyclopean foundation of stone. Fantastically grim the thing is, and grotesquely complex in detail; looking somewhat like a huge pagoda, of which the second, third and fourth stories have been squeezed down and telescoped into one another by their own weight. Crested at its summit, like a feudal helmet, with two colossal fishes of bronze lifting their curved bodies skyward from either angle of the roof, and bristling with horned gables and gargoyled eaves and tilted puzzles of tiled roofing at every story, the creation is a veritable architectural dragon, made up of magnificent monstrosities – a dragon, moreover, full of eyes set at all conceivable angles, above, below, and on every side. From under the black scowl of the loftiest eaves, looking east and south, the whole city can be seen at a single glance, as in the vision of a soaring hawk; and from the northern angle the view plunges down three hundred feet to the castle road, where walking figures of men appear no larger than flies.

The grim castle has its legend.

It is related that, in accordance with some primitive and barbarous custom, precisely like that of which so terrible a souvenir has been preserved for us in the most pathetic of Servian [sic] ballads, *The Foundation of Skadra*, a maiden of Matsue was interred alive under the walls of the castle at the height of its erection, as a sacrifice to some forgotten gods. Her name has never been recorded; nothing concerning her is remembered except that she was beautiful and very fond of dancing.

Now after the castle had been built, it is said that a law had to be passed forbidding that any girl should dance on the streets of Matsue. For whenever any maiden dance the hill Oshiroyama would shudder, and the great castle quiver from basement to summit.

### XIX

Over the Tenjin-bashi, or Bridge of Tenjin, and through small streets and narrow and densely populated districts, and past many a tenantless and mouldering feudal homestead, I make my way to the extreme south-western end of the city, to watch the sunset from a little sobaya [an inn where soba is sold] facing the lake. For to see the sun sink from this sobaya, is one of the delights of Matsue.

There are no such sunsets in Japan as in the tropics: the light is gentle as a light of dreams: there are no furies of colour; there are no chromatic violences in nature in this Orient. All in sea or sky is tint rather than colour, and tint vapour-toned. I think that the exquisite taste of the race in the matter of colours and of tints as exemplified in the dyes of their wonderful textures, is largely attributable to the sober and delicate beauty of nature's tones in this all-temperate world where nothing is garish.

Before me the fair vast lake sleeps, softly luminous, far-ringed with chains of blue volcanic hills shaped like a sierra. On my right, at its eastern end, the most ancient quarter of the city spreads its rooves of blue-grey tile; the houses crowd thickly down to the shore, to dip their wooden feet into the flood. With a glass I can see my own windows and the far-spreading of the rooves beyond, and above all else the green citadel with its grim castle, grotesquely peaked. The sun begins to set, and exquisite astonishments of tinting appear in water and sky.

Dead rich purples cloud broadly behind and above the indigo blackness of the serrated hills – misty purples, fading upward smokily into faint vermilions and dim gold, which again melt up through ghostliest greens into the blue. The deeper waters of the lake, far away, take a tender violet indescribable, and the silhouette of the pine-shadowed island seems to float in that sea of soft sweet colour. But the shallower and nearer is cut from the deeper water by the current as sharply as by a line drawn, and all the surface on this side of that line is a shimmering bronze – old rich ruddy gold-bronze.

All the fainter colours change every five minutes – wonderously change and shift like tones and shades of fine shot-silks.

xx

*At the market of the dead*
From the thirteenth to the fifteenth day of July is held the Festival of the Dead – the Bommatsuri or Bonku – by some Europeans called the Feast of Lanterns. But in many places there are two such festivals annually; for those who still follow the ancient reckoning of time by moons hold that the Bommatsuri should fall on the thirteenth, fourteenth and fifteenth days of the seventh month of the antique calendar, which corresponds to a later period of the year.

Early on the morning of the thirteenth, new mats of purest rice straw, woven expressly for the festival are spread upon all Buddhist altars and within each *butsuma* or *butsudan* – the little shrine before which the morning and evening prayers are offered up in every believing home. Shrines and altars are likewise decorated with beautiful embellishments of coloured paper, and with flowers and springs of certain hallowed plants – always real lotus-flowers when obtainable, otherwise lotus flowers of paper and fresh branches of *shikimi* (anise) and of *misohagi* (lespedeza). Then a tiny lacquer table – a zen – such as Japanese meals are usually served upon, is placed upon the altar, and the food offerings are laid on it. But in the smaller shrines of Japanese homes the offerings are more often simply laid upon the rice matting, wrapped in fresh lotus-leaves.

These offerings consist of the foods called *somen*, resembling our vermicelli, *gozen*, which is boiled rice, *dango*, a sort of tiny dumpling, eggplant, and fruits according to season – frequently *uri* and *sakiwa*, slices of melon and watermelon and plums and peaches. Often sweet cakes and dainties are added. Sometimes the offering is only *o-sho-jin-gu* (honourable uncooked food); more usually it is *o-rio-gu* (honourable boiled food); but it never includes, of course, fish, meats or wine. Clear water is given to the shadowy guest, and is sprinkled form time to time upon the altar or within the shrine with a branch of *misohagi*; tea is poured out every hour for the viewless visitors, and everything is daintily served up in little plates and cups and bowls, as for living guests, with *hashi* (chopsticks) laid beside the offering. So for three days the dead are feasted.

At sunset, the pine torches, fixed in the ground before each home, are kindled to guide the spirit-visitors. Sometimes, also on the first evening of the Bommatsuri, welcome-fires (*mukaehi*) are lighted along the shore of the sea or lake or river by which the village or city is situated – neither more nor less than one hundred and eight fires; this number having some mystic signification in the philosophy of Buddhism. And charming lanterns are suspended each night at the entrances of homes – the Lanterns of the Festival of the Dead – lanterns of special forms and colours, beautifully painted with suggestions of landscape and shapes of flowers, and always decorated with a peculiar fringe of paper streamers.

Also, on the same night, those who have dead friends go to the cemeteries and make offerings there and pray and burn incense, and pour out water for the ghosts. Flowers are placed there in the bamboo vases set beside each *haka*, and lanterns are lighted and hung up before the tombs, but these lanterns have no designs upon them.

At sunset on the evening of the fifteenth only the offerings called Segaki are made in the temples. Then are fed the ghosts of the circle of Penance, called Kakido, the place of hungry spirits; and then also are fed by the priests those ghosts having no other friends among the living to care for them. Very, very small these offerings are – like the offerings to the gods.

# 11

# Shikoku and the Inland Sea

As far as the eye can see on each pine top there
rests a crane –
Each crane to each pine, perhaps a faithful companion
these thousand years.

KI TSURAYUKI

Shikoku was for hundreds of years, very isolated and remote. It shields the Inland Sea, the Seto Naikai, the main route from Kyoto and Ōsaka, to Kyūshū and the garrison of Dazaifu. In ancient times ships would travel via Awajishima, the island on the way to Kyoto and the site of the whirlpools of Naruto. On the way back, this was also the route taken by those who had displeased the rulers in Kyoto. The poems in *The Man'yōshū* (see Nara chapter) describe the heart-wrenching moment of leaving the mainland behind.

*The Tosa Diary*, one of the most beautiful Japanese literary diaries, was written about a journey around Shikoku back to Kyoto by Ki Tsurayuki, the governor of Tosa (present-day Kōchi prefecture). Writing in 936, the author assumes the guise of a woman, as one of a party of travellers journeying over rough seas and often held up along the way as she journeys through Awajishima, Izumi and up to Naniwa, ancient Ōsaka, before proceeding towards the capital. Needless to say, this is an emotional as well as a physical journey, expressing love and loss. Writing a diary, the author says, 'equalizes the relationship between men and women'.

Before 1989, when the Seto Ōhashi bridge, linking Shikoku to the mainland was built, the island was very rural and both Shinto and Shingon sect Buddhism flourished there. Shingon (or True Word) Buddhism was propagated by Kūkai, also known as Kōbō Daishi, who was born near Takamatsu on Shikoku but studied classical Chinese in China (804–806). Shingon passes down the 'mysteries' of faith orally, and a lot of emphasis is thus placed on the relationship between master and disciple. Kōbō Daishi established an eighty-eight-temple pilgrimage, ending up in Moroto Misaki, a promontory of Tosa, where he is said to have gained enlightenment.

Shikoku is full of hidden delights including the largest garden in Japan at Ritsurin Kōen in Takamatsu, started in the seventeenth century and eventually owned by Lord Matsudaira and opened to the public in 1875. At Yashima near Takamatsu you can find the Shikoku Mura and visit the Isamu Noguchi garden museum. Plunging further inland there is the Iya valley and Ōboke gorge where the Taira were said to have come after their defeat at Dan no ura, putting down their swords to take up farming. Alex Kerr in his book, *Lost Japan*, describes restoring an ancient farmhouse here. He was charmed by the unmanaged, jungle-like forests.

All along the coast of Shikoku there are more sights including the whirlpools at Naruto, which look best at full moon, as well as turtles that come and lay their eggs at Hiwasa every summer. You can go whale watching in the Pacific Ocean off Kōchi, which is only accessible by sea due to the steep mountain range in the middle of Shikoku. In the summer you can see Bryde's whales, as well as Risso's dolphins. Kōchi is also home to Shikoku's political movements. For instance, Sakamoto Ryōma (1836–67), also from Kōchi, defied the rigid class system by setting up his own business in Nagasaki. He wrote a handbook on democracy for the Meiji period, although he was murdered at the age of thirty-one. He was so successful at instilling anti-feudal sentiments, that the ancient castle of Kōchi, his home town, was almost completely dismantled.

Then at Ashizuri Misaki there is the Kongōfukuji, a temple dedicated to Kannon, the goddess of compassion, the 38th temple of the eighty-eight-temple pilgrimage around the island. The Ashizuri Sea floor museum is where marine biologist Hirohito, Emperor Shōwa (ruled 1926–89), used to enjoy stepping over the coral beds to see the fish; and in Uwajima there is a castle, as well as a fertility and sex shrine and a bullfighting season. The bulls were said to have been

donated by thankful Dutch fishermen. At Uchiko there is a wax-
making town where everything is made from the crushed fruit of the
fern-like *sumach* tree.

Travelling clockwise around the island as Kōbō Daishi did, Matsuyama, on the shore of the *seto nakai*, the Inland Sea, is the largest city
in Shikoku. This was the home of Masaoka Shiki (1867–1902) (see
Nara chapter), the poet who freed haiku from its strict Japanese form
with freestyle haiku and *tanka*. Shiki's friend, Natsume Sōseki (1867–
1916), after graduating from college, was sent to Matsuyama to teach,
and his novel *Botchan* (which means 'master darling') is set here. At
Dōgo Onsen in Matsuyama, where Botchan takes a hot bath, there is
still a Botchan room. Donald Richie came in 1970, and wrote about
the people and the stories on many of the islands on the Inland Sea as
well as in the seaside towns, aware that the ancient fishing culture in
this remote district was dying out.

**Tajihi Kasamaro** – *when he went down to the land of Tsukushi*

> I set out
> For barbarian frontiers
> At the far reach of the heavens,
> Passing Awaji Island
> Directly before me
> And glancing back
> At Awashima behind
> Among pitched cries of sailors
> In the morning calm
> And the splash of oars
> In the evening calm,
> We have pushed through the waves
> And veered between the reefs,
> We have passed the rocky bend
> At Inabitsuma

And come across the seas
Like water fowl.
And now, at Ie Island,
Swaying lush on the rugged shore,
The *nanoriso* grass,
The 'name-telling':
O why have I come away
Without telling my wife?

**Ki Tsurayuki** from *The Tosa Diary*

*11 March, 4th day*

The steersman said that the wind-blown clouds looked very
threatening today, so the boat did not set out. However, the wind and
waves did not get up the whole day long; this steersman was not always
right in his forecasts of the weather. Beautiful shells of many kinds and
pebbles were plentiful on the shore where they camped; and with
reference to them somebody belonging to the ship composed this
verse in memory of one who was much loved:

Here the breaking waves
Come and go, as I lament
For my darling child;
Stooping I, to bid farewell,
Pick up a 'forgetting-shell'.

Such were her words; but 'a certain personage', unable to bear it
any longer, composed this, to give heart to the others in the ship:

Here no more we'll stray
Seeking for 'forgetting-shells';
But a dainty pearl
Pure and white might serve to tell
Of the child we loved so well.

Thus he spoke in memory of his little daughter, for a parent is apt
to become very childish. Some may object that she was not a pearl; be

that as it may, the child is dead, and it is no empty compliment to say that she had a beautiful face. A certain woman composed this verse in grief at the number of days spent in the same place:

> Long we've soaked our hands
> In Izumi's icy spring
> Dreading not the cold;
> Here though many days we waste,
> 'Tis a spring we never taste.

### 12 *March, 5th day*

This day with difficulty they hastened on through the Sea of Izumi to the Stopping-place of Ozu. To his eye the pine forests seemed never-ending, everything seemed to have gone wrong, and he composed this:

> Though we speed along,
> Yet the pine trees on the cliffs
> Never seem to pass;
> Long as thread is Ozu strand
> Spun out by a maiden's hand.

At these words and while they still travelled on, the steersman called to the sailors to pull hard, for the weather was about to improve: 'On this gallant ship my command must be obeyed; this is what I say – ere the morning north wind blow, get the rope ashore and tow,' said he. The poetic from of these words was quite unintentional on the part of the steersman; and, on being appealed to, he said he did not mean it for a verse; but on putting into writing the queer poetical sentence the man was heard to say, there proved indeed to be just over thirty syllables, i.e. thirty-one syllables. This day everyone prayed all day long that the waves outside might not arise; and in answer to their prayers the wind and waves did not get up. Soon (they arrived at) a place where flocks of seagulls sported about; in an excess of joy at getting so near the Capital, a child composed this:

> Though the wind has dropped,
> For the Gods have heard our prayers,
> In my dizzy brain

> Swooping seagulls look to me
> Like the ever surging sea.

While she recited this, they travelled on. The pine forest at a place called Iwatsu was very beautiful, but the shore seemed interminable. Once more, as they rowed past Sumiyoshi, 'a certain personage' composed this:

> Suminoye's pines,
> As I watch them, seem to be
> Younger far than I;
> I shall vanish from the scene,
> But the pines are evergreen.

And here, the mother of one now gone, whom she never forgets for a day, or even a moment:

> Urge the boat along,
> On to Suminoye beach,
> For I long to pick
> Some 'forgetting-grass', to see
> If it will come true with me.

This she said, not because she wished to forget really, but she hoped that her sorrow might find some short relief, in order that her love might return stronger than ever. With these words then they travelled on, while still gazing at the prospect. But suddenly the wind arose; and, though they rowed hard, they drifted quickly astern and nearly capsized, when they must all have been lost. The steersman said, 'This holy Deity of Sumiyoshi is a well-known God, and he desires some gift.' How like everybody else! Someone suggested that *nusa* should be offered; so accordingly an offering of prayer papers was made. But, though it was done chiefly for the wind to abate, it began to blow harder than ever and the waves rose accordingly, so that they were in great danger. Then the steersman spoke again, and said, 'As the august heart (of the God) has not been moved by the prayer-papers, the gallant ship cannot proceed; in making an offering, there-fore, something should be presented that will be thought of value.'

Accordingly, what was to be done? He had two eyes, but could offer only one mirror; so to his deep regret it was thrown into the sea. Well, immediately the sea became as calm as the looking-glass itself! And a 'certain personage' composed this:

> In the raging sea
> I have cast my looking-glass
> And the gift's result
> Shows the partiality
> Of the awful Deity.

Verily there are no Gods as kindly as the 'forgetting-grass' of Suminoye or the delicate pines upon its cliffs. Plainly in the mirror could his eyes see the august heart of the God – which was remarkably like the heart of the steersman!

### Oliver Statler from *Japanese Pilgrimage*

For three days, we walk along Tosa's bleak and craggy ramparts against the open Pacific. From the highway hacked into the cliff we look down on black rocks savaged for ages by a violent sea. The old path clung to the shoreline. There is no trace of it on today's maps but we wonder if some vestige remains. It was not an easy path; in the wash of waves the traveller scrambled over rocks that were 'jumping stones, bucking stones, tumbling stones.' Late in our third day of walking above the booming ocean, as we near the tip of the cape, we pass hundreds of stone statues of Jizo. Jizo is not only the guardian deity of children; he also stands between this world and the next to rescue souls on their way to hell. His images have been placed here and prayed to in memory of sailors and fishermen lost at sea.

'The sea is often stormy around Muroto,' the priest of the temple has said. 'There are a number of legends about sailors saved from the rocks by a vision of Kōbō Daishi. The danger isn't as great as it was when the boats were frailer but many of the temple's members are fishermen; they go out on long voyages after tuna or whales, and some of them don't come back.'

'Many of the typhoons that hit Japan hit Muroto first, at their most violent. They have battered the temple for twelve centuries; one of the major duties of the priest and the people is to repair the damage. During World War II the B-29 bombers used the cape as a landmark and then flew to their targets. When they attacked the prefectural capital I watched through my telescope as the city burned. The horror of that night is still with me.' And with a wry smile: 'Muroto sticks out like a hook and it catches trouble . . . But all that aside, this place is sacred because it was here that the young Daishi set his life's course.'

Just short of the tip of the cape we reach the caves where many believe that the Daishi invoked Kokuzo.

'He chose to get close to the sea, not to worship from the crest,' the priest says. 'The caves open to the southeast so that from them he could have seen Venus at dawn.' For Venus is considered a manifestation of Kokuzo. Affirming that in mediation at this cape he at last broke through to enlightenment he wrote: 'The planet Venus appeared in the sky.'

A massive rock, clutched by the roots of the banyan tree (Muroto is subtropical, brushed by the warm Black Current out of the South Pacific) separates grottoes large enough to give refuge from the wind and rain. Within, it is strangely hushed: the pounding of the breakers is muffled. All about are stones piled up by people who have carefully balanced one upon another as evidence of prayers offered.

Was it in this cave the young monk achieved enlightenment? Was it here he pledged his life?

'From that time on, I despised fame and wealth and longed for a life in the midst of nature. Whenever I saw articles of luxury – light furs, well-fed horses, swift vehicles – I felt sad, knowing that, being transient as lightning, they too would fade away. Whenever I saw a cripple or a beggar, I lamented and wondered what had caused him to spend his days in such a miserable state. Seeing these piteous conditions encouraged me to renounce the world. Can anyone now break my determination? No, just as there is no one who can stop the wind.'

> Muroto:
> The voice of Buddha
> Is heard –
> Yet day in, day out,
> Winds roar and waves surge

Winds and waves: the vicissitudes of life; despite them the voice of Buddha is within us if we but listen. He was insisting on that, as henceforth he always would.

A path rises steep to the temple above; its compound spreads over the flat crown of the promontory. We have climbed away from the sound of the ocean; at the main hall it is shady and still. We lower our packs and pray. This is the third and last temple where Kokuzo is enshrined. Here is memorialized the Daishi's enlightenment.

We leave the cover of the trees, walk to the tip of the headland, stand with the wind in our faces. Before us is the open Pacific, the limitless horizon. Suddenly I feel that I am standing where he stood when, having achieved enlightenment, he took the name he used for the rest of his life – Kūkai. It joins the *ku* of Kokuzo, meaning sky and the *kai*, meaning sea. It is a prayer for compassion as wide as the sky and as deep as the sea.

It is here that fully, finally committed to Buddhism, the young monk began the transition to great master.

## Masaoka Shiki

> *1891 Summer*
> Hydrangeas –
> And the rain beating down
> On the crumbled wall.

> *1891 Summer*
> In cleft on cleft
> on rockface after rockface –
> wild azaleas.

*1892 summer*
From the firefly
in my hands,
cold light.

**Donald Richie** from *The Inland Sea*

It is night. We pass islands that are great collections of shining standing tubes, clusters of enormous aluminium balls, covering the land with their metallic undergrowth, and whose purpose I do not know. They puff and sigh as we pass, reflect in the endless rows of perfectly spaced lights, the illumination for those straight industrial blocks, geometrical, perfectly spaced units of land in which I see nothing living, not a man, not a dog, not a tree.

I turn and walk to the stern. There lie other islands, forested islands, uninhabited islands, farming islands, fishing islands, stretching farther and farther into the sea. The nearer are now black, almost invisible. Just an hour ago, as afternoon faded they were dark, almost black but those behind were slate gray, separated by silver inlets leading to a farther island, dove-coloured. Then those behind turned blue, as island after island, like a range of peaks, stretched to the horizon, a faintest violet that was almost not a colour at all.

Now, at night, those islands far away are black shapes riding the lighter black of the waveless sea. Each is sprinkled with lights: a village, a town, a city – spots of light, tiny haloes no brighter than the overhead stars. Shikoku is a cloud in the distance, low on the horizon, dim lights at its base. Is it a city? What city?

The boat whistles, the wind is cool. At the port a new collection of aluminium stacks slowly rises, as though from the sea itself. I wonder what I am approaching, what I am leaving. The land is turning mineral. I look and see island after island approach, but all of them silver and illuminated to an almost hallucinatory clarity. Not a tree, not a bush, not a blade of grass. Extinguishing the stars, they rise like sculpture, sigh, blow smoke or steam, pass.

Is it all gone? I wonder as the cool wind reaches me, something sharp in it, like a knife wrapped in silk. I remember once, near my Tokyo house, some workmen were constructing a wall for an apartment house. They came to an old tree with a low overhanging branch. After some consultation they put a hole in the wall to accommodate the branch. It is still there – or was last month – a small and unthinking reminder of a way of thinking, a way of living that is right.

The Japanese are the last people who stand in reverence of the natural world. Rather than eradicate it, they have successfully adapted themselves to it. They have offered themselves to it, have come to terms with it. I am reminded of Robert Frost's words about those who 'found salvation in surrender'. There is something larger than man, though this the West denies. It is nature itself, the way things are, have been and always will be. The white man's most daring and foolhardy feat is mere rapine. All of his glory is merely brutality. He doesn't know how to live in the world he was born into and so he will destroy it and build another that will destroy him.

Japan has this gift of surrender. In backward sections of the land it has it still. But as I move from these islands nearer the shore I see that it is going, gone. Japan has learned all too well – the virus of glory is catching. *Shikata ga nai*, it can't be helped – that lovely and accepting phrase will soon be as extinct as the cry of the nightingale and the blinking of the fireflies on these shores. And with it will have gone a kind of hope.

# 12

# Kyūshū

And on the hillside I can see
The villages of Imari,
Whose thronged and flaming workshops lift
Their twisted columns of smoke on high,
Cloud cloisters that in ruins lie,
With sunshine streaming through each rift,
And broken arches of blue sky.

HENRY WADSWORTH LONGFELLOW

Kyūshū is the southernmost island of Japan and the closest to the
Asian continent. The landscape is filled with volcanoes, which give
rise to the famous *jikoku* or 'smoking hells'. The history of Kyūshū
reveals one of the oldest cultures in the world, with pottery being
made from around 10,000 years ago in the Jōmon period. The
archaeology also reveals a wave of foreign influences – no wonder,
since it is a shorter trip to Korea across the waters of the East China
Sea than to Tokyo. The island's past is steeped in legend and history,
from the ancient Jōmon people who made rope pattern pottery and
started to cultivate rice, to Emperor Jimmu who conquered Yamato
(the area around Nara) in 667BC and Empress Jingu, another
legendary figure who established a colony in Korea in AD369.

Recent centuries have also been eventful, with rebellions breaking
out frequently. Dazaifu on the north of the island was built as a
garrison for an early disastrous campaign against the Koreans. It is
still preserved high up in the wooded hills and it was from here that
many officials wrote to their loved ones back in Nara or Kyoto
during their seemingly endless garrison duty.

One of the greatest writers and politicians to occupy the Dazaifu

post was Sugawara no Michizane (845–908), otherwise known to the
Japanese as Tenjin or 'The god of scholarship'. He wrote beautiful
classical Chinese but, by rising too high in court circles, fell out with
the ruling Fujiwara clan. He was punished with two years of garrison
duty. There are Tenmangu (god of scholarship) shrines throughout
the country including at Ueno park in Tokyo. At the Tenmangu
shrine in Dazaifu, there is a little plum tree, said to be an offshoot of
the one that the scholar grew in his garden at court in Kyoto.

Chinese embassies travelled to Kyoto through Kyūshū in the
twelfth century, and later, Zen Buddhist priests passed this way on
their way to the capital in the following years. The next waves of
foreigners came from further afield, from 'Barbary'. The first wave
of *namban*, or 'Southern Barbarians' were Portuguese traders who
were shipwrecked off the coast of Kyūshū in 1543, an accidental
event that stands on a level with Columbus's discovery of America.
They were followed by Jesuit missionaries and by St Francis Xavier,
who arrived from the Malaccas in 1549 and started to preach in
Kagoshima on Kyūshū's southern tip. Helped by an interpreter
named Anjiro, within ten months he converted about one hundred
and fifty people, according to the Jesuit Luis Frois. Xavier even made
friends with the head of a local Zen monastery, Ninjitsu, initiating
one of the first Buddhist-Christian dialogues, including being shown
Zazen meditation. He wrote back to his Jesuit masters about his
meetings with the local lords. He met with Otomo Sorin, the King
of Bungo (a region just south of Kagoshima in Kyūshū ) who wanted
Xavier's assistance with keeping the trade with the Portuguese.
Xavier's vivid letters show how much he was in awe of his Japanese
hosts, and how much the Europeans had to learn about Japanese
customs and manners. Jesuits also had a hard task ahead of them: to
convert the people to Christianity despite their lack of knowledge of
the language and local customs.

Xavier and the missionaries that followed him converted many
thousands of Japanese (see Nagasaki chapter), to the extent that the
sixteenth century is known as the 'Krishitan' (Christian) century in
Japan. Kyūshū's volcanic landscape saw some dreadful battles and
persecutions. The Shimabara peninsula on the other side of Nagasaki

Bay was where 23,000 peasants and *rōnin* (independent soldiers) led by an unarmed fourteen-year-old, Amakusa Shiro, rebelled against the shogun's anti-Christian edicts in 1637. The siege was one of the greatest in history, lasting eighty days, and was brutally suppressed by the Tokugawa shogunate with 120,000 men and the help of Miyamoto Musashi (the greatest swordsman in Japan and author of *The Book of Five Rings*).

The sufferings of the Christians at Shimabara were reimagined by Shusaku Endo in his short story 'Unzen', which is set in these parts and describes the famous *jikoku*.

With 37,000 Christians massacred by the shogunate, all foreign entry into Japan was stopped and Kyūshū became a backwater; its only trading point was at Dejima, where the Dutch were allowed to dock two ships a year, while the Chinese were allowed two junks per year. Ihara Saikaku, a famous Edo period writer, depicted the remoteness of Kyūshū villages with a story about how a village came to worship an umbrella. Kyūshū nevertheless remained the source of some of the finest pottery in Japan and Imari porcelain, which Longfellow describes in his poem, was made in the town of Arita in Hizen (the porcelain is known as Aritayaki in Japan), and exported specifically for the European market.

But rebellion returned in the nineteenth century. Saigo Takamori, (1828–1877) part of the Meiji restoration government, who, like other Kyūshū samurai, joined the '*sanno joi*' or 'Revere the Emperor, Expel the Barbarian' movement against the Tokugawa shogunate. He then realised that the Meiji government was Westernising the country rapidly and undermining the traditional samurai class system. He returned to Satsuma and set up paramilitary academies, leading the Satsuma rebellion against his overlords in 1877. He even besieged government forces at Kumamoto Castle. As Alan Booth points out, Kumamoto is one of the three largest castles in Japan, and he compares the Japanese and European castles as follows:

The strongest point of a European castle is almost always the central keep. (The walls of the white Tower of London are twelve feet thick). But the *donjon* of a Japanese castle such as Kumamoto is almost invariably its weakest point. Often, this part of the castle is constructed, not of stone, but of wood and plaster (the present donjon at Kumamoto was rebuilt in ferroconcrete in 1960), and its elaborate tiled roofs and temple-like facades give it the appearance of a fragile bird poised for flight, or of a decorative plum on a suit of stone armour. The Japaense *donjon* by itself is indefensible. The strongest point is invariably the outermost of the concentric walls and the builders of such castles must have known that once the last of these walls was breached the *donjon* would very quickly fall – most likely to an attack by fire.

## Sugawara no Michizane

Now that I have become
Mere scum that floats upon the water's face
May you, my lord, become a weir
And stop me in my downward flow!
Your sisters must all stay at home,
Your brothers are sent away.
Just we three together, my children,
Shall chat as long as we go along.
Each day we have our meals before us
At night we sleep all together.
We have lamps and tapers to peer in the dark
And warm clothes for the cold.
Last year you saw how the Chancellor's son
Fell out of favour in the capital
Now people say he is a ragged gambler
And call him names in the street
You have seen the barefooted wandering musician
The town people call the Justice's Miss –
Her father too was a great official; –
They were all in their day exceedingly rich.
Once their gold was like sand in the sea;
Now they have hardly enough to eat.

When you look, my children, at other people,
You can see how gracious Heaven has been.

**St Francis Xavier** – *excerpts from a letter to the Society of Jesus in Rome from St Francis Xavier about his activities in Japan, 1552*

Japan is a very large empire entirely composed of islands. One language is spoken throughout, and it is not very difficult to learn. This country was discovered by the Portuguese eight or nine years ago. The Japanese are very ambitious of honours and distinctions, and think themselves superior to all nations in military glory and valour. They prize and honour all that has to do with war, and all such things, and there is nothing of which they are so proud as weapons adorned with gold and silver. They always wear swords and daggers both in and out of the house, and when they go to sleep they hang them at the bed's head. In short, they value arms more than any people I have ever seen. They are excellent archers, and usually fight on foot, though there is no lack of horses in the country. They are very polite to each other, but not to foreigners, whom they utterly despise. They spend their means on arms, bodily adornment, and on a number of attendants, and do not in the least care to save money. They are, in short, a very warlike people, and engaged in continual wars among themselves; the most powerful in arms bearing the most extensive sway. They have all one sovereign, although for one hundred and fifty years past the princes have ceased to obey him, and this is the cause of their perpetual feuds. When I was at Yamaguchi with Father Cosmo Torres and Joam Fernandez, the King of Bungo, one of the most powerful of the country, wrote to ask me to go to him; a Portuguese vessel had come into his harbour, and he wished to talk with me on certain subjects. So, both to find out how he was affected towards our holy religion, and to pay a visit to the Portuguese, I set out at once for Bungo, leaving Cosmo and Joam with the Christians. The King gave me a most gracious reception, and it was a great pleasure to me to meet with the Portuguese.

The King of Bungo commands numerous and very war-like troops, and as things go with Japanese kings, has vast dominions to govern.

He has a great liking for the Portuguese. No sooner was he informed of the power and character of the King of Portugal than he wrote to him asking to be admitted into the number of his friends, and sending him a rich suit of armour as a token of friendship. He has also sent an envoy to the Viceroy of India, offering him with many compliments his friendship, alliance, and good offices; this messenger, who came to India with me, has been most honourably and liberally received by the Viceroy. Before I left Japan, the King of Bungo promised the Portuguese and myself to take Cosmo Torres and Joam Fernandez under his protection. The sovereign elect of Yamaguchi bound himself in the same way, when he enters into the possession of his kingdom […]

**Shusaku Endo** from 'Unzen'

Halfway down the mountain he had a glimpse of the dark sea. Milky clouds veiled the horizon; several wan beams of sunlight filtered through the cracks, Suguro thought how blue the ocean would appear on a clear day.

'Look – you can see a blur out there that looks like an island. Unfortunately, you can't see it very well today. This is Dango Island, where Amakusa Shiro, the commander of the Christian forces, planned the Shimabara Rebellion with his men.'

At this the passengers took a brief, apathetic glance towards the island. Before long the view of the distant sea was blocked by a forest of trees.

What must those seven Christians have felt as they looked at this ocean? They knew they would soon be executed at Shimabara. The corpses of martyrs were swiftly reduced to ashes and cast upon the seas. If that were not done, the remaining Christians would surreptitiously worship the clothing and even locks of hair from the martyrs as though they were holy objects. And so the seven, getting their first distant view of the oceans from this spot, must have realized that it would be their grave. Kichijiro too would have looked at the sea, but with a different kind of sorrow – with the knowledge that the strong ones in the world of faith were crowned with glory, while the cowards had to carry their burdens with them throughout their lives.

When the group reached Shimabara, four of them were placed in a cell barely three-feet-tall and only wide enough to accommodate one *tatami*. The other three were jammed into another room equally cramped. As they awaited their punishment, they persistently encouraged one another and went on praying. There is no record of where Kichijiro stayed during this time.

The village of Shimabara was dark and silent. The bus came to a stop by a tiny wharf where the rickety ferry-boat to Amakusa was moored forlornly. Wood chips and flotsam bobbed on the small waves that lapped at the breakwater. Among the debris floated an object that resembled a rolled-up newspaper; it was the corpse of a cat.

The town extended in a thin band along the seafront. The fences of local factories stretched far into the distance, while the odour of chemicals wafted all the way to the highway.

Suguro set out towards the reconstructed Shimabara Castle. The only signs of life he encountered along the way were a couple of high school girls riding bicycles.

'Where is the execution ground where the Christians were killed?' he asked them.

'I didn't know there was such a place,' said one of them, blushing. She turned to her friend. 'Have you heard of anything like that? You don't know, do you?' Her friend shook her head.

He came to a neighbourhood identified as a former samurai residence. It had stood behind the castle, where several narrow paths intersected. A crumbling mud wall wound its way between the paths. A drainage ditch was as it had been in those days. Summer *mikans* poked their heads above the mud wall, which had already blocked out the evening sun. All the buildings were old, dark and musty. They had probably been the residence of a low-ranking samurai, built at the end of the Tokugawa period. Many Christians had been executed at the Shimabara grounds, but Suguro had not come across any historical documents identifying the location of the prison.

He retraced his steps, and after a short walk came out on a street of shops where popular songs were playing. The narrow street was packed with a variety of stores, including gift shops. The water in the drainage ditch was as limpid as water from a spring.

'The execution ground? I know where that is.' The owner of a tobacco shop directed Suguro to a pond just down the road. 'If you go straight on past the pond, you'll come to a nursery school. The execution ground was just on the side of the school.'

Though they say nothing of how he was able to do it, the records indicate that Kichijiro was allowed to visit the seven prisoners on the day before their execution. Possibly he put some money into the hands of the officers.

Kichijiro offered a meagre plate of food to the prisoners, who were prostrate from their ordeal.

'Kichijiro, did you retract your oath?' one of the captives asked compassionately. He was eager to know if the apostate had finally informed the officials that he could not deny his faith. 'Have you come here to see us because you have retracted?'

Kichijiro looked up at them timidly and shook his head.

'In any case, Kichijiro, we can't accept this food.'

'Why not?'

'Why not?' The prisoners were mournfully silent for a moment. 'Because we have already accepted the fact that we will die.'

Kichijiro could only lower his eyes and say nothing. He knew that he himself could never endure the sort of agony he had witnessed at the Valley of Hell on Unzen.


**Ihara Saikaku** from *The Umbrella Oracle*

Commendable indeed is the spirit of philanthropy in this world of ours!

To the famous 'Hanging Temple of Kwannon' in the Province of Kii, someone had once presented twenty oil-paper umbrellas which, repaired every year, were hung beside the temple for the use of any and all who might be caught in the rain or snow. They were always conscientiously returned when the weather improved – not a single one had ever been lost.

One day in the spring of 1649, however, a certain villager borrowed one of the umbrellas and, while he was returning home, had it blown out of his hands by a violent 'divine wind' that blew up suddenly from the direction of the shrine on Tamazu Isle. The umbrella was blown completely out of sight, and though the villager bemoaned its loss there was not a thing he could do.

Borne aloft by the wind, the umbrella landed finally in the little hamlet of Anazato, far in the mountains of the island of Kyūshū. The people of this village had from ancient times been completely cut off from the outside world and – uncultured folk that they were – had never even seen an umbrella! All of the learned men and elders of the village gathered around to discuss the curious object before them – reaching agreement, however, only upon the fact that none of them had ever before seen anything like it.

Finally one local wise man stepped forth and proclaimed, 'Upon counting the radiating bamboo ribs, there are exactly forty. The paper too is round and luminous, and not of the ordinary kind. Though I hesitate to utter that august name, this is without doubt the God of the Sun, whose name we have so often heard, and is assuredly his divine attribute from the Inner Sanctuary of the Great Shrine of Ise, which has deigned to fly to us here!'

All present were filled with awe. Hurriedly the salt water of purification was scattered about the ground and the divinity installed upon a clean reed mat; and the whole population of the village went up into the mountains and, gathering wood and rushes, built a shrine that the deity's spirit might be transferred hence from Ise. When they had paid reverence to it, the divine spirit did indeed enter the umbrella.

At the time of the summer rains the site upon which the shrine was situated became greatly agitated, and the commotion did not cease. When the umbrella was consulted, the following oracle was delivered: 'All this summer the sacred hearth has been simply filthy, with cock-roaches boiled in the holy vessels and the contamination reaching even to my Inner Shrine! Henceforth, in this entire province, let there not be a single cockroach left alive! I also have one other request. I desire you to select a beautiful young maiden as a consolation offering for me. If this is not done within seven days, without fail, I will cause the rain to fall in great torrents; I will rain you all to death, so that the seed of man remains no more upon the earth!'

Thus spake the oracle.

The villagers were frightened out of their wits. They held a meeting, and summoned all the maidens of the village to decide which one should serve the deity. But the young maidens, weeping and wailing, strongly protested the umbrella god's cruel demand. When asked the reason for their excess of grief, they cried, 'How could we survive even one night with such a god?' – for they had come to attach a peculiar significance to the odd shape which the deity had assumed.

At this juncture a young and beautiful widow from the village stepped forward, saying, 'Since it is for the god, I will offer myself in place of the young maidens.'

All night long the beautiful widow waited in the shrine, but she did not get a bit of affection. Enraged, she charged into the inner sanctum, grasped the divine umbrella firmly in her hands and screaming, 'Worthless deceiver!' she tore it apart, and threw the pieces as far as she could!

# 13

# Nagasaki

In Nagasaki Bay where sky and sea meet to the West
At heaven's edge, a little dot appears.
The cannon of the lookout tower sounds once;
In twenty-five watch stations, bows are bared.
Through the streets on all sides, the cry breaks forth:
'The redhaired Westerners are coming!'

RAI SANYŌ

The Portuguese were shipwrecked off the coast of Kyūshū in 1543 and searched for a suitable place to settle. Several places were tried but Nagasaki, with its deep bay and surrounding hills, became their favoured port.

The early letters and reports by Jesuit priests were filled with wonder and admiration and local lords often became friends of the Portuguese merchants for the purposes of commerce as the Portuguese traded between China and Japan at a time when the two countries had broken off trade relations. The Portuguese introduced gunpowder weaponry in the form of arquebuses as well as new-fangled cuisine. Many Japanese words date back to this time including *pan* – bread, *tempura* – battered food, and *kasutera* – Castillian sponge cake. Known as *Nanbanjin* or Southern Barbarians, their arrival affected every area of Japanese life and copies of their arquebuses were quickly made. The Portuguese traded Chinese silk for Japanese silver, a profitable trade.

The fashion for things foreign affected the ruler Hideyoshi (see Kyoto chapter), who started to eat beef and eggs, as well as the artists who started the *Namban* or foreigner style of art and painted screens (which depict the arrival of the Portuguese in colourful array and even watching local theatre performances). Christian accoutrements were also fashionable, a kind of accretion and absorption of Western style that the Japanese are so good at even to this day. The Jesuits introduced the first movable type pieces to print bibles. Only some of the aristocracy actually adopted Christianity sincerely, others paid court to the missionaries for Portuguese trade. But it was a Roman Jesuit priest, Alessandro Valignano, the first official Jesuit visitor to Japan, who along with Sumitada, the local lord, laid out the plan for Nagasaki with its still-recognisable grid plan of streets for four hundred houses for foreigners in 1570, along with a joint Roman and Japanese system of law. This was the first foreign community in the historical record to establish itself in Japan. But Valignano left in 1582, without much hope that this harmony would survive and indeed in 1596, the *daimyo* started the first persecution: the crucifixion of twenty-six martyrs.

Will Adams was the first-known British man to arrive, in 1600. Supposedly blown off course, he witnessed some of the more wild attempts of the Spanish friars, who had arrived more recently, to prove the divinity of Christ. Miura Anjin, as Adams was known, quickly became the shogun's appointed shipbuilder and he obviously found it in his interest to praise them: 'The people of the island of Japan are good of nature, courteous above all measure, valiant in war, their justice is severely executed without any partiality upon transgression of the law.'

The Japanese were equally impressed by European ships and artist Araki Genkei wrote this appreciation to accompany his idealised picture of one of the ships:

> Human intelligence and the skilful adaptation of means to ends have discovered a way whereby, by the power of man, the waters may be crossed and the seas navigated, as is evidenced by the man of rare intelligence who built the first vessel and whose intellect did not become dulled by the making of it. It is also evidenced every day by those whom shipping enriches.[36]

In 1613, the Portuguese traders lost their ascendancy in Japan after

36  Araki Genkei d.1799 was a Nagasaki painter and Dutch interpreter.

squabbling with the *daimyo* lords about the supply of trade with King Arima of the Malaccas. The East India Company arrived at about this time under John Saris (see Kyoto chapter), attempting to set up an English factory at Hirado in Kyūshū. Only a decade later, after heavy losses of about £4,000 per year, Saris's successor Richard Cocks had to close the East India Company factory in Hirado. Cocks' descriptions of his time in Japan show the skulduggery that was rife on the ships of Hakata bay and his summary of ten years' hard grind on the island as he hoisted sail in 1624 were summed up in the line 'Warry! Warry! Warry!' [Worry! Worry! Worry!].

Although the early seventeenth century was a time of great cultural mixing with Dutch, Chinese, British and Spanish around Maruyama-shi and Shianbashi areas – only the Dutch and Chinese were given leave to remain after 1641, when *sakoku*, the policy of isolation was enforced. The Chinese remained cloistered within a compound, finished for them in 1689, although they were allowed to celebrate their festivals, including the famous dragon dance which became part of the yearly Shinto Okinchi festival (see below). The Chinese also influenced Nagasaki cuisine – the famous *shippoku ryōri* is a hybrid of Japanese and Chinese food.

In 1641 a special factory island called Dejima was constructed just off the mainland of Nagasaki for the Dutch, who were allowed to send two ships a year, for trading purposes only. The *seisatsu* or notice board in front of Dejima was very strict:

Anyone breaking the law will be denounced. Bribing an official is forbidden, informers in cases of bribery will be promised a reward double of that which was offered, only courtesans can enter the prescribed area, neither Buddhist priests nor Yamabushi (Shinto priests) can enter. None may go further out to sea than the harbour beacon – no one may pass under the entrance bridge. Dutch residents are forbidden to go out without giving their intention of doing so. No boat is allowed to pass this beacon. Prohibition boats will approach from the sea.[37]

37  From Dejima Museum, Nagasaki

The Edo period (1603–1867) is often seen as a period of stagnation – except at Dejima where a few Japanese scholars were allowed to come and study Western subjects such as anatomy and astronomy, painting and physics. Thus many novelties in science and the arts percolated through to Japan, including anatomy, Copernicus' theory of the sun-based universe, and the English dictionary. One interpreter, Hiraga Gennai (1728–80), advocated practical observation and electrical appliances known as *erekiteru*. The interpreters studied under the factors of Dejima, who have given their names to modern Japanese institutes as well. Famous visitors were Engelbert Kaempfer (who came to Nagasaki in 1690), followed by Charles Thurnberg (who came in 1775 and travelled Japan disguised as a native, drawing the flora) and Philip Franz Siebold, who came in 1824 to set up a medical school in Nagasaki, but was expelled for drawing a map of the country.

The interpreters of Japan were daring men who dodged the shogun's penalties to write and draw as much as they could. Kaempfer's *History of Japan* is a massive work complete with detailed drawings of the trips to pay tribute to the shogun. When the treaty ports opened in the 1850s, all of this changed. The bay of Nagasaki received 20,000 tons of trade within a few months of the opening. As Admiral Christopher Pemberton Hodgson, the British Consul to Nagasaki who arrived there in June 1859, wrote:

> Japan had hitherto been a self-supporting country but here was a sudden draining on her resources, here occurred demand upon the internal produce of a state scarcely open to trade, fifteen thousand tons of shipping already supplied. Sake, tea, wheat, rice (though forbidden yet exported in quantities), wax, oil, peas and other products of Kyūshū were never known to be so dear. The sudden and enormous drain on their home consumption terrified this patriarchal government and caused them, in shortsightedness perhaps, to adopt precautions, and without alleviating the evil at home, embittered the foreigners.[38]

38 *A residence at Nagasaki and Hakodate in 1859–1860: with an account of Japan generally by C. Pemberton Hodgson; with a series of letters on Japan by his wife.* London, 1861

Pierre Loti, the orientalist master of disguises, rushed to sample the pleasures of the Maruyama licensed quarters, where previously foreigners had not been allowed to visit, crossing Shianbashi – the *Should I or Shouldn't I* bridge of temptation – which led to the quarter. He wrote *Mme Chrysanthème* as an ironic skit on Japan and was roundly criticised by fellow writers such as Felix Régamy, who said that Loti's understanding of Japan was as superficial as that of a geisha's sandal. Nagasaki became a cosmopolitan community once again, this time focussed almost completely on trade, with merchants like Thomas Glover (who married into the Maruyama geisha), Frederick Ringer, Johnny Walker and William Alt who supplied arms, tea, railroads steam ships and even deep sea fishing. The feel of that cosmopolitan period stayed around until the 1930s when print maker Ken Tagawa lived on the hillside where Glover lived:

> I spent five years in Minami Yamate before and after 1935. It was the good days of foreign settlement. Gigantic camphor trees grew densely, stone pavements were wet, many Western-style buildings were solid and people, including foreigners, lived there comfortably. Of course, these Western-style buildings can only be seen in Nagasaki. [39]

This world disappeared forever in a split second at 11.01 a.m. on August 9th 1945, when Little Fat Boy, the second atomic bomb, was dropped on Japan. Takashi Nagai, who was a doctor and leukaemia researcher at the time, witnessed the dropping of the bomb from his hospital. His book, *The Bells of Nagasaki*, is dedicated to the thousands of practising Christians who died in Urakami Cathedral, the epicentre of the bomb explosion. The Cathedral was founded on the site of one of the oldest Christian communities in Japan, a hidden group of *kakure* Christians. These were Christians from Hirado, Gotō, Shimabara, Amakusa and Urakami who had hidden their faith after the end of the Shimabara rebellion. Every single member of the congregation was killed.

39 Source: The Glover Museum, Nagasaki

The story of his birthplace's destruction must have haunted British novelist Kazuo Ishiguro, who left Nagasaki aged six. More than sixty years on, however, the city of Nagasaki has been rebuilt, and a great Okunchi lantern and float festival founded in the seventeenth century by the Suwa Jinja, a Shinto shrine has been revived.

**Anthony Thwaite** On Dejima: 1845

A turn around the yard, then back again:
A pint of gin, a game of dice, to bed

Knocked out, locked in. Twenty-two exiled men
Marooned like ghosts who do not know they're dead.

Krieger talks rubbish. Blomhoff wants a whore
And says so, endlessly. Van Puyck adds up

Consignment figures for the umpteenth time.
Wail of a *shakuhachi*[40] from the shore.

Tomorrow night, some fiefling in to sup;
Adam the cook prepares a fishy slime

Fit for outlandish palates, and sweet wine
To tilt his brains indulgently our way

('Your eminence, do take another cup') –
Turn a blind eye to Rahder's escapade

Last week (a scuffle on the landward side,
A bloody nose or two): we cover up

For one another like a gang of boys,
Distrust and honour shiftily in turn

Keeping the balance. Distantly, a noise
Of drum and cymbals marking out some rite

40  A Japanese flute

Pickled in superstition. Candles burn
Down to each dish, spit smoke, and then go out.

The hills of Nagasaki ring the night,
Our dark horizon where we cannot go.

Each day creeps by, each minute labours slow.
A hundred years from now, perhaps some light

Will fall upon this heathen harbour town –
But let the gin take over, let me row

My numbed, thick, sleepy body out to sea.
Let me go easy. Let me sink and drown

Far from this fan-shaped offshore prison where
Seabirds screech alien words in alien air.

**Pierre Loti** from *Madame Chrysenthème*

We have spent the day – Yves, Chrysanthème, Oyouki and myself,
wandering through dark and dusty nooks, dragged hither and thither
by four quick-footed djinns, in search of antiquities in the bric-a-brac
shops.

Towards sunset Chrysanthème, who has wearied me more than
ever since morning, and who doubtless has perceived it, pulls a very
long face, declares herself ill, and begs leave to spend the night at her
mother's, Madame Renoncule.

I agree to this and with the best grace in the world; let her go,
tiresome little *mousume* (young lady)! Oyouki will carry a message to
her parents, who will shut up our rooms; we shall spend the evening,
Yves and I, in roaming about as fancy takes us, without any *mousume*
dragging at our heels, and shall afterwards regain our own quarters on
board the Triomphante, without having the trouble of climbing up
that hill.

First of all, we make an attempt to dine together in some

fashionable tea house. Impossible, there is not a place to be had; all the absurd paper rooms, all the compartments contrived by so many ingenious dodges of slipping and sliding panels, all the nooks and corners in the little gardens are filled with Japanese men and women eating impossible and incredible little dishes! Numberless young dandies are dining tête-à-tête with the lady of their choice, and sounds of dancing girls and music issue from the private rooms.

The fact is that today is the third and last day of the great pilgrimage to the Temple of the Jumping Tortoise, of which we saw the commencement yesterday, and all Nagasaki is this time given over to amusement.

At the Teahouse of the Indescribable Butterflies, which is also full to overflowing, but where we are well-known, they have had the bright idea of throwing a temporary flooring over the little lake – the pond where the goldfish live, and it is here that our meal is served, in the pleasant freshness of the fountain which continues its murmur under our feet. After dinner, we follow the faithful and ascend again to the temple.

Up there we find the same elfin revelry, the same masks, the same music. We seat ourselves, as before, under a gauze tent and sip odd little drinks tasting of flowers. But this evening we were alone, and the absence of the band of *mousumes*, whose familiar little faces formed a bond of union between this holiday-making people and ourselves, separates and isolates us more than usual from the profusion of oddities in the midst of which we seem to be lost. Beneath us lies always the immense blue background: Nagasaki illumined by moonlight, and the expanse of silvered, glittering water, which seems like a vaporous vision suspended in mid-air. Behind us is the great open temple, where the bonzes officiate to the accompaniment of sacred bells and wooden clappers, looking, from where we sit, more like puppets than anything else, some squatting in rows like peaceful mummies, others executing rhythmical marches before the golden background where stand the gods. We do not laugh tonight, and speak but little, more forcibly struck by the scene than we were on the first night; we only look on, trying to understand.

**Takashi Nagai** from *The Bells of Nagasaki*

Chimoto-san was cutting grass on Mount Kawabira. From where he worked, he could see Urakami three kilometers down to the southwest. The hot summer sun was shining lazily over the beautiful town and its hills. Suddenly Chimoto-san heard the familiar, still faint sound of a plane. Sickle in hand, he straightened his body and looked up at the sky. It was more or less clear, but just above his head there floated a big cloud the shape of a human hand. Yes, the sound of the plane came from above that cloud. And as he watched, out it came. 'It's a B-29.' From the tip of the middle finger of the hand-shaped cloud, a small, flashing silver plane appeared. It must have been eight thousand meters up in the sky. 'Oh! It's dropped something. A long, narrow, black object. A bomb! A bomb!' Chimoto-san threw himself to the ground. Five seconds. Ten seconds. Twenty seconds. One minute. As he held his breath, eternity seemed to pass.

Suddenly there was a blinding flash of light; an awful brightness but no noise. Nervously Chimoto-san raised his head. 'A bomb! It's at Urakami.' And in the area above the church he saw an enormous column of white smoke float upward, swelling rapidly as it rose. But what struck terror into his heart was the huge blast of air like a hurricane that rushed toward him. It came from under the white smoke and rolled over the hills and fields with terrifying speed and power. Houses and trees and everything else collapsed.

It was as though a huge, invisible fist had gone wild and smashed everything in the room. The bed, the chairs, the bookcases, my steel helmet, my shoes, my clothes were thrown into the air, hurled around the room with a wild, clattering noise, and all piled on top of me as I lay helpless on the floor. Then the blast of dusty dirty wind rushed in and filled my nostrils so that I could scarcely breathe. I kept my eyes open, looking always at the window. And as I looked, everything outside grew dark. There was a noise like the sound of a stormy sea, and the air everywhere swirled round and round. My clothes, the zinc roof, pieces of wood, and all kinds of other objects were performing a macabre dance in that dark sky. Then it gradually became cold, as at the end of autumn, and strange and silent emptiness ensued. Clearly this was no ordinary event.

I again came to the conclusion that a bomb of at least one ton had fallen at the entrance to the hospital. There would probably be about a hundred wounded. Where could we send them? What could we do with them? We must get the teachers together. But probably half of them were dead or wounded.

But I must first get myself out of this wreckage in which I was trapped. I moved my knees and with difficulty stretched out my body. As I did so, everything became black. Were both my eyes completely blind? What a mess I was in! At first I thought that since I had wounds around my eyes there must be a cerebral hemorrhage there. But when I tried to move my eyes I succeeded in doing so. I was not blind.

And, strange to say, when I reached the conclusion that I was not blind, I was, for the first time, struck with horror. The building had collapsed and I was buried alive! What a weird and grotesque death I was destined to meet. Anyhow, let me do what I can, I thought. And underneath the pieces of debris I continued to struggle with all my might. But I was flattened like a rice cracker lying in a toaster. I couldn't imagine what part of my body I could move or in what direction.


**Kazuo Ishiguro** from *A Pale View of the Hills*

Shortly after breakfast, Ogata-san suggested we should go and look around Nagasaki – 'like the tourists do', as he put it. I agreed at once and we took a tram into the city. As I recall, we spent some time at an art gallery, and then, a little before noon, we went to visit the peace memorial in the large public park not far from the centre of the city.

The park was commonly known as 'Peace Park' – I never discovered whether this was the official name – and indeed, despite the sounds of children and birds, an atmosphere of solemnity hung over that large expanse of green. The usual adornments such as shrubs and fountains, had been kept to a minimum, and the effect was a kind of austerity; the flat grass, a wide summer sky, and the memorial itself – a massive white statue in memory of those killed by the atomic bomb – presiding over its domain.

The statue resembled some muscular Greek god, seated with both arms outstretched. With his right hand, he pointed to the sky from where the bomb had fallen; with his other arm – stretched out to this left – the figure was supposedly holding back the forces of evil. His eyes were closed in prayer.

It was always my feeling that the statue had a rather cumbersome appearance, and I was never able to associate it with what had occurred that day the bomb had fallen and those terrible days which followed. Seen from a distance, the figure looked almost comical, resembling a policeman conducting traffic. It remained for me nothing more than a statue, and while most people in Nagasaki seemed to appreciate it as some form of gesture, I suspect the general feeling was much like mine. And today, should I by chance recall that large white statue in Nagasaki, I find myself reminded primarily of my visit to Peace Park with Ogata-san that morning.

**Richard K. Nelson** from *A Year in the Life of a Shinto Shrine*

One thing about Okunchi – it is relatively 'new'. Flooded as Nagasaki was by foreigners and the accoutrements of their cultures in its formative years as an international trading centre, the participating neighbourhoods had no inhibitions about trying innovative ideas in making their floats. And as competition for prizes and recognition increased, so did the daring. The guiding principle was 'If it looks impressive, let's use it!' Thus we have today, as legacies from that upstart beginning, the 'Hollanders' dance (satirizing the 'barbarians' from Europe); the Kokodesho, or 'let's do it here!' dance (taught to locals by businessmen from Ōsaka); and the Jaodori, or dragon dance (reflecting the city's Chinese links and custom); as well as some curious chants used by the bearers of the portable shrines instead of the typical *'wasshoi, wasshoi'* heard elsewhere in Japan. One neighbourhood, fascinated with the logo of the East India Trading Company, decided to turn the symbol on its head (a bit like *fumie* turning Christ on his head), and include it as part of the insignia for their *machi*.

The morning is overcast and balmy, and carries with it traces of the Typhoon Fifteen's extraordinary clouds that dumped three inches of rain on Southwestern Kyūshū. Here on the backside of the ridge of mountains running down the Nagasaki peninsula, where a caravan of cars from Suwa Shrine has parked beside one of Ariake Bay's beaches, the farmers and fishermen take their clouds very seriously. Early-warning systems installed after the three disastrous typhoons of mid-August, in which fifteen fishermen drowned, prevented further loss of life and property in what has been a particularly turbulent year. This morning though, there is a rich texture to the mottled greens of the loquat and tangerine groves blanketing steep hillsides, and the sand of Miyazuri Beach looks smooth and washed, as if a gardener had tended it all through the rainy night.

But typhoons and weather systems are the last things on the minds of a group of half-naked men who stand huddled together on the beach, awaiting the completion of an opening prayer. In just a moment these bearers of the festival's portable shrines (*mikoshi*) must be thoroughly purified in the most ancient, efficacious style – total immersion in saltwater – before they can even approach the *kamis'* palanquins. Framed by the distant volcano of Unzen on the other side of the bay's grey waters and the long expanse of beach stretching away on either side, the men look fragile and insignificant in their white loincloths and headbands, not at all sure that going into the sea is something human beings are supposed to do on the first of October. Although being selected to carry the *mikoshi*, is a once-in-a-lifetime opportunity and honour, the lapping waves and great silence behind them are more than enough to make this distinction appear dubious. Most Japanese will tell you that swimming in the ocean is simply not possible after August 15 because by then not only has the typhoon season started in earnest, churning up the water and letting the sea show its violent side, but also the jellyfish have found their way into the warm currents, and leave nasty welts for those foolish enough to go even wading. (Never mind that the jellyfish are gone in two weeks, and that during all of September the water is mild and warm.)

When the final bows are made before the portable altar loaded with offering dishes, *sake* vessels and *sakaki* branches, the priest picks up the wand of purification and waves it above the bowed heads of the group. Then, hesitantly, each man slowly wades into the water up to his armpits, pauses an instant to silently recite the formula for purification while looking at the blue outline of the volcano of Mount Unzen and, joining his palms together, disappears beneath the waves. It is an eerie sight how completely they are 'gone' for there is no sign whatsoever that they even existed at all. For that instant, the participant is no longer a human being but has become the ancient deity Izanagi (see Ise chapter), who had no choice but to purify himself in the water after seeing the rotting corpse of his wife in the netherworld. It was from this purification that numerous *kami* were born from his body, among them Amaterasu, the supreme Sun *kami*, who sprang into the world from Izanagi's left eye. But it was also this ritual that provided Shinto with one of its most fundamental and powerful orientations to the world: that of *misogi*, or purification by cold water.

# 14

# Okinawa

Waves be still
And quiet, Wind,
The king from Shuril comes –
And we must pay him reverence.

ONNA NABE

Okinawa (meaning Rope on the Sea) is the collective name for the archipelago of islands off the coast of Kyūshū, in the South China Sea. It was first written about as a dream or mythical island destination. Marco Polo had heard of thousands of islands in the South China Sea (or 'Sea of Zin', as he calls it) – where 'in all these there grows no tree which is not agreeably fragrant, and also useful, being equal or superior in size to lignum aloes'.[41] On the islands, the aloe is harvested for its juice as well as its all round medicinal properties to this day.

Okinawa was linked to both Japanese and Chinese culture. Jōmon period as well as Yayoi period pottery has been found here. Okinawan and Japanese dialects are also linked. An exiled Minamoto warrior is credited with coming here in the twelfth century and marrying the daughter of the local *anji* or chief, while his son Shunten subsequently built his castle, Shuri-jō, near the present-day capital, Naha. From that point onwards, the island grew in prosperity, first establishing trading links with China and sending tribute under the leader Shō Hashi, who unified south, north and central islands in 1429. Shō Hashi also introduced Chinese style arts such as the three-stringed lyre or *shamisen*, and Chinese stone cutting techniques, stone bridge

---

41  *The Travels of Marco Polo*, published 1844, Oliver and Boyd, Edinburgh, ed. Hugh Murray.

building and castle building and other Chinese innovations, followed by exotic Indonesian turbans and tie-dying through trade with southeast Asia. In the sixteenth century, Shōen of the second Shō dynasty ushered in a period of peace. Chieftains vied for goods not arms. This was when the *Omori Shoshi*, a body of poems paying homage to the ancient culture was written down, including the *waka* poem by Onna no Nabe (above).

But when the rest of Japan was unified under the Tokugawa, the Japanese made Okinawa a vassal state ruled from Satsuma on Kyūshū. The Satsuma *daimyo* forced all sorts of strange rules on the Okinawans, as he was keen to exploit the precious Chinese trade – numerous Chinese junks could land on Okinawa every year, whereas only two were allowed into Nagasaki. The Satsuma *daimyo* also levied heavy taxes. At one point the Okinawans were forbidden from speaking Japanese and made to wear Chinese dress so as not to discourage the Chinese from visiting. The opportunities for trade in Ryūkyū (or Loochoo as the islands were known to Europeans in the eighteenth century), were quickly spotted, so French, Russian and then British ships landed here seeking trading agreements, leaving the locals feeling rather overwhelmed. Captain Basil Hall of the *Lyra* arrived here in 1814 and he and his surgeon John Mcleod delighted in the hospitality they received.

But the Japanese took a tougher stance after the Edo period. A later visitor, a Japanese official, Sasamori Gisuke (1845–1915), who was sent to Okinawa during the Meiji period to see if increased sugar cane production could be encouraged there, observed the much-deteriorated conditions of the island. Sasamori treated a lot of malaria as he went around the dilapidated villages, noting how the samurai 'were not concerned with the lives of others'.[42] Although the Japanese introduced cash crops such as cane and sweet potatoes, colonial rule had depleted the island's health and wealth. Sasamori observed that Chinese culture had had a major influence on the island, that Confucian temples were still standing and the Okinawans were

---

42 *The Japanese at Home and Abroad as Revealed through Their Diaries*, ed. Donald Keene, Exploration of the Southern Islands, p. 164

resentful of the fact that their king Sho Tai had been forced to give up his throne in 1879, and that the Japanese had made their kingdom a 'prefecture' of Japan.

The high taxes continued after the Japanese had annexed the island. Emigration from Okinawa steadily increased during this period, encouraged by the Tokyo government, with tens of thousands moving to Hawaii or to the United States, until Okinawa fell victim to one of the worst battles in the Second World War, when the Americans destroyed first the capital of Naha (where the Shuril castle had already been destroyed by the Japanese in 1879) and then, from April 1st, 1945, they went on to destroy the rest of the island in the only land battle fought on Japanese soil. Chizuko Oyasato bore witness to the event as a young girl. The US kept the islands until 1972, and there is still a huge American military base there.

**George Kerr** from *Okinawa, the History of an Island People*

Captain Hall of the *Lyra* comments on the individual character of the Okinawans who became friendly companions during the autumn sojourn. The narrative of Dr John Mcleod, surgeon on the *Alcester*, supplements Hall's account with wide ranging remarks on the character of the countryside, the habits and customs observed during the long rambles in the wooded hills and fields near Naha. He notes the innate dignity and cultivated manners displayed by the ranking men of Okinawa. Americans who have become acquainted with the ravaged island since 1945 find it difficult to credit Mcleod's description of the landscape:

> They seemed to enjoy robust health, for we observed no diseased objects, nor beggars of any description, among them ... Cultivation is added to the most enchanting beauties of nature. From a commanding height . . . the view that is, in all directions, picturesque and delightful . . . To the South is the city of Napafoo (Naha) and in the intermediate space appear numerous hamlets scattered about on the banks of the rivers, which meander in the valley beneath; the eye being in every direction, charged by the varied hues of the

luxuriant foliage around their habitations. Turning to the east, the houses of Kintching (Shuri) the capital city, built in their peculiar style, are observed, opening from among the lofty trees which surround and shade them, rising one above another in a gentle ascent to the summit of a hill, which is crowned by the king's palace; the intervening grounds between Napafoo and Kintching, a distance of some miles, being ornamented by a continuation of villas and country houses. To the North, as far as they can reach, the higher land is covered with extensive forests.

This island also boasts its rivers and secure harbours; and last, though not least, a worthy, friendly and a happy race of people.

Many of these islanders displayed a spirit of intelligence and genius, which seemed the more extraordinary, considering the confined circle in which they live; such confinement being almost universally found to be productive of narrowness of mind. Our friends here were an exception to the general rule: Maddera (i.e. Maedera) Cosyong, one of our most constant and intimate friends, acquired such proficiency in the English language, in the course of a few weeks as to make himself tolerably understood.

He was gay or serious, as occasion required, but was always respectable; and of Maddera it might be truly said, that he was a gentleman, not formed upon this model, or according to that rule, but 'stamped as such by the sovereign hand of Nature'.

They all seemed to be gifted with a sort of politeness which had the fairest claim to be natural; for there was nothing constrained – nothing stiff or studied in it.

Captain Maxwell having one day invited a party to dine with him, the health of the king Lewchew was drank in a bumper: one of them immediately addressing himself with much warmth and feeling to the interpreter, desired him to state how much they felt gratified by such a compliment; that they would take care to tell it to everybody when they went on shore; and proposed, at the same time, a bumper to the king of the *Engelees* (English). A Chinese mandarin, under the like circumstances, would, most probably, have chin chinned, (that is clenched his fists) as usual; he would have snivelled and grinned the established number of times and bowed his head in slavish submission to the bare mention of his tyrant's name; but it would never have occurred to him to have given, in his turn, the health of the sovereign of England.

The superiority of manner brought to our recollection the boorishness of the Chinese near the Pei-ho. Certain mandarins who were not sufficient button (rank) to be entertained in the company of the ambassador, were invited to dine with the officers, and some of them, after gnawing the leg of a fowl would without any ceremony thrust the remains of it into any other dish near them.

[...]

The following lines, written by Mr Gillard on leaving our hospitable friends at Grand Lew Chew, speak not only his own, but the general feeling on that occasion:

> While friendship thus was shown to all
> Congenial minds attached a few;
> And Memory oft will pleased recall
> The names of 'Madd'ra' and Ge Roo.
> Farewell dear Isle! – on thee may ne'er
> The breath of civil discord blow!
> Far from your shores be every fear,
> And far – oh far – the invading foe!

**Chizuko Oyasato** from *Okinawa 1945: A child's perspective*

*The first air raid*

'See you later, Mother,' I waved to my mother who came to the door to see me off to school. It was the morning of October 10, 1944.

I was wearing my favourite *mompe* (pantaloons) my mother had made from her old *kasuri* (splash pattern) kimono. I had my emergency pouch and my lunch and carried my *boku zukin* (padded hood) on my shoulder. A white nametag with my name, address, and blood type was sewn on the front of my pouch.

My family name is Maeshiro and we originally come from Naha City on the main island of Okinawa. My father's company transferred him to Kitadaito Island, 360 km east of Okinawa on the Pacific side. I was born in Kitadaito. Later, my grandmother on my father's side injured her leg in an automobile accident. Because of this, my mother and I moved back to Naha to take care of Grandma Maeshiro.

My father stayed in Kitadaito, my two older brothers went to school in Tokyo, and my sister Yoko who returned to Naha before us lived with our grandmother and great grandmother in Tomari, Naha. I was in the sixth grade at the time.

My mother, who used to work as a schoolteacher, quit her job and was home all day. That made me very happy.

In April 1944, I enrolled in the Second Prefecture Girl's School that was located in Naha. We were able to attend classes all day only for the first two or three months. After that emergency sirens that signalled us to gather our things immediately and go home regularly interrupted our classes. Soon classes were dropped altogether and we were sent to help build military facilities.

First we helped dig emergency shelters in Haebaru; later we were assigned to do volunteer work at the antiaircraft artillery base at Gajanbara, located south of Naha port. We would sing uplifting nationalistic songs like 'Until the Day of Triumph' as we toiled in the scorching sun all day. I had to walk through the city of Naha, from one end to the other for an hour to get to my duty station.

Our main duty was to transport the soil that the soldiers dug out. We worked in pairs and carried out the soil in baskets. Sometimes we would hang the basket on a pole and carry it over our shoulders. Other times, we would stand in a line and pass the baskets from one to the other.

That day, I had walked about twenty minutes and reached the Miebashi district of Naha when I spied two or three warplanes pierce the morning calm with their metallic roar and circle the skies.

'Masa-chan, did you notice something strange about those planes?' I asked. Masa-chan was a neighbourhood girl who was the same age as me.

'I know something is fishy,' she answered, as she looked up into the sky.

Soon we noticed small puffs of smoke appear around the planes and disappear quickly. We stood there and stared upward.

Someone in uniform came running and shouted into a bullhorn, 'This is an aerial attack! Return to your homes.'

'It is an air raid.'

Men on their way to work, ladies in aprons; everyone was running here and there. We decided to return home too.

'Mother I'm back!' I called out, as I entered my house without bothering to remove my shoes. My mother was busy packing all our belongings.

My grandmother had lost one leg in the car accident and my great-grandmother, who was now over ninety years old, couldn't move her legs because of rheumatism.

When I came home from school, they would be in their favourite spots in the family room next to the kitchen. My white-haired great-grandmother was usually napping while sitting hunch-backed on the floor, or she would be busy inspecting a cabinet drawer full of her things. Grandmother would remove stitches from an old kimono, sort good black-eyed peas from the bad, or snap off the tops from bean sprouts for dinner.

'Where are the grandmas?' I asked as I looked for my grandmothers who weren't in their usual spots.

'Our neighbour Mr Ikeymiya came to take them to our neighbourhood emergency shelter,' Mother replied. She was moving all our household goods to our shelter in the back yard and the furniture to a corner in the yard to avoid fires from a possible air raids. I helped as much as I could. I realized that I was stronger than usual and I was able to carry heavy boxes that I usually couldn't even lift.

[...]

Shortly, the warplanes came, one after the other, and started bombing the area. Mother and I put on our *boku zukin* to protect our heads and fled to the shelter in our yard. From the entryway on the south side, I had a view of the city of Naha.

All morning the bombers came, scattered across the skies like a swarm of horseflies. They would take a sudden dive over the anti-aircraft artillery base in Gajanbira (where I worked), drop a bomb and ascend just as abruptly as they came. Later they attacked the Oroku airfield (the

present Naha terminal). Scenes that I have seen only on newsreels at
movie theatres were now unfolding right before my very eyes. I trembled
in my mother's arms as I watched the nightmare before me. Tears rolled
down my cheeks as I pictured the artillery field in Gajanbira, which I
helped to build under the blazing sun, being destroyed into rubble.

I saw pillars of fire everywhere quickly turn into columns of smoke
that enshrouded the sky. The warplanes descended in an almost
leisurely manner and bombarded the city. Now and then I could see
puffs of white smoke rising. I wondered if that was the Japanese forces
retaliating: they didn't seem to hit their targets much. It was a dis-
comforting sight.

[…]

The city of Naha continued to burn, dyeing the skies red and
making loud crackling noises. Though the district of Tomari where
we live was spared, the waterfront and uptown areas had burned down
and were covered with a layer of steam and smoke.

I went to check the front gate of our house to check out the damage.
Maemichi Street (the present Songenji) that runs adjacent to the river
was filled with people with all their earthly belongings, running helter-
skelter to find a safe place to hide.

Because all the buildings had burned down, I had a clear view of the
area around me. Over the fires destroying the city, I saw the sun about
to set. I was terrified and dumbfounded as I gazed at this eerie
spectacle. It is a sight I remember distinctly to this day.

The grandmothers decided to spend the night at the neighbourhood shelter. In the evening, my sister who worked at the artillery
command came home.

'Yoko-chan, you were all right,' Mother sobbed as she held my
sister tightly.

Mother delivered dinner to our grandmothers at the shelter. We
had a light supper and then went to the centre room with the ancestral
altar, to sleep together, still in our *mompes*. Was it because I was so
tense or because of the constant buzzing sound in my ear? I was so
afraid that the enemy would return with new weapons that I could
hardly fall asleep.

This was the first air raid of Okinawa. Naha was not the only place under siege. Most of Okinawa including the islands of Miyako and Yaeyama and neighbouring Amami Island was bombarded by over 900 warplanes and casualties were approximately 1,500. Naha City was the most heavily attacked, especially in central regions, and 90 per cent of the city was destroyed.

*After this Chizuko journeyed with her elderly great-grandmother and grandfather through the island to Kunigami, a safe place, while others left for mainland Japan. Once the American invasion started in April 1945, she escaped death by hiding in an Okinawan tomb, she then crossed enemy lines and became a prisoner of war.*

# 15

# Hokkaidō

Amid the brilliance of the fresh green fields, cattle and horses play and students, guiding their ploughs, cultivate the pasturage that bends like waves in the wind. The clean beauty makes a magnificent panorama that one could not find elsewhere in Japan, no matter where one looked ...

ARASHIMA TAKEO

Hokkaidō is a pastoral idyll to most Japanese, a place to escape from the fetid heat that hits the main areas of Honshū and Kyūshū in July and August, with wide open pastures and mountain peaks with *rotemburo onsen* hotsprings and alpine flora and fauna. Hokkaidō cows adorn the milk cartons and cheese triangles sold in convenience stores across Japan.

The Ezo, as the Ainu people of the north were called historically, posed a threat to the early rulers of Japan, and were pushed up to Hokkaidō during the seventh and eighth century. After the 1669 uprising, which was brutally suppressed by the shogun, the Ainu have been in retreat. Their culture was suppressed through de facto Japanese land grabs, settlement and intermarriage during the nineteenth century. The Japanese compared the Ainu to *tsuchigomo* or earth spiders because they dug houses underground for themselves during the winter time. Only around 25,000 Ainu survive, although Ainu activist and Diet representative Kayano Shigeru (1926–2006) fought hard to promote Ainu rights; largely as a result of his efforts, the 1993 UN Year of Indigenous People took place.

One benefactor and friend of the Ainu was Sir John Batchelor, who joined the missionary society in order to go to Japan in 1879, and remained there until 1924. At that time, the Ainu were more numerous and lived on Hokkaidō as well as what are now the Russian Sakhalin Islands. John Batchelor studied the Ainu and entertained them with Aesop's fables while they told him their folklore. As opposed to attempting to impose an alien religious system on them, he listened to their stories of cosmology through his interpreter, Parapita. He described their animistic beliefs:

> Whatever has life moves and whatever moves has life. The religion of the people is a very present and deep one, it is coextensive with the universe . . . and pervades everyone and everything . . . all are bound by it and there is no possible way of escaping it.[43]

The land and culture is different from Japan. In winter there are *yuki matsuri*, snow festivals, in the city of Sapporo and people eat a Mongolian barbecue style of dish called a *jingisukan*, or 'Genghis Khan'. The hills and forests are filled with wildlife, including Blakiston's fish-owl (*bubo blakistoni*), the *ezo higuma*, the Hokkaidō brown bear, and the *tancho* or red-crowned crane.

The Hoppo Minzoku Shiryoshitsu (Batchelor Museum) in the middle of the botanical gardens in Sapporo is filled with Ainu culture, artefacts, photographs, textiles and items from the Sakhalin and Gilyak tribes (of Siberia), to whom the Ainu are said to be related. Batchelor also describes the Ainu hunting quail and duck and bear, driven by hunger rather than any other motivation such as sport or championship.

The rural Japanese explorer Matsuura Takeshiro (1818–88), visited each one of the sixty-eight provinces of Japan as well as the Chishima (Kuril) islands to the north. Originally self-funded, his expeditions were so successful that the Government seconded him to explore the interior, including a trip with eight Japanese and Ainu across from Soya in Hokkaidō to Sakhalin, the island now owned by Russia (which was one of the causes of the Russo-Japanese war in 1904–05). Matsuura's experience of hunting a bear was recorded in his *Shiribeshi Nisshi* (*Daily Record of Shiribeshi*) of 1858.

Stretching between the two horn-like tips of Hokkaidō is the great sea of Ohkotsk, which washes Hokkaidō's north-eastern shore as well

---

43  *Ainu Life and Lore*, Jonson reprint, New York, 1971

as the coast of Siberia. In the middle of this sea lie the Kuril Islands, whose occupancy has long been disputed (Japan is still officially at war with Russia over the issue). Of a population of 23,000, a third are Russian soldiers. Kenji Miyazawa, poet of Iwate (see Northern Honshū chapter), wrote an ode to the Sea of Okhotsk.

As international interest grew during the 1850s, Hokkaidō became one of the first sites for modern Meiji (1868–1912) experiments in industrialisation. A visiting American noticed the climate was right for growing hops and so the first brewery was established. Sapporo beer and Asahi beer (named after one of Hokkaidō's volcanos, Asahidake), were brewed here. The first Hokkaidō agricultural college was also founded here by American educator William Smith Clark. Now a university, its motto is 'Boys be ambitious!' This is where novelist and short story writer Arashima Takeo (1878–1923) worked at the turn of the century.

Hakodate is a rocky headland sticking out into the sea where, in 1740, the Russian ships first weighed anchor and for a brief period, Hakodate became an open city. It then became a major port for Hokkaidō and the centre of international – especially Russian – interest in 1854, when the ports of Japan first opened. In 1864, Tokugawa shogunate loyalists retreated here and declared an independent republic. Ishikawa Takuboku (1886–1912) was a young *tanka* and *jiyushi* (freestyle) poet and a member of the *shintaishi* naturalist school, who took up residence in Hakodate and wrote moving poems about the place. Will Ferguson picked up the more cosmopolitan feel of modern day Hakodate, after he had hitch-hiked all the way from Kyūshū.

**Sir John Batchelor** from *Ainu Life and Lore*

In our very early days in Hokkaidō there were times when we could get no animal food to eat. We found this very trying in the winter. I therefore determined to buy a gun and try to better matters in this respect. After the gun came, I was able to keep our larder well-stocked with such things as wild duck, snipe, woodcock, tree grouse, hares, and now and then wild geese.

One day, an English gentleman and his wife came to visit us at Sapporo. They were supporters of missions and it was my pleasure to take the gentleman with me to some of the rougher places of the interior. Just before starting, my friend saw me cleaning my gun, when he informed me that he was very sorry to see that I shot, and that he did not consider it right for a missionary to shoot birds and animals. So, in order not to offend one of our supporters, I put my gun out of sight. His dear good wife also, being of like opinion, had the grace to tell my spouse, who had a couple of very pretty duck wings in her hat, that she did not think ladies ought to wear feathers!

My friend and well-wisher soon started off with me on our tour, and in a few days we arrived at a hamlet in the interior, where an old Ainu friend had put up two nice rooms in his house, in which I always stayed. As it happened, I had not brought a very big supply of tinned provisions with me, so it was not long before we ran out of animal food.

[...]

Within forty yards of our rooms, a quail got up at my feet. He rose with a startling whirl from under my very nose. 'Bang!' went my gun and I forthwith picked up my breakfast. I had no sooner secured my bird than I heard a loud voice coming from the window. 'There goes another! Look! Quick!' The poor man saw his breakfast flying away and was evidently afraid of losing it! 'Bang' sounded my gun again and down came my friend's breakfast also. And he was very much pleased. Out he rushed and said, 'Ah, I think it is all right to shoot for food, but I do not like shooting for mere sport.' 'Come along,' said I, 'let us go and pick up a few dinners if we can.' Away we went and returned with a bag of seven or eight fine, fat tree-grouse and a few quails. These lasted for us for some time, and when they were eaten up, we went and got more, and a few duck as well. So my companion saw that whether clergy or laymen 'a man's a man for a' that' and must be fed.

It is supposed among ourselves that the fox is the most wily animal of the forests, but the Ainu say 'No, not so. The bear is the most artful of all.' That may be true, but I think all animals have their little tricks, which they play when hard pressed. One day an Ainu friend and I went out to try and shoot something to eat, for I was very tired of nothing but millet and vegetables. As we were going along, we chanced to hit upon the tracks a fox had made in the snow, and I asked my friend whether we should go and see if we could get its skin. 'No,' he said very emphatically, 'not if you wish to shoot a hare or some ducks.' 'But why?' I asked. 'What has that got to do with it?' Then he said, 'If you kill a fox, the first thing you will be certain not to get, is any good game today.' 'I don't see why,' I replied. 'Oh,' he returned, 'that is because you do not understand how to hunt. If you kill a fox, his spirit will immediately come out of his body and travel round and tell all the other animals and the birds also that you are after them.' So we left the fox alone and got on to a hare. My friend told me that in olden times, whenever the men killed a fox while hunting, they always tied his mouth up tightly so as to prevent his spirit from getting out and going off to spread the news.

Another incident happened very near our home in Sapporo one afternoon. It was winter and I put on a pair of broad Canadian snow-shoes and went out to find our dinner for the next day. It was not long before I discovered the tracks of a hare, which I followed up for some time. I saw the animal before me but after about an hour of patiently following him in hope, lost him completely. I then returned home and reported my failure. The next day I went again to the same place and as a little more snow had fallen during the night, quickly found his new foot prints. I put the animal up and again followed him, but once more lost him. As I was returning home along my snow shoe track, I was surprised to find that the hare had been following me on the very path I had made! I wondered at his sagacity and returned home once more empty-handed. The next morning I got up and went again to have it out with him. I put him up and followed him. We went in a big circle, but after a time, I was in front and he behind! I actually saw him hopping along steadily after me. I therefore got behind a big tree and waited. By-and-by along he came, but he stopped just out of gunshot, sat up on his hind quarters, looked about, and then proceeded to wash his face with his paws exactly like a cat! After about ten minutes of waiting and looking round, he came on again along my tracks, and I got him as he was passing. I carried him home, where we jugged him, and found him fine eating. He was indeed a wily hare.

Hares are not looked upon by the Ainu with favour, for they are supposed to be witches. They are said to enter people's dwellings with the intention of bewitching the family residing there. When their tracks are discovered in the snow near a house, they must be scooped up with a water ladle and carefully turned upside down, in order to prevent evil. While doing this, the person must say, 'A hare has come to bewitch us, but with this ladle, I turn his track upside down and thereby bury his soul under the snow. Therefore, although there are people living in this house, they will not now be bewitched. Let the hare himself sicken and die.'

**Matsuura Takeshiro** from *Travels to the North*

I climbed up to a high place about forty or fifty yards away and watched. The men thrust pointed sticks into the cave, but the bear remained inside, roaring in anger. The dogs wagged their tails joyfully, two of them dancing around as if they meant to enter the cave; but the Ainu, restraining them, fired three or four poison arrows inside. This made the bear roar all the more furiously, until I thought that the cave would collapse under the reverberations. Then the men, clearing a path in the snow, drove the dogs into the cave. The bear grew all the more crazed as the poison started to take effect, and came roaring out of the cave, heading directly at Tonenbaku. But he, not in the slightest perturbed, cried out, 'Damn you, *heureho*.' (The natives call a bear cub a *heureho*, and always use this word when confronting a bear.) He got his arm firmly around the neck of the bear which, though its strength was visibly failing, continued to shake and roar. Tonenbaku drew his knife and thrust the point in from under the bear's legs all the way to the ribs. His skill was really astonishing.

When the other Ainu saw that Tonenbaku had killed the bear, they at once set about cutting up the meat. First they offered some to the gods of the mountains and sea, next, they dragged the carcass into the cave where they had spent the previous night, and proceeded to devour the meat, raw or grilled. The fresh blood froze to their beards, and their hands were stained with blood. They looked exactly like devils in paintings. It was a terrifying sight.

**Kenji Miyazawa** from 'Ohkotsk Elegy' [44]

The sea is rusted by the morning's carbon dioxide.
Some parts show *verdigris*, some azurite.
There where the waves curl, the liquid is fearfully emerald.
The ears of the timothy, grown so short,
are one by one blown by the wind.
    (They are blue piano keys
    pressed one by one by the wind)
The timothy may be a short variety.
Among dewdrops, morning-glories bloom,
the glory of the morning-glories.
    Here comes the steppe cart I saw a moment ago.
    The head of the aged white draft horse droops.
    I know the man is all right
    because on that empty street corner
    when I asked him, Where's the busiest section of the shore?
    he said, It must be over there
    because I've never been there.
    Now he looks at me kindly from the corners of his eyes.
    (The small lenses he wears
    Surely reflect the white clouds of Karafuto)
They look more like peonies than morning-glories,
those large blossoms of beach roses,
those scarlet morning blossoms of beach eggplant.
    These sharp flower scents
    must be the elves' work
    bringing forth numerous indigo butterflies.
    Here again, tiny golden lance-like ears.

---

44 Ohkotsk, Karafuto, Saghalien (Sakhalin in Russian) and Eihama: Saghalien is
an island in the Sea of Okhotsk. Divided between Russia and Japan in 1905,
the southern half became known as Karafuto. The island has been wholly
Russian since Russia joined the war and captured the island in August 1945.
Eihama, now called Starodubskoe, is a port town in Karafuto.

Jade vases and blue screens.
And since the clouds dazzle so,
this joyous violent dizziness.

    Hoof marks, two by two
    Are left on the wet quiet sand.
    Of course not only the horse has passed.
    The wide tracks of the cart wheels
    form a soft series.

Near a white thin line waves have left
three tiny mosquitoes stray
and are being lightly blown off.
Piteous white fragments of seashells,
blue stalks of day lilies half buried in the sand.
The waves come, rolling the sand in.
I think I'll fall upon the pebbles of white schist,
hold in my mouth a slice of seashell
polished clean by the waves
and sleep for a while.
For now, from the sound of these waves,
the moist fragrant wind and the light of the clouds
I must recover the transparent energy that I gave
to the morning elves of Saghalien
while I lay on the fine carpet of
blue huckleberries bearing black ripe fruits
among the large red blossoms of beach roses
and mysterious bluebells.
Above all, because of exhaustion
my imagination has paled,
becoming a dazzling golden green.
In the sun's rays and the sky's layers of darkness
I hear a mysterious steady sound of tin drums.
[...]

**Ishikawa Takuboku** Three poems

> Dune flowers on a northern beach
> reeking of the sea –
> I wonder will they bloom again this year . . . ?

> \*     \*     \*

> Ah, Aoyagi in Hakodate!
> How sad it was!
> My friend's love song . . .
> The wild cornflowers . . .

> \*     \*     \*

> When I breathe in
> there is a sound in my body
> sadder than the winter wind.

**Will Ferguson** from *Hokkaidō Highway Blues*

Early morning in Hakodate. Even the very air was drowsy. I walked down among some brick warehouses as the dawn slowly filled with sounds and smells; traffic, trolley bells, car exhaust. I ended up in the city's morning market, a large, low-ceilinged building stuffed with stalls and wet smells. You could buy anything you wanted at the Hakodate market, as long as it had gills or was made of polyester.

A woman in a rubber apron, rubber gloves, rubber boots and – for all I know – rubber underwear was hosing down a sheaf of freshly caught fish. There was that smell – the smell of fish. It fills your mouth and nearly suffocates you. It's like breathing cod liver oil. 'Tasty, *ne!*' exclaimed an old lady behind me, scanning the fish with a greedy eye.

Right next to the fish stall was a stand selling sweets. Is that bad market research or what? Kind of like putting a perfume factory downwind from a sewage treatment plant. I had a cup of green tea at the sweet shop, but it tasted like fish.

The further I ventured into the market, the thicker became the crowds and the narrower the lanes between the stalls. Women examined floppy octopi with the critical gaze of connoisseurs. I saw every sort of slimy sea creature imaginable slopped up on tables and carefully appraised. Voices rattled in echoes under the corrugated tin roof, voices haggled, endlessly haggled, and bodies pushed past me on every turn. For the most part, Japanese markets are sorely disappointing. They are too restrained, too orderly, too reserved. But here in the clutter and clutch of Hakodate, was a market worthy of the name. It was almost *Korean* in its exuberance and bad manners. I wandered through the smell – sodden air like a sensory voyeur, taking in the sights, sounds and malodorous tastes that hung in the air.

[...]

The heart of Hakodate is the historic, time-battered Motomachi District, which curves around the base of Mount Hakodate. Mr Saito, the innkeeper, insisted I borrow his wife's bicycle to go sightseeing, and it was a good thing too. The Old Town is spread out over a far enough distance to make walking tiresome.

'Just make sure you lock the bike whenever your park it. The Russians are in port today.'

'The Russians?'

'They steal bicycles. They take them back to Russia and sell them. Sometimes they even steal the tires off of cars. We have to be very careful whenever they are in town.'

Jeez. From thermonuclear superpower to bicycle thieves; no wonder the Russian hardliners are so pissed off. I assured Mr Saito that I would indeed watch out for nefarious bands of spanner wielding Russkies and I set off.

What a wonderful place. Cobblestone streets. A beautiful Greek Orthodox Church, rising up in onion domes and spires. Winding alleyways. Faded glory. Knocked-about, meandering – Hakodate wore its past like an old sweater. Even better, I now had a choice of three gears: slow, very slow, and really very slow. This was a vast improvement over the previous rent-a-bikes I had used.

I bicycled down to a crumbling old wharf where the smell of the sea permeated the very wood and where houses were falling into ruin, the windows cracked, the walls patched up. It was as though the Japanese had moved into an Eastern European city en masse. As though Belgrade had been foreclosed by the bank and sold to Japanese investors. I wobbled up and down the side streets. Parked the bike and wandered into alleyways. Got lost. Got unlost. Got lost again. It was like playing hide-and-seek with yourself.

A Russian man was having a futile conversation with a Japanese store clerk over some sort of purchase. Russian is not an international language, nor is Japanese – neither is spoken much beyond their borders – and this forced the two men to meet on neutral ground: English. Or at least something that resembled something that might have been mistaken for English.

Q: 'How much this is being two for each?'
A: 'That good tension for you. It gives four.'
Q: 'Four? I am asking two for each.'
A: 'Yes, yes. Many good for you.'

I stood near by eavesdropping on their increasingly surreal dialogue and tried to decide who was the worse speaker of English, the Russian sailor or the Japanese clerk. It was hard to say. Kind of like comparing infinity with infinity plus one.

Hakodate's prime cherry-blossom-viewing spot was the city's star-shaped fortress, where four thousand cherry trees were now coming into bloom. More than one person heartily encouraged my attendance in much the same way that people root for their home team. 'Hakodate cherry blossoms rule! Go Hakodate!'

Even better, for the most time since I set out, for the first time ever, I was not assumed to be a Mormon or an American. Here in Hakodate, everyone mistook me for Russian. I thought this was splendid and to help it along I began speaking Japanese *with a Russian accent*. This was more difficult than you'd think. Shop owners would narrow their eyes and ask me questions that were tinged with suspicions waiting to be confirmed.

'Are you a sailor?' they'd ask.

'I am being from Vladivostock,' I would say in what I hoped was a suitably Slavic manner.

'Here on business?'

'*Nyet, nyet*. I am, how you say – ' and my voice would drop ' – shopping.'

'Shopping?'

'For bicycles.'

It was all very entertaining, and I like to think I helped escalate international tensions ever so slightly, for which I am suitably proud.

# 16

# Northern Honshū

Even while I was getting ready, mending my torn trousers, tying a new strap to my hat, and applying *moxa* to my legs to strengthen them, I was already dreaming of the full moon rising over the islands of Matsushima. Finally I sold my house, moving to the cottage of Sampū for a temporary stay. BASHŌ

The road north of Tokyo is still the least travelled in Japan. This is Japan's rural heartland. During the war, children were sent to stay with families in the northern hills to escape the bombings. More recently, the 2011 Great Tōhoku earthquake has set the region back severely. The trunk road, the Oshukaidō, built by the Tokugawa shogunate, stopped at Nikkō, where shogun Tokugawa Ieyasu (1543–1616) was buried in a huge shrine. The land further north remained largely unexplored except by Bashō and other pilgrims, until Victorians like Isabella Bird came along, when foreigners were granted diplomatic passes to see Japan for the first time after the Edo closure.

## NIKKŌ

The air of secrecy and mystery that surrounds this site must have made it particularly desirable for foreigners in the Meiji period. The intrepid traveller Isabella Bird made Nikkō the first destination of her arduous journey around the north of Japan in 1878. She describes the harshness of her journey in great detail, starting out through the paddy fields outside Tokyo and then the hemp growing towns of Tochigi and Kasukabe. The first part of her journey borders on hilarity, as she visited the *chaya* (teahouses) and the *yadoya* (hostels) of ordinary folk along the way, suffering flea-ridden stretchers that collapsed in the night, the noisy hostels full of geisha and loud shamisens, as well as the locals who kept on sliding open the shōji screens to take a look at this peculiar foreigner, despite the watchful eyes of Ito, her ever-faithful manservant.

'All of this serves as a great contrast to the experience of Nikkō, which is so beautiful and well-looked after with its dolls' house streets – so painfully clean that I should no more think of walking over it in muddy boots than over a drawing-room carpet,' she wrote.

Nikkō was originally the sight of Buddhist monasteries at the sacred mountain Nantai-san (founded by the Tendai Buddhist priest Ennin in 848). Tokugawa Ieyasu (1543–1616) founded his *tōshōgū* or mausoleum here. Ieyasu in some ways founded modern Japan when he defeated his rival clans, the supporters of *daimyo* Hideyoshi, at the battle of Sekigahara and made himself shogun or supreme military ruler. His line was then established for another two hundred and fifty years, and, appropriately enough, for such an ambitious man, he wished to become *gongen* (protector) or *kami* (god). So Ieyasu is still worshipped at Nikkō, where Tendai priests are installed. The shrine bears his inscription, 'Light of the East, great Incarnation of the Buddha'. Tokugawa Ieyasu's grandson and protégé, Iemitsu (1604–51), the shogun who suppressed Christianity and expelled the foreigners, is also buried at the shrine. The cost of building the shrine was levied from the samurai fiefdoms so, for instance, the Date clan in Sendai were rendered almost penniless by the endeavour.

Isabella was one of the first foreigners to set foot across the Shinkyo, the Red Bridge, built in 1636 and forbidden to all except the Imperial court. She also saw Nantai-san, the volcano which towers above Chūzenji – known in Japanese as 'the Sea of Happiness'. The lake spills over into the beautiful Kegon *shiraito no taki*, white thread waterfalls, which are famous for suicides.

A later visitor, Kipling, who came here in 1889, was stunned by the vast, high cryptomeria avenue which leads up to the shrine 'with cypress trees eighty feet high with red or dull silver trunks'. The town and shrine now receives millions of visitors per year.

**Isabella Bird** from *Unbeaten Tracks in Japan*

Nikkō, June 13. – This is one of the paradises of Japan! It is a proverbial saying, 'He who has not seen Nikkō must not use the word *kekko*' (splendid, delicious, beautiful); but of this more hereafter. [...] I have been at Nikkō for nine days, and am therefore entitled to use the word 'Kek'ko!' Nikkō means 'sunny splendour', and its beauties are celebrated in poetry and art all over Japan. Mountains for a great part of the year clothed or patched with snow, piled in great ranges round Nantaizan, their monarch, worshipped as a god; forests of magnificent timber; ravines and passes scarcely explored; dark green lakes sleeping in endless serenity; the deep abyss of Kegon, into which the waters of Chuzenjii plunge from a height of 250 feet; the bright beauty of the falls of Kiri Furi, the loveliness of the gardens of Dainichido; the sombre grandeur of the passes through which the Daiyagawa forces its way from the upper regions; a gorgeousness of azaleas and magnolias; and a luxuriousness of vegetation perhaps unequalled in Japan, are only a few of the attractions which surround the shrines of the two greatest shoguns. To a glorious resting-place on the hill-slope of Hotoke Iwa, sacred since 767, when a Buddhist saint, called Shodo Shonin, visited it, and declared the old Shinto deity of the mountain to be only a manifestation of Buddha. Hidetada, the second shogun of the Tokugawa dynasty, conveyed the corpse of his father, Iyeyasu, here in 1617. It was a splendid burial. An Imperial envoy, a priest of the Mikado's family, court nobles from Kyoto, and hundreds of daimiyos, captains, and nobles of inferior rank, took part in the ceremony. An army of priests in rich robes during three days intoned a sacred classic 10,000 times, and Iyeyasu was deified by a decree of the Mikado under a name signifying 'light of the east, great incarnation of Buddha'. The less important shoguns of the line of Tokugawa are buried in Uyeno and Shiba, in Yedo. Since the restoration, and what may be called the disestablishment of Buddhism, the shrine of Iyeyasu has been shorn of all its glories of ritual and its magnificent Buddhist paraphernalia; the 200 priests who gave it splendour are scattered, and six Shinto priests alternately attend upon it as much for the purpose of selling tickets of admission as for any priestly duties.

All roads, bridges, and avenues here lead to these shrines, but the grand approach is by the Red Bridge, and up a broad road with steps at intervals and stone-faced embankments at each side, on the top of which are belts of cryptomeria. At the summit of this ascent is a fine granite torii, 27 feet 6 inches high, with columns 3 feet 6 inches in diameter, offered by the daimiyo of Chikuzen in 1618 from his own quarries. After this come 118 magnificent bronze lanterns on massive stone pedestals, each of which is inscribed with the posthumous title of Iyeyasu, the name of the giver, and a legend of the offering – all the gifts of *daimyo* – a holy water cistern made of a solid block of granite, and covered by a roof resting on twenty square granite pillars, and a bronze bell, lantern, and candelabra of marvellous workmanship, offered by the kings of Corea and Liukiu. On the left is a five-storied pagoda, 104 feet high, richly carved in wood and as richly gilded and painted. The signs of the zodiac run round the lower story.

The grand entrance gate is at the top of a handsome flight of steps forty yards from the *torii*. A looped white curtain with the Mikado's crest in black, hangs partially over the gateway, in which, beautiful as it is, one does not care to linger, to examine the gilded *amainu* in niches, or the spirited carvings of tigers under the eaves, for the view of the first court overwhelms one by its magnificence and beauty. The whole style of the buildings, the arrangements, the art of every kind, the thought which inspires the whole, are exclusively Japanese, and the glimpse from the Ni-o gate is a revelation of a previously undreamed-of beauty, both in form and colour.

Round the neatly pebbled court, which is enclosed by a bright red timber wall, are three gorgeous buildings, which contain the treasures of the temple, a sumptuous stable for the three sacred Albino horses, which are kept for the use of the god, a magnificent granite cistern of holy water, fed from the Somendaki cascade, and a highly decorated building, in which a complete collection of Buddhist Scriptures is deposited. From this a flight of steps leads into a smaller court containing a bell-tower 'of marvellous workmanship and ornamentation', a drum-tower, hardly less beautiful, a shrine, the candelabra, bell, and lantern mentioned before, and some very grand bronze lanterns. From this court another flight of steps ascends to the Yomei gate, whose splendour I contemplated day after day with increasing astonishment. The white columns which support it have capitals formed of great red-throated heads of the mythical Kirin. Above the architrave is a projecting balcony which runs all round the gateway with a railing carried by dragons' heads. In the centre two white dragons fight eternally. Underneath, in high relief, there are groups of children playing, then a network of richly painted beams, and seven groups of Chinese sages. The high roof is supported by gilded dragons' heads with crimson throats. In the interior of the gateway there are side-niches painted white, which are lined with gracefully designed arabesques founded on the botan or peony. A piazza, whose outer walls of twenty-one compartments are enriched with magnificent carvings of birds, flowers, and trees, runs right and left, and encloses on three of its sides another court, the fourth side of which is a terminal stone wall built against the side of the hill. On the right are two decorated buildings, one of which contains a stage for the performance of the sacred dances, and the other an altar for the burning of cedar wood incense. On the left is a building for the reception of the three sacred cars which were used during festivals. To pass from court to court is to pass from splendour to splendour; one is almost glad to feel that this is the last, and that the strain on one's capacity for admiration is nearly over.

In the middle is the sacred enclosure, formed of gilded trellis-work with painted borders above and below, forming a square of which each side measures 150 feet, and which contains the *haiden* or chapel. Underneath the trellis-work are groups of birds, with backgrounds of grass, very boldly carved in wood and richly gilded and painted. From the imposing entrance through a double avenue of cryptomeria, among courts, gates, temples, shrines, pagodas, colossal bells of bronze, and lanterns inlaid with gold, you pass through this final court bewildered by magnificence, through golden gates, into the dimness of a golden temple, and there is simply a black lacquer table with a circular metal mirror upon it. Within is a hall finely matted, 42 feet wide by 27 from front to back, with lofty apartments on each side, one for the shogun and the other 'for his Holiness the Abbot'. Both, of course, are empty.

The roof of the hall is panelled and richly frescoed. The shogun's room contains some very fine *fusuma*, on which *kirin* (fabulous monsters) are depicted on a dead gold ground, and four oak panels, 8 feet by 6, finely carved, with the phoenix in low relief variously treated. In the Abbot's room there are similar panels adorned with hawks spiritedly executed. The only ecclesiastical ornament among the dim splendours of the chapel is the plain gold *gohei*. Steps at the back lead into a chapel paved with stone, with a fine panelled ceiling representing dragons on a dark blue ground. Beyond this some gilded doors lead into the principal chapel, containing four rooms which are not accessible; but if they correspond with the outside, which is of highly polished black lacquer relieved by gold, they must be severely magnificent.

But not in any one of these gorgeous shrines did Iyeyasu decree that his dust should rest. Re-entering the last court, it is necessary to leave the enclosures altogether by passing through a covered gateway in the eastern piazza into a stone gallery, green with mosses and hepaticae. Within, wealth and art have created a fairyland of gold and colour; without, Nature, at her stateliest, has surrounded the great shogun's tomb with a pomp of mournful splendour. A staircase of 240 stone steps leads to the top of the hill, where, above and behind all the stateliness of the shrines raised in his honour, the dust of Iyeyasu sleeps in an unadorned but Cyclopean tomb of stone and bronze, surmounted by a bronze urn. In front is a stone table decorated with a bronze incense-burner, a vase with lotus blossoms and leaves in brass, and a bronze stork bearing a bronze candlestick in its mouth. A lofty stone wall, surmounted by a balustrade, surrounds the simple but stately enclosure, and cryptomeria of large size growing up the back of the hill create perpetual twilight round it. Slant rays of sunshine alone pass through them, no flower blooms or bird sings, only silence and mournfulness surround the grave of the ablest and greatest man that Japan has produced.

The shrines are the most wonderful work of their kind in Japan. In their stately setting of cryptomeria, few of which are less than 20 feet in girth at 3 feet from the ground, they take one prisoner by their beauty, in defiance of all rules of western art, and compel one to acknowledge the beauty of forms and combinations of colour hitherto unknown, and that lacquered wood is capable of lending itself to the expression of a very high idea in art. Gold has been used in profusion, and black, dull red, and white, with a breadth and lavishness quite unique. The bronze fret-work alone is a study, and the wood-carving needs weeks of earnest work for the mastery of its ideas and details. One screen or railing only has sixty panels, each four feet long, carved with marvellous boldness and depth in open work, representing peacocks, pheasants, storks, lotuses, peonies, bamboos and foliage. The fidelity to form and colour in the birds, and the reproduction of the glory of motion, could not be excelled.

Yet the flowers please me even better. Truly the artist has revelled in his work, and has carved and painted with joy. The lotus leaf retains its dewy bloom, the peony its shades of creamy white, the bamboo leaf still trembles on its graceful stem, in contrast to the rigid needles of the pine, and countless corollas, in all the perfect colouring of passionate life, unfold themselves amidst the leafage of the gorgeous tracery. These carvings are from 10 to 15 inches deep, and single feathers in the tails of the pheasants stand out fully 6 inches in front of peonies nearly as deep.

[...]

The details fade from my memory daily as I leave the shrines, and in their place are picturesque masses of black and red lacquer and gold, gilded doors opening without noise, halls laid with matting so soft that not a footfall sounds, of room whose twilight the sunbeams fall aslant on richly arabesqued walls and panels carved with birds and flowers, and on ceilings panelled and wrought with elaborate art, of inner shrines of gold, and golden lilies six feet high, and curtains of gold brocade, and incense fumes, and colossal bells and golden ridge poles; of the mythical fauna, kirin, dragon, and howo (phoenixes), of elephants, apes, and tigers, strangely mingled with flowers and trees, and golden tracery, and diaper work on a gold ground, and lacquer screens, and pagodas, and groves of bronze lanterns, and shaven priests in gold brocade, and Shinto attendants in black lacquer caps, and gleams of sunlit gold here and there, and simple monumental urns, and a mountain-side covered with a cryptomeria forest, with rose azaleas lighting up its solemn shade.

## SHIRAKAWA

Bashō was the most famous traveller to the north during the Tokugawa period, and his literary travel diary *Narrow Road to the Deep North* (*Oku no Hosomichi*) 1689, became one of the first famous pieces of world travel literature when it was translated into English. Bashō spent six months travelling the great arc of the northern route – from the Oshukaidō to the Hokurikudō – and published his literary diary five years later, so it is definitely a work of art rather than a simple diary.

Bashō's first destination was the Shirakawa barrier, the famous gateway to the north. Now a sleepy country town, this was the physical barrier of high mountains where many lords of Japan had passed on their way to quell the Ezo (Ainu), who had been a major threat to the capitals of Nara, Kyoto and Edo. Sakanoue no Tamuramaro (758–811), was a lord who served Emperor Kammu during the Heian period, and routed the Ezo through ingenious tricks such as the lighting of lanterns. Subsequently Minamoto no Yoshiie, otherwise known as the Eldest Son of the God of War (1039–1106), was revered as a protector of the land and wrote poems longing for home. The Ezo continued to be much feared, and were brutally put down in 1669 during the rule of Tokugawa Ietsuna. Noin Hoshi wrote a famously banal poem ridiculing the nostalgia for the north: 'I left Kyoto in the spring mist/By the time I reached Shirakawa Barrier/The fall wind was blowing.' Bashō's lines are slightly more evocative of the place.

**Bashō** from *Narrow Road to the Deep North*

After many days of solitary wandering, I came at last to the barrier-gate of Shirakawa, which marks the entrance to the northern regions. Here, for the first time, my mind was able to gain a certain balance and composure, no longer a victim to pestering anxiety, so it was with a mild sense of detachment that I thought about the ancient traveller who had passed through this gate with a burning desire to write home. This gate was counted among the three largest checking stations and many poets had passed through it, each leaving a poem of his own making. I myself walked between trees laden with thick foliage, with the distant sound of autumn wind in my ears and the vision of autumn tints before my eyes. There were hundreds and thousands of pure white blossoms of *unohana*[45] in full bloom on either side of the road, in addition to the equally white blossoms of brambles, so that the ground, at a glance, seemed to be covered with early snow. According to the accounts of Kiyosuke,[46] the ancients are said to have passed through this gate, dressed up in their best clothes:

> Decorating my hair
> With white blossoms of *unohana*
> I walked through the gate
> My only gala dress.
>
> Written by Sora[47]

## SENDAI AND MATSUSHIMA

When Bashō travelled north towards his beloved Matsushima, he went first to Sendai, the northern capital of Miyagi prefecture, which is famous for making *kōkeshi* or wooden dolls as well as for being the home of the Date family, the supreme lords of Tōhoku during the sixteenth and seventeenth centuries. Date Masamune (1567–1636) was a right-hand man of both *daimyo* Hideyoshi Toyotomi and shogun Tokugawa Ieyasu. Shusaku Endo's novel *Samurai* is set in 1613 when Date, a Christian, sent his samurai envoy Hasekura Tsunenaga, also a Christian, to deliver a letter to Pope Paul V in Rome seeking friendship and further Christian missionaries. Hasekura was the first Japanese to set foot in the Americas as well as at several European courts and journeyed back across Mexico, sailing

---

45  Latin name of this is *deutzia crenata*
46  The *fukuro zoshi* accounts of Fujiwara no Kiyosuke (1104–77), scholar of the Heian period
47  Bashō's fellow poet and companion on this journey

to Manila and then back to Japan. He returned empty-handed in 1620, because the Jesuits had reported to Rome the hostility of the Tokugawa towards Christianity. When he returned to Japan the country had witnessed more persecutions. A few Date Christian relics such as silver candlesticks are in the Sendai City Museum as well as in Matsushima's Zuigan-ji Museum, which suffered in the 2011 tsunami.

The best time to come to Sendai is for the Tanabata festival on July 7th, the famous firework star festival when a weaving girl and a herdsman, represented by the stars Vega and Altair, usually on opposite sides of the Milky Way, meet once a year. Nowadays people string thousands of decorations, made out of bamboo, paper and vinyl from huge bamboo poles decorated with a crane for wishes for a long life, a purse for wealth, a fishnet for a good catch or a basket for savings, or simply a strip of paper with a poem.

James Kirkup, the British poet, who took a position at Sendai University in 1959, went for a weekend jaunt to the famous Matsushima islands off the coast and to Kinkazan or Mount Golden Flower.


**Shusaku Endo** from *Samurai*

Three days later the missionary took the Korean with him and set out to the Trade Adviser's residence to express gratitude for his release. Knowing that the Japanese officials enjoyed wine, he brought with him several bottles intended for use in the Mass.

Although the trade adviser had a visitor when they arrived, they were ushered into his room without having to wait in a separate chamber . . .

'Lord Velasco, have you ever heard the names of Shiogama or Tsukinoura? They are especially seeking to find harbours in the North-East.'

'Do you intend to make them into ports like Uraga?'

'That is part of our plan. But in those harbours we might also build great ships like the ones you Europeans have.'

For a moment the missionary was speechless. To his knowledge at that time the Japanese had only shogunate licensed vessels modelled on Siamese and Chinese sailing boats. They possessed neither shipyards nor the expertise to produce galleons capable of crossing the wide oceans at will. Even if they were able to build such a ship, there was little likelihood that they would have the skill to sail it.

'Would they be built by Japanese?'

'Perhaps. Shiogama and Tsukinoura face the ocean, and large quantities of good lumber can be cut there.'

The missionary wondered why the Adviser was discussing such secret matters so openly in his presence. Quickly, he studied the expressions on both men's faces and groped for a response.

That must mean they will use the crew from that ship . . .

The previous year, the ship carrying the Spanish emissary from Manila for whom Velasco had interpreted at Edo castle had encountered a storm on his return voyage and been driven ashore in Kyūshū. Repairs were out of the question, so the boat had been detained at Uraga. The emissary and ship's crew were still in Edo, waiting patiently for another ship to come for them. Perhaps the Japanese were planning to use the sailors to help them build a galleon just like their own.

'Has all this been decided?'

'No, no. It is just one idea that has been mentioned.'

The Adviser turned his gaze towards the garden. The missionary knew that this was a sign for him to retire, so after uttering a few words of gratitude for his release, he left the room.

As he stooped and bowed to the retainers in the antechambers, he thought, 'So at last the Japanese plan to cross the Pacific on their own and make their way to Nueva España.'

These people are like ants. They will try anything! When ants are faced with a puddle of water, some of their number will sacrifice their own lives to form a bridge for their comrades. The Japanese were a swarm of black ants with those very instincts.

**Bashō** from *Narrow Road to the Deep North*

Crossing the river Natori, I entered the city of Sendai on May the
fourth, the day we customarily throw fresh leaves of iris on the roof
and pray for good health. I found an inn and decided to stay there for
several days. There was in this city a painter named Kaemon. I made
special efforts to meet him, for he was reputed to be a man with a truly
artistic mind. One day he took me to various places of interest which
I might have missed but for his assistance. We first went to the plain of
Miyagino, where fields of bush clover were waiting to blossom in
autumn. The hills of Tamada, Yokono, and Tsutsuji-ga-oka were
covered with white rhododendrons in bloom. Then we went into the
dark pine woods called Konoshita where even the beams of the sun
could not penetrate. This darkest spot on the earth had often been a
subject of poetry because of its dewiness – for example, one poet says
that his lord needs an umbrella to protect him from the drops of dew
when he enters it. We also stopped at the shrines of Yakushido and
Tenjin on our way home. When the time came for him to say good-
bye this painter gave me his own drawings of Matsushima and
Shiogama and two pairs of straw sandals with laces dyed in the deep
blue of the iris. In this last appears most clearly perhaps the true
artistic nature of this man.

> It looks as if
> Iris flowers had bloomed
> On my feet –
> Sandals laced in blue.
> [...]

The following morning I rose early and did homage to the great
god of the Myōjin Shrine of Shiogama. This shrine had been rebuilt
by a former governor of the province with stately columns, painted
beams and an impressive stone approach, and the morning sun shining
directly on the vermillion fencing was almost dazzlingly bright. I was
deeply impressed by the fact that the divine power of the gods had
penetrated even to the extreme north of our country, and I bowed in

humble reverence before the altar. I noticed a lantern in front of the shrine. According to the inscription on its iron window, it was dedicated by Izumi no Saburo,[48] killed by his brother who betrayed him and Yoshitsune. My thought immediately flew back across the span of five hundred years to the days of this most faithful warrior. His life is certain evidence that if one performs one's duty and maintains one's loyalty, fame comes naturally in the wake, for there is hardly anyone now who does not honour him as the flower of chivalry.

It was already close to noon when I left the shrine. I hired a boat and started for the islands of Matsushima. After two miles or so on the sea, I landed on the sandy beach of Ojima Island.

Much praise had already been lavished upon the wonders of the islands of Matsushima. Yet, if further praise is possible, I would like to say that here is the most beautiful spot in the whole country of Japan, and that the beauty of these islands is not in the least inferior to the beauty of Lake Dōtei, or Lake Seiko.[19] The islands are situated in a bay about three miles wide in every direction and open to the sea through a narrow mouth on the south-east side. Just as the River Sekkō in China is made full at each swell of the tide, so is this bay filled with the brimming water of the ocean and innumerable islands are scattered over it from one end to the other. Tall islands point to the sky and level ones prostrate themselves before the surges of water. Islands are piled above islands, and islands are joined to islands, so that they look exactly like parents caressing their children or walking with them arm in arm. The pines are the freshest green, and their branches are curved in exquisite lines, bent by the wind, constantly blowing through them. Indeed the beauty of the entire scene can only be compared to the most divinely endowed of feminine countenances, for who else could have created such beauty but the great god of nature himself? My pen strove in vain to equal the superb creation of divine artifice.

48  Fujiwara no Tadahira (1167–89)
49  Seiko is in the Chekiang province of China

**James Kirkup** from *These Horned Islands*

The Japanese, impressed by my modest six feet, sometimes call me
'the fire-bell stealer'. This is the name they give to tall people, because
in towns and villages the firebell is hung at the top of a tall metal
tower, painted white and looking somewhat like a miniature Eiffel
Tower. The one at Matsushima is opposite the Park Hotel where
there is a waitress with a face like a white anemone.

One of the most interesting islands in the Matsushima group is
called Oshima, joined to the mainland by a humpbacked vermilion
bridge. On this island are stone lanterns carved with crescent moon,
bamboo sprays, deer. The sun's head today is thrown up like liquid
fire from the languid water under the little vermilion bridge. The
pines, leaning from the cliff-tops sweep down to screen the dazzling
water, to frame the white-shirted fishermen in their long boats with
pointed prows, the throng on the quay sides, the large white steamers
hung with yellow awnings. One called Matsushima maru departs for a
tour of the islands and then on to Shiogama; the twittering and
melodious voice of the guide floats clearly over the bay as she describes,
with many a gay *gozaymasu*, the passing sights, which include oyster
beds, seaweed and eel-beds, and of course, the islands of pines.

As Chamberlain writes, each island, down to the least, has received
a separate name, many of them fantastic, as 'Buddha's Entry into
Nirvana', 'Question and Answer Island', 'The Twelve Imperial
Consorts', and so on; and no less fantastic than the names, are the
shapes of the islands themselves. In almost every available nook, stands
one of those thousand pine-trees that have given name and fame to
the locality. The quaintest and most Japanesey spot of all, is the island
of Oshima, which is connected to the shore by tiny bridges [... ]

Today, only one small bridge exists. I run through a tunnel bored
right through the island to catch another glimpse of the departing
steamer, turning and twisting as it moves between the islands. It gives
three farewell hoots for 'sayonara'. There are some interesting small
statues on the island set in long, open tunnels carved in the rock.
There is a poem by Bashō here too, on a slab of rock. It was Bashō

who wrote an 'absurd' haiku about Matsushima which runs something like this:

> Oh Matsushima,
> Oh, Oh, Matsushima, Oh
> Matsushima Oh!

I bought a baby doll in a circular straw basket, the kind that was once used here as a cradle. Grumbling of lions in the tatty zoo, and in the children's fairground, the Ferris Wheel is slowly revolving, with no one in it, against an evening sky all green and salmon-pink, white and grey. High pagoda-like hotels, for New Moon Viewing, are silhouetted against the sky. In the darkening waters, the bamboo poles squiggle their ideograms in the reflections lit by the last light.

There is a keen fizzling of crickets, grasshoppers' stridulation – their fiddling vibration is regular in beat as a small motor; it is, in fact, exactly the same rhythm as that of the outboard motor on a belated water-skier's boat. The water-skier of course has to fall into the water [...]

Back in Sendai, I watched some basket weavers, using mouth and feet as well as all fingers making the split bamboo woven balls, of varying sizes, which are the frameworks used for mounting brilliant artificial flowers or bunches of paper and streamers for the Tanabata Festival.

The breathless stillness of the stars.

The chime of patterns on stones. At night, the fierce headlights of passing cars illuminate the cloudlet of dust raised by each slurring step.

First of August. Yesterday was the hottest in Sendai for thirty years with a temperature of 36 degrees centigrade. Today the bright chugging of crickets in the bamboos sounds like a clockwork toy engine.

## MORIOKA AND IWATE

Morioka is an old castle town where the Lord of Nambu, as this part of the north was known, lived. It is a well-preserved town noted for its artistic activities, full of quaint old Japanese temples, merchant quarters, crafts, traditional arts and provincial contests. Many traditional crafts such as silk dying (Konya-chō or 'dyers town' is based along the river), and bamboo, rice cracker making, *washi* paper making and other skills as well as selling *tetsubin* or iron kettles blackened with the same substance such as tooth blackening used to be made. The poet Kenji Miyazawa (1896–1933) was a native of Iwate prefecture, which means rocky outcrop. He returned from Tokyo to his home province in 1921, because of the sickness of his sister Toshiko, working as a teacher, a quarryman and as an engineer. He was completely committed to raising the lot of the local people in his area and turned his hand to this poem in praise of pine needles.

**Kenji Miyazawa** *Pine Needles*

Here's the beautiful pine branch
I took the snow from.
Oh, you almost leap to it,
Pressing your hot cheeks to its green leaves.
The way you let the blue needles
Sting your cheeks fiercely,
The way you covet them with such greed,
How it surprises us!
You have wanted so much to go to the woods.
While you burned with fever,
While you writhed in sweat and pain,
I was happy, working in the sunlight,
I was strolling in the forest, thinking of someone else.
Like a bird, like a squirrel
You longed for the woods.

How you must have envied me!
Oh my sister, you are going to leave before the day ends,
Can you be going alone?
Ask me to come with you.
Please ask me.
    Your cheeks
    How beautiful they are!
    Let me put the fresh pine branch
    On the green curtain.
    Soon drops will fall from it.
    And look,
It's fresh.
Can you smell the fragrance of turpentine?


## HIRAIZUMI

Almost directly north of Sendai on the Tōhoku *shinkansen* (bullet train) is the town of Hiraizumi, a ruined site, which was built as a rival to Kyoto. The Northern Fujiwara ruled here from 1090 to 1189. Lesley Downer, who followed the footsteps of Bashō, describes the construction of the famous gilded palace of Chūson-ji and the building of Hiraizumi by its first lord, Fujiwara no Kiyohira, who had been named Governor of the Northern Provinces. Yoshitsune, the victorious hero of the battle of Dan no ura (1185), took refuge in the Northern capital after his jealous half-brother, the fearsome Minamoto no Yoritomo, swore to take vengeance on him for his increased popularity. Having bribed the Northern Fujiwara to kill Yoshitsune, Yoritomo then betrayed his promise to the Fujiwara and sent a huge army to destroy the city. By the time that Bashō came to Hiraizumi, five centuries had obliterated almost all traces of the once-glorious golden Fujiwara capital, so he wrote:

        The summer grass –
        All that's left
        Of the ancient warrior's dream.

Both the gilded hall, the Konjiki-dō as well as the Kyōzō or sutra library are still preserved as well as the Mōtsū-ji, where you can find more wonderful irises than the ones that Bashō describes at Sendai.

### Lesley Downer from *On the Narrow Road to the Deep North*

The further we got from Sendai, the greener the place became, until we were chugging gently along between fields bursting with rice shoots, dazzlingly emerald green, with tidy round hills on each side. By this time, everyone but me was asleep sprawled as innocently as children in an assortment of undignified Hogarthian postures, mouths gaping, legs splayed. Every now and then, we rolled past a farmer working out in the fields, up to his knees in water, plucking out weeds and throwing them into the plastic basket on his back or drew up at a little station in the middle of nowhere, grass and vines spilling across the platforms. [...]

Everyone seemed to know by some sixth sense that we were approaching Hiraizumi. By the time we had trundled past a few small grey sheds and were pulling into the station, they were all wide awake, on their feet and standing in line at the door, ready to shuffle off as soon as the train stopped; even these little country trains didn't stop for long.

Hiraizumi looked sleepy enough, a nondescript little country town of faded wooden houses strung along dusty streets, with sunlight sparkling on the paddy fields just behind – hard to imagine that it had once been the Ezo capital, the centre of Ezo civilisation. On three sides were hills, covered in thick forest, while the fourth, bound by a wide river, opened out into a shimmering plain of rice fields which stretched away to the hills, hazy on the horizon. It was a spectacular setting for such a dozy little town.

The air seemed cleaner – the hills, with their untamed forest, closer, the paddy fields somehow less tidy – as if I had managed at last to shake off the deadening influence of Tokyo and the concrete which smothers the surrounding countryside for hundreds of miles around it.

I watched my fellow passengers disappearing purposefully along the dusty street which led up the hill from the station. A few lingered, settling down on the bench at the bus stop.

[...]

It was still early so I left my bag at the station and ambled off down the road which ran between the river and the railway line. It turned out to be the main shopping area of town, lined with open-fronted shops and trestles loaded with vegetables, fruit and fish.

I stopped to watch the *tatami*-maker, in white vest and longjohns, cross-legged on the earthern floor of his shop, hand-stitching the straw mats. Then the fishmonger, an old fellow in vest, wellington boots and a long black apron right to the ground, beckoned me over, his enormous grin revealing a mouthful of teeth all bound at the roots with gold.

'Fresh in this morning!' he said, holding up a huge gleaming fish on a hook.

Next stop was the tofu shop to buy a block of freshly made beancurd for the next day's breakfast. It was dark and blissfully cool inside.

'What is your country, dear?' enquired the fat tofu lady as she scooped a slab of it out of the water. 'All the way from England?' She sighed with amazement. 'Such a long way, just to see our little town,' and took fifteen yen off the price.

[...]

'The glory of three generations of Fujiwaras has passed like an empty dream.' Long before Bashō came, Hiraizumi was a great city, the City of Gold, capital of the North, home to a magnificent culture. But it was to last no more than a hundred years. For a hundred years, they say, its marvels outshone Kyoto – then vanished, as completely as the cherry blossoms.

Marco Polo knew about it, though by his time Hiraizumi and its wonders were no more than a memory. In the land of Zipangu, Japan, he wrote, 'they have gold . . . in measureless quantities. The ruler of the island has a very large palace entirely roofed with fine gold. Just as we roof our houses or churches with lead, so this palace is roofed with fine gold. And the value of it is almost beyond calculation. Moreover all the chambers of which there are many, are likewise paved with fine gold to a depth of more than two fingers' breadth. And the halls and

the windows and every other part of the palace are likewise adorned
with gold. All in all I can tell you that the palace is of such incalculable
richness that any attempt to estimate its value would pass the bounds
of the marvellous.'

Admittedly Marco Polo is one of the most unreliable of reporters.
He added for good measure that the people of Zipangu not only had
idols with the heads of cattle, pigs, dogs and sheep, too horrible to
speak of and 'no fit hearing for Christians' but were also cannibals.

In the matter of Japan's gold, however, he was not far off the mark.
But it was not the Emperor in Kyoto who had palaces roofed with
gold but the Fujiwara Lords in Hiraizumi.

A few centuries later, Christopher Columbus, inspired by tales of
Hiraizumi's gold, set off to sail to the West, thinking that if he went
far enough, he would circle the world and 'come across the island of
Zipangu' with its fabulous riches. His quest for gold took him to
another small island, Cuba, which he thought was Japan and on until
he finally reached the New World, America.

The City of Gold . . . Long before Sakanoue no Tamuramaro
marched North to subdue the Ezo, they found gold here, in 749.
They began mining the Oshu mountains and panning the rivers. The
gold for the entire country – to make shrines, Buddha images, shrine
furnishings, decoration for temples and palaces – all came from Oshu
and so did horses and falcons; and generally the conquered Northern
lands became very rich.

By the eleventh century, a hundred years before Yoshitsune, the
Ezo were becoming unruly again. The governors of Oshu at that
time were six Ezo brothers called the Abé lords, a remarkable bunch,
according to the *Gikeiki*. One 'could make fog and mist or stay under
water all day long' and all of them were 'taller than the Chinese' –
and much taller than the little men of Yamato. 'Sadato was nine feet
five inches tall, Muneto eight feet five inches and every one of the
brothers at least eight feet. Sakai Kanja's height was ten foot three
inches.'

The Abé were supposed to travel down to Kyoto every year to pay
tribute to the Emperor (a considerable journey – six hours on the
bullet train, weeks by foot or on horseback). But one year, they sent a

message saying that they would only go if the Emperor would pay their travelling expenses – 'the cost of the journey there and back'.

Not surprisingly, the Emperor was displeased and dispatched a force of Minamoto warriors. They fought the Ezo 'day and night for seven years' and were all either killed or wounded. Then another force was sent North, led by the thirteen-year-old Minamoto Yoshiie, Yoshitsune's great-great-grandfather (like Yoshitsune he began his career young). But they too were beaten.

Finally they had a bright idea. Every time a new Emperor is crowned, a new era begins and each era has a name. Perhaps they thought 'the era designation might be at fault'. He rechristened the year, 'The first year of Kohei', 'Year 1 of the Peace and Tranquility Era.' Things were simpler in those days. It was the last time anyone ever won a war simply by changing the name of the year.

It was 1058. That year the Ezo fortresses were all taken, one by one, and the nine-foot five-inch Sadato, 'mortally wounded, lay down for the last time on the water moorland, dressed in a yellow robe.' The Emperor appointed Fujiwara Kiyohira, Yoshiie's second-in-command to govern the Northern provinces. Kiyohira had chosen to side with the Minamoto, but in fact he was at least half Ezo, for his mother was an Abé. He took the title 'Head of the Ezo race' and set about creating a magnificent Ezo kingdom in the North, using Oshu's gold to build a capital that would rival Kyoto.

The site he chose for his capital mirrored the site of Kyoto and satisfied the rules of classical geomancy: mountains on three sides, water – the great River Kitagami, like Kyoto's Kamo River in front, 'purple hills, crystal streams'. The city faced to the south, its streets laid out in a grid like a giant chessboard, and the greatest artisans of the day were commissioned to work on its palaces and temples.

Artists, poets and craftsmen – masters of lacquerware, gold leaf, wood and metal work, masons, dyers, weavers – flocked to Hiraizumi. The hills glittered with golden temples and jewel-like palaces and thronged with a brilliant crowd of monks, courtiers, artists and warriors; and even the smallest of Oshu's ten thousand villages boasted an image of the Buddha, of pure gold.

The sun sets early, even on these hot summer nights. At dark,

I trudged up to Motsuji Temple. I left my bags in the pilgrims' hall, had some iced noodles, then went outside to explore the temple grounds.

It was dark and silent. The moon had not yet risen and even the insects had stopped chattering. I took a few steps out of the pool of light around the open door of the hall, then thought better of it. The air was thick with the ghosts of all those courtiers and warriors of a thousand years ago. I could feel them at my back, muttering balefully (as Japanese ghosts do) '*Urayamashii! Urayamashii!*' – 'Envious! We are envious!' My spine was prickling. I hurried back inside, grateful for the clatter of chopsticks on bowls and the pilgrims' voices.

## TONO

Travelling east of Hiraizumi you will find Tono, a well-preserved town lying in one of the most remote and inaccessible parts of Honshū. This was where Kunio Yanagita (1875–1962), a wealthy bureaucrat in the ministry of agriculture, a friend of the novelist Shimazaki Tōson (see Nagano chapter), came to take down the beliefs and folklore of the locals, in the early 1900s. He was recording a dying generation in an attempt to preserve the spirit of animist Japan. As he writes:

> the word *furusato* means 'one's native place'. But you can hear city people use the word when they see apples for sale in baskets woven from bamboo rather than stamped out of green plaster, when they taste homemade pickles from a country store, or when they come across a thatched roof farmhouse tucked into a cove behind a green rice paddy. Tono basin is the *furusato* of all Japan. The traces of pure Japan can be found in Tono, reminders of primitive Japan that existed before the Chinese brought over Buddhism in the sixth century, once isolated area's ancient customs, folk beliefs and legends, there are few places like Tono left in Japan.

The legend here is about the famous *kappa*, the ugly spirits with dish-shaped heads that live in mountain pools ready to catch a runaway child or to make love to lonely women.

**Kunio Yanagita** from *The Legends of Tono*

*Legend Number Fifty-five, the Kappa*

Across the highway from the old torii is a road leading to the temple Jokenji and Kappabushi, the water imp pool. Approach the Kappa pool with caution lest you should run into one of the ugly water creatures that exist in bodies of water all over Japan. Since they have been known to pull babies and small children as well as horses, make liberal uses of kappa stories to keep children away from dangerous bodies of water – a kappa can be described as slippery skinned and sharp beaked with webbed hands and feet at the end of long human like arms and legs and of course a unique dish shaped concavity at the top of his head.

The rivers in this district are rich in kappa – an imaginary river animal supposed to drown people – above all in the river of Sarugaishi. In the house by the river in the village of Matsuzaki, two women over two generations running have been with a child by kappa. The child was cut in pieces, put in a cask of sake and buried in the earth. The shape of the child was very ugly and strange. The house of this woman was also by the river in the village of Niibari. The master of this house once told as follows:

One day the family of the woman were about to return home from the fields in the evening and then, the woman was found crouching with a smile on the bank of the river. The next day while they were resting at noon she was also found crouching with a smile on the bank of the river. The next day while they were resting at noon, she was also found crouching just as she had been before. Thus day after day passed, until the rumour spread that a man in the same village would often visit the woman at night. At first he came only when her husband was out driving the pack-horse to the coast, but soon afterward she would come even when her husband was in bed in the same room with her. The rumour that he must be kappa was so much spread day by day that all the relatives gathered together to watch and guard her, but all in vain. Mother of the husband also went to the house and slept beside her. When at midnight she heard the woman laughing, she could notice that a man was there beside the woman, but she could not move herself at all. All the people there could not know what to do.

She had a very laborious delivery, but they tried as some one had said that if the woman was put in a manger full of water the delivery would be much easier, and she could give birth to a child as easily as expected. The child has web-hands. The mother of this woman had also given birth to a child of a kappa.


## YAMAGATA

Bashō travelled west from Sendai towards the mountainous Yamagata region, where he went to see the Yamadera or mountain temple. Bashō calls it Ryushakuji or the temple of jutting rocks, due to its highly dramatic setting. The temple was founded by the Tendai sect priest Ennin in 860. Ennin was also known as 'Jikaku Daishi' and studied under the great Tendai sect founder Saichō (see Kyoto chapter).

Yamagata, an old castle town where safflower red dye was produced, stands on the road to the Dewa Sanzan or holy mountains, including Gassan, Yudosan and Hagurosan, which were opened by the seventh-century prince Hoshi who dedicated the mountains to the extreme Shugendō sect of Shinto. The *yamabushi*, or mountain priests, became very powerful over the next four hundred years, and they helped Yoshitsune and his faithful servant Benkei as they were fleeing from Yoshitsune's jealous brother Yoritomo on their way to Hiraizumi (see above). Bashō was a consummately good traveller, engaging with the priests, writing verse for fellow poets and talking to a swordsmith, also called Gassan, as he went. On Mount Gassan he even wore the *yamabushi*'s clothes. He finishes his journey to Dewa Sanzan with a trip down the Mogami river, which flows north to the Sea of Japan. Lesley Downer, who followed Bashō's footsteps three hundred years later, describes her own experience of the stillness of the holy mountains but she, more prosaically perhaps, takes the bus to join a tourist trip down the very same Mogami river to the very same white thread falls.

**Lesley Downer** from *On the Narrow Road to the Deep North*

*Down the Mogami*

I woke early and heaved open the wooden shutters. Outside it was still cool. Mist hung low in the valley, parting here and there to reveal a great gnarled rock, a clump of dark twisted pines, a glimpse of ghostly white crags looming over the paddy fields, wisps of cloud curling at the foot.

In the silence the plaintive strains of an *enka* drifted across the fields. Somewhere not far away, hidden in the mist, a woman was singing, one of those sad sobbing ditties that Japanese love so much. A small figure in blue, head swathed in a white scarf, hurried past in front of the meeting house. Further along, children in pinnies and grubby trousers were playing in the road. It was so medieval, it wouldn't have surprised me if two figures dressed in black like priests, with straw hats slung on their back and staffs in their hands, had appeared around a corner, scuffing along in their straw sandals down the valley towards the river.

I would happily have stayed a few more days. But I had loitered long enough. It was time to rejoin Bashō. From here on there would be no more interruptions. I wasn't going to stop again until I reached the sacred mountains.

Early though it was, everyone else had been up for hours. My breakfast was waiting on the table, covered in a wire mesh to keep off the flies: rice, *miso* soup, *aomidzu* (a green celery-like wild vegetable) and a brown gooey mass which slithered from the bowl into my mouth; it turned out to be the fat brown root which Ocaasan had dug up on the mountain, grated raw.

'Going by bus, aren't you?' said Ocaasan. I had told her I was going to walk, but she still hoped I would see reason. 'You can go on the eight o'clock with Grandad.' He was off to Shinjo as usual, to 'work'.

As the road curved around a corner and the house vanished from sight, I turned for a last look. They were all standing watching and waved and bowed when they saw me stop. There was Granny in her pinny, all bent; pale, grinning Father with his big stomach; Ocaasan with her brown berry face; and Naoko hovering behind, elegant in her red skirt, waving feverishly. That was the trouble with all this travelling – having to say goodbye.

| | |
|---|---|
| *okuraretsu* | Now being seen off |
| *okuritsu hate wa* | Now seeing off – the end of all this? |
| *Kiso no aki* | Autumn in Kiso |

Or in my case, summer in Mogami.

Still, I was excited to be on my way and set off in high spirits, my back nearly as bent as Granny's under the weight of all the *onigiri* (rice balls), home-made *mochi* (rice cakes), pickles and plums which they had insisted I take. A few minutes later, the bus overtook me with a roar. Through the window Grandad gave a regal wave.

Then I was on my own. The road wound off, clinging to the edge of the mountain, following in and out along its curves.

Every now and then I came to a tiny remote village, nothing more than a few tattered houses perched forlornly on outcrops of land high above the fields, with thin cows tethered, cropping the scrubby grass. Some of the houses looked as if no one had lived in them for years. The roofs were falling in and grass and lilies sprouted from the thatch. There were no shops, of course. But in each village there was a fire tower and a tumbledown shack with the characters for 'Meeting House' written on the rusting iron wall.

Mainly there was nothing to see but stepped paddy fields and steep wooded hills soaring up on each side of the valley. The rice must have been about a foot high, glowing green, and the wind which rushed up between the hills sent long ripples across it like waves. Down in the fields some peasants in straw hats and wellingtons were weeding. Somehow they no longer seemed alien now, but like the people that I knew.

Gradually the valley grew wider and the hills lower and the road began to wind uphill. The top of the pass was marked by a small wayside shrine, two rocks one on top of the other. In the lower one was an indentation, a natural basin brimming with rain water. Some-one had left a rusting tin ladle laid neatly across it. Some characters like a prayer were carved on the upper one.

I sat down on the grass and looked back at the valley, wishing I could have stayed longer. Water was splashing noisily along irrigation channels on each side of the road and a *semi* [cicada] was shrilling on the rocks. Then I heard music, a tinny little tune somewhere in the distance, coming closer and closer. Finally I made out the words: 'Ladders, washing poles, ladders, washing poles', again and again. A blue truck bristling with ladders and long broom handles – the second vehicle I had seen that day – appeared over the top of the hill and trundled off down the valley the way I had come.

Reluctantly I picked up my pack and trudged off. Ahead was an endless sea of rice, broad and flat, greenly rippling. The mountains on the horizon looked as far away as ever.

But now there were shops. First there was one, all alone at the side of the road, an old wooden house badly in need of rethatching, with sacks of seeds and rice stacked outside and flower pots tied together in bundles. Inside were dark shelves with a few dusty packets of crackers and biscuits and a fridge full of icecream and cold drinks. Then came more and more until there was a whole village of them, even a bicycle shop and a chemist's, lined-up along the road with the sparkling paddy fields just behind, stretching away to the horizon

I was tramping through one of these small villages, feeling the sun on my head and wishing I had a hat like everyone else, when a woman on an outsize tricycle pedalled slowly by, calling out 'Where to?' as she passed. She had a round button face and a warm smile and baggy country clothes – a long loose pinny, baggy brown trousers and a white scarf knotted round her head. On the back of her tricycle was a wire basket with a large blue bucket wedged into it.

'Furukuchi,' I called back.

'On foot? It's a long way,' she shouted. She was well ahead by now.

Fifteen minutes later we met up again. She was on her way back, the lid of the bucket propped in the basket. I asked what she had had in it.

'Tofu,' she smiled, stopping this time – beancurd. She had been up since four in the morning, preparing a special order of it 'for those people there,' gesturing to a large house set back from the road among trees. 'They're having a party.'

'Not from the Philippines, then, are you,' she added. It was a statement not a question.

Rather mystified, I agreed that I wasn't.

'Knew you weren't Japanese,' she beamed, pleased with herself. 'Thought you must be one of those Filipina brides. That's why I said hello. But your Japanese is too good. "Good morning", "Good after-noon" "Thank you", that's all they can manage. Friendly girls, though.'

I was still puzzling over this half a mile later when I came to a signpost. There was the name of the village – Okura, where unmarried girls were so rare that they had had to send to the Philippines for brides.

On the other side of Okura, the road began to climb. Below, the paddy fields spread into the distance like a giant chessboard of brilliant green squares outlined in darker green, as flat as a well-tended lawn. A narrow river meandered between sandbanks on the far side of the plain. I stopped to rest and gaze at the pale line of mountains on the horizon. Which, I wondered, was Gassan, the highest of the three sacred mountains?

I struggled on. It was well past midday and the sun was blazing.

At the top of the hill, in the shadow of a grove of pine trees, was a coffee machine, offering hot and cold drinks. I suppose at another time it might have seemed incongruous, this gleaming metallic obelisk in perfect working order, in the middle of remote countryside. But today it seemed quite natural, quite appropriate, just what one would expect to find all alone at the top of a hill – and delightfully Japanese. I put in my coins and the machine rewarded me with a little tune as I took my Vitamin C Juice (properly chilled, of course) and a woman's voice thanked me politely for my custom.

Around the next corner, on the other side of the grove was some-thing stranger. It was a huge painting of the moon, enormous and pock-marked, and some planets against a black sky full of stars. I pondered it for a while, then trekked around it (it was the size of a small house). In fact it seemed, it was a screen, like the screens the Okinawans build in front of their doors to ward off evils spirits. Behind it was the entrance to a forlorn holiday camp of concrete chalets with alternating red and blue slate roofs, huddled between the woods and a field full of rice. Then I noticed a sign, *Tsuki sekai*, 'Moon World', in yellow neon on blue and underneath two smaller signs, 'Rooms Available' (green) and 'Rooms Full' (red). 'Rooms Available' was lit up.

Of course, it was a love hotel, probably used quite innocently by young farmers and their wives – maybe even some of the people I knew – when the perpetual presence of their parents became too inhibiting. Despite the grim exterior, the interiors of the chalets, I was sure, were as gorgeous as any other love hotel: plaster statuary, a fountain perhaps, a revolving bed with mirrors above it and red velvet drapes, a pink spangled bathtub, 'adult videos', and a karaoke machine in case the lovers became bored before their two hours were up.

By now – five hours after leaving the village – I was nearly at the river. Another turn in the road and I had my first sight of it, high and brown, rolling ponderously between wide banks, dark forested cliffs soaring behind.

| *samidare o* | Gathering the rains of June |
| *atsumete hayashi* | Swift rushing – |
| *Mogami gawa* | Mogami river. |

Then it disappeared and the road plunged into a shanty town of decaying tin shacks, littering the hillside right to the river bank. This, according to my map, was a town, dignified enough to have a name. Though, looking at the torn walls, flimsy as cardboard, and rusting roofs, it was hard to believe that anyone lived here. I walked slowly, tired now and saddened by the squalor. I guessed that it meant I was not far from the main road. My private escapade along some truly narrow roads was over.

Down a side turning between the tin roofs, I caught a glimpse of stone pillars. They stood guarding the edge of the water, two of them, massive and imposing, wide at the base and tapering towards the top with four faceted sides – evidence that at one time the place had been more important and prosperous than it was now. They must once have flanked a boarding pier, though now there was no sign of it, not even steps down to the river. The road came jaggedly to an end above a precipitous drop to the pebbly shore and the sluggish brown river, a good thirty feet below.

Beside them, engraved on an old wooden signboard, faded but still legible, was the name of the place: Motoaikai. I deciphered the characters, suddenly full of excitement. Purely by chance, I had stumbled on the precise place where Bashō boarded the river boat to go down the Mogami.

I sat down on a rock beside the pillars and opened Sora's diary. Bashō didn't mention the long trek to Motoaikai. He left his readers to assume that the two travellers took the boat from the great river port of Oishida. As I pored over Sora's antiquated Japanese, I was remembering the lively evenings around the table in Obanazawa; it had been only a few days ago, but already it seemed like another world.

'Don't forget,' Kawashima had said, helping me with the difficult sentences, 'that it was five years ago before Bashō wrote the *Narrow Road*. He sorted through everything that happened on the journey and selected the most interesting and poetic things. That's why he doesn't mention Motoaikai. It's a poetic creation, not an accurate record.' Though, he added, shaking his head over the old poet's perversity, the travellers should have taken a boat from Oishida; it would have been the best place to board.

Bashō and Sora were held up for three days at Oishida. On the first, wrote Sora, there was heavy rain. 'Tired, so wrote no haiku,' he added. On the second it rained a little in the evening, on the third it was cloudy in the morning and brightened up after the hour of the dragon.

The following day was the first of the sixth month by the old calendar, July 17th 1689. The two travellers left Oishida early in the morning and took horses along the Amida-do, the broad 'Amitabha Road'. They ambled past Obanazawa, through a long valley to Funa-gata, then across a wooded pass and down to Shinjo, the metropolis full of coffee shops and department stores, where, three hundred years later, Grandad was even now slotting coins into a pachinko machine. At that time too Shinjo was a sizeable city, *jokamachi*, a castle town, with a community of poets. The travellers arrived in the evening and went to stay with Furyu, a pupil of Bashō's.

They rested here a couple of days. The local poets, excited at the chance of pitting their wits against the famous master from Edo, flocked to meet him. They spent the afternoon together, composing a round of linked verse. Sora meanwhile was delegated to collect permits for the next section of their journey.

Finally I came to the words I had been looking for: '3rd. Weather fine. Left Shinjo. One-and-a-half *ri*. Motoaikai.' I was right. It was the same characters that were written on the sign board. At that time this jumble of tin shacks, tumbling down the river bank as if someone had discarded a lorry load of boxes, had been an important port, a boarding station for the Mogami. Here – perhaps just here where I was sitting – the travellers showed their permits, then scrambled down the steps to the river and clambered into one of the long wooden rice barges. There was a big group of them by now. Bashō and Sora in their black robes, some of the Shinjo poets, even a couple of Zen monks who joined them for the boat ride.

After one-and-a-half *ri*, they reached Furukichi, the village that I was headed for. Here there was a barrier. Everyone had to disembark and present their papers to the burly guards, who checked them thoroughly before allowing them to change on to another boat to cross into the territory of the Sakai lord, Saemon. One of the group, Heshichi, had forgotten to get a permit and despite their pleas, they had to leave him behind.

Bashō described their journey: 'With mountains overhanging to left and right, in the midst of dense foliage we went down the river. We took a boat used for transporting rice, called a "rice boat", apparently. *Shiraito no taki*, White Thread Falls, tumbled through spaces between the young leaves, Sennin-do, the Hermit's Hall, stood on the bank facing the water. The river was swollen with the rains and our boat was in constant peril.'

# 17

# Niigata and Sado Island

'Winter comes quite quickly in that Northern region and it
was impossible to hunt for alluvial gold in that deep snow.'

IHARA SAIKAKU

Niigata is the largest port on the Sea of Japan and was once a rich rice-growing state on the banks of the Shinanogawa river. Originally a remote city whose main claim to fame was as gateway to Sado island in the Sea of Japan, it is now linked to Tokyo by the *shinkansen* bullet train.

This is the region where they drape the shrines of the temples with straw during winter. Yasunari Kawabata's novel *Yukiguni*, or *Snow Country* (started in 1935 but not completed until much later), set in the famous hot springs of Yuzawa in Niigata prefecture, follows the love affair of a Tokyo dilettante, Shimamura, with a local geisha, Yoko. The opening is one of the most famous in Japanese literature, and the feeling of remote isolation is emphasised by the fact that Shimamura arrives through the famous Shimizu tunnel, which runs for about a kilometre under the border mountains of Gunma (Kozuku no kuni) and Niigata (Echigo no kuni). The northern winds from the Sea of Japan come up against these mountains and deposit a lot of snow here. One of the things that Shimamura observes is the spinning of fine silk cloth that resembles crepe with artificial wrinkles called *chijimi*. The thread is spun and bleached in snow. It is said that this kind of cloth remains cool to the skin even during the hot Tokyo months.

Sado island is just off the coast of Niigata, a famous place for exile. First silver and then gold was mined here, right up until 1989. The hero of Ihara Saikaku's first popular novel, *The Life of an Amorous Man*

(1682), comes to Niigata because he intends to hunt for gold on the 'golden island of Sado'. Emperor Juntoku was also exiled here in 1221 and died in 1242. The Buddhist monk Nichiren, who revived the Buddha's teaching of the Lotus Sutra as a teaching for all people (see Kamakura chapter), was also exiled to Sado island in 1271–4. In 1434 Noh playwright Zeami (1364–1444), was also exiled here by shogun Yoshinori for seven years. The new exiles, the Kodo drummers, a group that brought Japanese drumming to the world and who organise the annual Earth festival on the island, have come here voluntarily.

**Yasunari Kawabata** from *Snow Country*

The train came out of the long tunnel into the snow country. The earth lay white under the night sky. The train pulled up at a signal stop.

A girl who had been sitting on the other side of the car came over and opened the window in front of Shimamura. The snowy cold poured in. Leaning far out of the window, the girl called at the station master as though he were a great distance away.

The station master walked slowly over the snow, a lantern in his hand. His face was buried to the nose in a muffler, and the flaps of his cap were turned down over his ears.

It's that cold is it, thought Shimamura. Low, barrack-like buildings that might have been railway dormitories were scattered here and there up the frozen slope of the mountain. The white of the snow fell away into the darkness some distance before it reached them.

'How are you?' the girl called out. 'It's Yoko.'

'Yoko is it. On your way back? It's gotten cold again.'

'I understand my brother has come to work here. Thank you for all you've done.'

'It will be lonely, though. This is no place for a young boy.'

'He's really no more than a child. You'll teach him what he needs to know, won't you?'

'Oh but he's doing very well. We'll be busier from now on, with the snow and all. Last year we had so much that the trains were always being stopped by avalanches, and the whole town was kept busy cooking for them.'

'But look at the warm clothes, would you. My brother said this in his letter that he wasn't even wearing a sweater yet.'

'I'm not warm unless I have on four layers, myself. The young ones start drinking when it gets cold, and the first thing you know they're over there in bed with colds.' He waved his lantern toward the dormitories.

'Does my brother drink?'

'Not that I know of.'

'You're on your way home now, are you?'

'I had a little accident. I've been going to the doctor.'

'You must be more careful.'

The station master, who had an overcoat on over his kimono turned as if to cut the freezing conversation short.

'Take care of yourself,' he called over his shoulder.

'Is my brother here now?'

Yoko looked out over the snow-covered platform. 'See that he behaves himself.' It was such a beautiful voice that it struck one as sad. In all its high resonance it seemed to come echoing back across the snowy night.

The girl was still leaning out the window when the train pulled away from the station. 'Tell my brother to come home when he has a holiday.' She called out to a station master, who was walking along the tracks.

'I'll tell him,' the man called back.

Yoko closed the window and pressed her hands to her red cheeks.

Three snow ploughs were waiting for the heavy snows here on the Border Range. There was an electric avalanche-warning system at the north and south entrances to the tunnel. Five thousand workers were ready to clear away the snow, and two thousand young men from the volunteer fire departments could be mobilized if they were needed.

Yoko's brother would be working at this signal stop, so soon to be buried under the snow – something about that fact made the girl more interesting to Shimamura.

**Angus Waycott** from *Sado: Japan's Island in Exile*

A little way inland from Sawada are two temples associated with a powerful Buddhist sect whose founder was a thirteenth-century priest named Nichiren. Exiled to Sado in 1720, Nichiren underwent an initial period of deprivation but was then 'adopted' by a sympathizer and allowed to live at his home. This place is now a temple complex called Myosho-ji complete with ornate gardens, gateways, tall slabs of stone inscribed with quotations from the master, and clear pools of water planted with lilies and spanned by tiny stone bridges. But Myosho-ji lies enclosed by trees in a hollow on the mountainside, with no view in any direction, so every morning, it's said, the exile would walk half a mile down the track to the edge of a steep escarpment overlooking the Kuninaka plain. Here he would perform his devotions as the sun rose over the mountain ridge to the East and flooded the plain with light. A second temple, Jisso-ji, now stands on this escarpment, and I spent some time exploring the grounds. In the middle of a large gravelled area bordered by neat flowerbeds stood a massive statue of Nichiren set up on a concrete plinth. The plinth was inscribed, in English and Japanese, with the words 'May Peace Prevail on Earth'.

[...]

Exile has a long history in Japan, and, like the expulsion of Adam and Eve from the Garden of Eden, traces its authority to divine precedent. According to an early history called the Kojiki (Record of Ancient Matters), the dispositions made by the country's original creator, the god Izanagi, included directing his capricious son Susano-wo to assume responsibility for the tides, currents, and living creatures of the oceans; but the son had other plans, and set off instead to visit the land of his mother, leaving 'the mountains to wither away and the rivers and seas to dry up'. In anger at this disobedience, his father expelled him from the high Celestial Plain with a 'divine expulsion'.

Before the coming of Buddhism to Japan in the seventh century, serious crimes were normally punished by death, but contemporary Chinese historical records mention that their island neighbours made frequent use of banishment and flogging as well. The first systematic code of Japanese law, which was promulgated in 668, specified three grades of *tsuiho*, or banishment – near, medium and far, for differing degrees of offence. Much later, in feudal times, the shogunate's stricter social regime extended these categories to seven, ranging from *tokoro-barai*, which barred the criminal only from his own village or community, to a kind of blanket ban that expelled him from all the fifteen provinces around Edo and Kyoto, and, for good measure, denied him the use of major highways as well. Persons condemned to death could also have their sentences commuted to banishment as a result of intervention by influential third parties. Islands, which offered security as well as isolation, were ideal destinations, and Sado's first exile, a poet called Hozumiason-no-oi, arrived as early as the year 722.

As Buddhist influence continued to grow, particularly the belief that the ghost of an executed person could return to exact revenge, use of the death penalty as a judicial instrument declined. In fact, from 818 to 1156, it was abolished altogether, although lawbreakers still faced other severe punishments. Exile became the maximum sentence, and not only for transgressions of the law: individuals who fell from official favour could be effectively banished by being appointed to some post in a distant province. Others became exiles by choice, to put themselves and their families beyond the reach of powerful enemies.

In 1185, the Heian Period ended and authority passed from the Imperial court into the hands of the military clans, who were much less squeamish about taking life. Common law was strict and categories of criminals were numerous. But for Japan's pickpockets, murderers, arsonists, rapists, adulterers, blackmailers, and disturbers of public order, plenty of harsh summary punishments were available. Relatively few such people were reckoned to merit the extra administrative work involved in dispatching and supervising an exile. The new growth area was in the category of political exiles, once-powerful individuals removed for backing a wrong horse, for ideological deviation, or for belonging to outlawed sects or organizations. Far from being tough, street-hardened villains, these were often persons of culture and education, well-born, intellectual, with artistic or professional skills. No wonder that when they arrived at their place of exile they weren't feared or scorned, but admired and respected as bringers of new knowledge.

Exiles were allowed a good deal of freedom within their assigned area. The highest classes could even bring goods and servants with them, build homes, and pass their time much as they liked. Although they were supposed to work for local people, doing fishing and farming chores, in practice they lived however they could. As a result, remote, backward Sado had a more or less permanent pool of teachers, actors, and musicians as well as craftsmen like masons, carpenters and builders.

But most of Sado's exiles had a full-time job just staying warm and getting enough to eat. Food was short even for the islanders, and new arrivals without land to plant or skills to gather often went hungry. What was available was poor in quality: there were a few starchy root species, a notorious soup based on seawater, and rough gruels made of pounded millet, barley or vegetables. Sweet potatoes, which grow well even in poor soil, were not introduced until the early eighteenth century. Rice would have been a rare treat, probably available only at festivals and even then only to the rich and privileged. Edible wild plants were another possible food source, and so were the fruits of the sea; but sometimes, in their ignorance of local conditions, exiles sickened on poisonous berries or slipped off slick wet rocks and drowned while foraging on the shore in bad weather.

It was midmorning now, and I was getting hungry myself, so I walked back to Sawada to find something to eat. The main street ran parallel to the shore, and was lined with nondescript shops. At a dusty little grocery store I bought some rice balls, a couple of apples, and a small bag of cherries. The old woman at the till, observing my stick, warned me off the mountains. 'Take care if you go up there,' she said. 'The weather today could turn nasty – please make sure to come back safely.' This sounded like good advice so I carried my purchases down to the beach, and ate them sitting on the sand as the wind gusted around me and blew wreaths of murky coloured cloud on and off the tops of the distant mountains.

Someone else who spent time on this beach at Sawada, and described it in his *Kintosho* (*Book of the Golden Island*), was another famous exile, Zeami. Zeami was one of the founding geniuses of Japan's Noh theatre, a brilliant actor, playwright and critic who was born into a distinguished Kyoto family in 1363. As a teenager he became a protégé of the ruling shogun, who encouraged the boy's education and advised him to make a study of Zen. He is credited with having written about ninety Noh plays, including several that were rewrites of earlier pieces, and such critical works as the seven-part *Fushi Kaden (Transmission of the Flower of Acting Style)* and *Shikadosho (Essay on the Way to the Flower)*. Zeami often used the term 'flower' to denote the invisible genius of performance, the ability to act out something familiar yet make the audience feel and see it as if for the first time.

Zeami dominated the development of Noh theatre until 1422, when he retired and took up the contemplative life of a Soto Zen monk. The theatrical mantle passed to his gifted elder son, Motomasa. Soon afterwards, things began to go wrong. A new shogun took power and made known his preference of the Noh interpretations of Zeami's nephew, a man called On'ami. Zeami and Motomasa were barred from the shogun's court, and when Motomasa died in 1432, On'ami became supreme in the world of Noh. Two years later, Zeami was banished to Sado. The precise charge is not known, but he may have angered the shogun by disdaining the nephew who had supplanted his beloved son. Some believe that he died on the island, others that he eventually returned to Kyoto.

Coincidentally, Sado itself has long been closely associated with Noh, more closely than almost any part of Japan. This has less to do with Zeami than with the discovery of gold at Aikawa and the government's dispatch of Okubo Nagayasu to take charge of its exploitation. The Okubos were a family of actors and the newly appointed *bugyo* brought a troup of performers with him as part of his entourage. With its dramatic recitals and subtle, mannered enactments of scenes from famous tales and legends, Noh caught on in a big way. Before long, villages all over Sado were competing among themselves to build their own stages and put on their own plays. To cover the costs, each village set aside the income derived from one community-owned rice field. This system lasted until after World War II, when government reforms lumped the old irregular landholdings together and then redistributed them among the former tenants. This undermined the financing system, pushing Noh into decline, and posing the danger that it might one day disappear from Sado altogether. For the moment, tradition is holding the line and there are still thirty or forty stages in active use.

[...]

Exile-as-punishment ended in the mid-nineteenth century, and Sado's isolation, once so dreaded, is now one of the main attractions for those outsiders who choose to make their homes on the island – like the famous Kodo drummers. The seeds of this remarkable musical community were sown some twenty five years ago, when the youth of Japan was gripped by the spirit of the 1960s. It was a time of social and political ferment: there were demonstrations against the continuing American occupation of Okinawa, more demonstrations against the Vietnam War, and a general atmosphere of protest against the growing national obsession with material success. Art, theatre, film and literature all provided fertile ground for trying out the new theories of alternative culture, and oddball social experiments were sprouting up all over the country like toadstools.

In 1970, an entrepreneur called Tagayasu Den came up with the idea of conducting a summer music school on Sado. As well as attracting musicians, he hoped it would generate interest in the island itself, perhaps create some work for a few of the islanders and help to stem the steady flow of youngsters leaving to look for jobs on the mainland. Fifty or so people took part in the summer school, and by the time it was over, a core group of about a dozen young men had made up their minds to stay on Sado and set up a permanent community. They planned to live a spartan, frugal existence and devote themselves to studying the ancient art of the drum. Ondekoza was the name they chose for their group, *ondeka* being island dialect for 'Demon Drum'.

Taking up residence in a former school building, the community embarked on a lifestyle that was as spartan as any of them could have wanted, and then some. At twenty years older than the others, Den was the natural leader, and the regime he established was strict. Tobacco, alcohol and personal relationships with the opposite sex were all banned. So was personal money; any assets belonging to group members were pooled. On top of the rigorous program of musical study, there was plenty of physical exercise, including long cross-country runs before breakfast every morning.

While other experimental communes bloomed and then quickly withered all over Japan, Ondekoza hung in there and survived. Den, however, became more and more autocratic and was finally ousted in 1981. The remaining members recast their community in a more democratic form and adopted a new name – Kodo, which means 'heartbeat'.

The departure of their leader was a painful experience, but it unlocked precisely the blend of community spirit, dedicated professionalism and musical excellence that he himself had wanted to build. The new group made its debut at the 1981 Berlin Festival and went on to perform before packed houses in Japan and overseas – New York, London, Paris, Madrid, Rio. Today, having given something like two thousand concerts in thirty different countries, Kodo has become Japan's most widely travelled and acclaimed musical ensemble, with an international reputation that sells thousands of recordings and brings invitations from any and all of the world's most prestigious concert halls.

# APPENDIX 1

# Timeline of Japanese historical periods and events

**Jōmon period 10,000–300BC**

**Yayoi period 300BC–AD300**
369AD Japan formalises relations with Kaya also known as 'Mimana' in present day Korea

**Kofun 300–710**
538 Buddhism arrives in Japan
607 Prince Shōtoku constructs Horyūji
645 The Fujiwara clan overthrows the Soga clan and sets up centralised bureaucracy along Chinese lines, known as the Taika reforms

**Nara period 710–784**
710 Capital first established at Nara
752 Great Buddha of Nara completed at Tōdaiji
794 Kyoto becomes the capital, Heian Kyō (Capital of Peace)

**Heian period 794–1185**
805 Voyages of monks Saichō (Dengyō Daishi) and Kūkai (Kōbō Daishi) to China
894 Official missions to China stopped by the Emperor
995 Fujiwara no Michinaga is regent
1156–60 Taira no Kiyomori rebels against the Minamoto
1180 Minamoto no Yoritomo establishes his military capital at Kamakura

1185  Minamoto led by Yoshitsune defeat the Taira at the battle
        of Dan no ura

## Kamakura period 1185–1333

1195  Tōdaiji rebuilt at Nara
1199  Yoritomo's death, first Hōjō regent, Tokimasa, installed
1268  Kublai Khan sends ambassadors to Kamakura government
1274  Mongols land at Hakata in Kyūshū
1281  Kublai Khan sends 100,000 men. After seven weeks'
        fighting, a 'divine wind' pushes the Mongols back
1331–33  Emperor Godaigo's rebellion against the Hōjō

## Muromachi period 1333–1573

1338  Ashikaga Takauji defeats Godaigo and becomes shogun in
        Kyoto
1392  Ashikaga Yoshimitsu reopens trade with China
1467–77  The Ōnin wars devastate Kyoto, followed by *sengoku
        jidai*, a century of anarchy
1482  Ashikaga Yoshimasa finishes the Ginkakuji, the Silver
        Pavilion
1543  Portuguese shipwrecked off Kyūshū at Tanegashima;
        Japanese adopt European firearms
1549  Francis Xavier enters Japan

## Momoyama period 1573–1600

1573  Oda Nobunaga reunifies Japan, defeating the Ashikagas
1576  Oda Nobunaga builds Azuchi castle
1582  Nobunaga assassinated and Toyotomi Hideyoshi rises
        to power
1588  Hideyoshi sets up fixed social classes
1592  Hideyoshi begins abortive Korean campaigns
1598  Death of Hideyoshi
1600  Tokugawa Ieyasu defeats his rivals at the Battle of
        Sekigahara, becoming shogun

## Edo Period 1603–1867

1615  Ieyasu defeats Hideyoshi's son at Ōsaka

1636  Tokugawa Iemitsu builds Ieyasu's *tōshōgū* mausoleum at Nikkō

1637–38  Shimabara rebellion and *sakoku* closing of Japan

1688–1703  Genroku Era – the rise of *ukiyo-e* prints, plays and novels

1853  Arrival of US Commodore Matthew Perry at Edo

1858  Townsend Harris signs treaty of Commerce and Navigation with Japanese

## Meiji period 1868–1912

1868  Emperor Mutsuhito enthroned, known as Meiji Restoration

1869  Imperial Court moved from Kyoto to Edo, now renamed Tokyo

1889  Meiji Constitution is adopted, with advice from Itō Hirobumi

1894  Japan wins Sino-Japanese war; China cedes Fomosa (Taiwan) to Japan

1905  Japan wins Russo-Japanese war

1910  Korea annexed by Japan

1912  Death of Emperor Meiji

## Taishō period 1912–26

1914  Japan is an ally of Great Britain's during the First World War (1914–18)

1921  Crown Prince Hirohito is a guest of George V at Buckingham Palace

1923  Great Kantō Earthquake

## Shōwa period 1926–1989

1931  Manchurian incident, army officers occupy Northern China and install puppet Emperor

1932  Assassination of Finance Minister and Prime Minister Tsuyoshi Inukai

1937  Japan invades China, Rape of Nanking
1941  Japanese enter World War II, launching a surprise attack
      on Hawaii's Pearl Harbour
1942  Battle of Midway, US wins significant victory, turning the
      tide of Japanese victories
1945  America firebombs Tokyo and other cities and drops atom
      bombs on Hiroshima and Nagasaki; General Macarthur
      leads occupation of Japan
1950  Outbreak of Korean war
1952  American occupation of Japan ends
1964  Tokyo Olympics
1970  Ōsaka World Expo
1972  Okinawa returned to Japan
1989  Emperor Hirohito dies

**Heisei period 1989–present**

1989  Emperor Akihito ascends the throne
1993  Crown Prince Naruhito marries Owada Masako, a career
      diplomat
1995  Great Hanshin Earthquake (at Kōbe)
1995  AUM Shinrikyō Sarin Gas attack
2001–6  Junichirō Koizumi is Prime Minister of Japan
2002  Korea and Japan jointly host the FIFA world cup
2008  Taro Aso is Prime Minister of Japan
2011  Great Tōhoku earthquake and tsunami
2012  Shinzō Abe is Prime Minister

# APPENDIX 2

# Biographies of the authors

### Arashima Takeo (1878–1923)

Arashima Takeo was a novelist, short story writer and critic, the son of a samurai and a companion to the future emperor Taishō. He studied at Sapporo Agricultural College. In 1903 he obtained a position as foreign correspondent with the Mainichi shimbun and in the US he enrolled at Haverford College, near Philadelphia. He published his best known book *Aru Onna, A Certain Woman*, in 1909 followed by *The Descendants of Cain* (1917) about a tenant farmer. Arashima renounced his own tenant farm in Hokkaidō. He committed double suicide or *shinjū* in 1923.

### Ariwara no Narihira (825–880)

Ariwara no Narihira is considered to be the author of *The Tales of Ise*, a collection of short stories with poems. In the first section of most of the tales, a young man who has just come of age flirts with two beautiful sisters at the Nara capital. Two hundred and nine of the poems are on the theme of Japanese court poetry and love.

### Pat Barr

Pat Barr lived in Japan for three years in the 1960s; since then she has lived in London and Norwich. She wrote two books about western settlements in Japan, *The Coming of the Barbarians* and *The Deer Cry Pavilion* as well as other works of non-fiction *Taming the Jungle, To China with Love, The Memsahibs* and a biography, *A Curious Life for a Lady*. She has written four novels, *Chinese Alice, Uncut Jade, Kenjiro* and *Coromandel*.

### John Batchelor (1854–1944)

Batchelor went to Japan in 1877 and, in 1879, joined the church missionary society. He remained in Hokkaidō until 1924. He recorded the myths and beliefs of this vanishing way of life through an elder and interpreter, Parapita. *Ainu Life and Lore* (Kyobukwan, Tokyo, New York, London) is still the major reference book on the island and there is a museum filled with his collection in Sapporo.

### Bashō Matsuo (1644–94)

Born Matsuo Kinsaku, the son of a low-ranking samurai, Bashō became a servant to Tōdō Yoshitada from whom he learnt *haikai no renga*, cooperative poetry composition. By 1680, after studying under Kitamura Kigin (1624–1705), he had a full-time job teaching twenty poetic disciples, but then he moved out of the public eye to Fukagawa. In 1684 he went to Kyoto, beginning the first of four major literary journeys around Japan, most famously in 1689, which he wrote up as *Oku no Hosomichi, The Narrow Road to the Deep North*. The travel diary was an instant bestseller when published posthumously in 1702.

### Isabella Bird (1831–1904)

The daughter of a clergyman, Isabella Bird suffered from a spinal complaint as a young woman and was sent by her father to America and Canada to improve her health. She continued travelling and writing for the rest of her life, completing great journeys across the globe. She felt very at home in Japan where she visited twice. *Unbeaten Tracks in Japan* was published in 1880.

### Edmund Blunden (1896–1974)

Blunden joined the 11th Royal Sussex Regiment in 1916, serving at the Somme and Passchaendaele. He became a writer for *The Nation* and the *TLS*. His poetry collection, *The Shepherd* (1922), won the Hawthornden Prize and *Undertones of War* followed (1928). He was the post-War British cultural advisor in Japan and in 1956 he was awarded the Queen's Gold Medal for Poetry.

### Alan Booth (1924–93)

Journalist and travel writer, Alan Booth moved to Japan to study Noh theatre and worked for the Asahi Evening News. He wrote *The Roads to Sata*, an account of his 2000-mile walking tour of Japan, and *Looking for the Lost: Journeys through a Vanishing Japan* following famous characters and events in Japan.

### Nicolas Bouvier (1929–98)

Bouvier made his first journey from his native Geneva to Japan in a Fiat Toppolino, setting out in 1953 with no intention of coming back, he finally arrived in Japan in 1955. He was to visit again during the 1960s and 1970s and he also became a photographer in Tokyo. He published *The Japanese Chronicles* in 1975. His most famous book, *The Way of the World*, an account of his travel to the East was republished by Eland in 2008.

### Basil Hall Chamberlain (1850–1935)

One of the first experts in Japan studies, Chamberlain translated the *Kojiki*, the *Record of Ancient Matters* for the first time. He is also considered to be a 'father' of Japanese linguistics, his books include: *Things Japanese, Aino Folktales* and *The Classical Poetry of the Japanese*. His *Handbook for Travellers in Japan* was the standard travel guide at the turn of the century.

### Setsuko, Princess Yasuhito Chichibu (1909–95)

Setsuko was the wife of Prince Chichibu (Yasuhito – a brother of Emperor Hirohito of Japan) and the daughter of Tsuneo Matsudaira, Japanese ambassador to the United States and later to Great Britain. She was born in Britain and in her youth she travelled extensively with her father, a life which was interrupted when Empress Sadako chose her to marry her second son Prince Chichibu, the brother of Emperor Hirohito. Throughout her life she visited Britain and in fact received the Order of the Dame Grand Cross of the Order of the British Empire and the Order of St Michael and St George.

### Lesley Downer

Lesley Downer was born to a Chinese mother and Professor of Chinese father. She has written several non-fiction books on Japan including *On the Narrow Road to the Deep North, Geisha: The Secret History of a Vanishing World, Madame Sadayakko: The Geisha who seduced the West, The Brothers: the Hidden World of Japan's richest family,* as well as presenting television programmes on Japan for Channel 4, the BBC and the NHK. She recently wrote a novel, *The Last Concubine* (2008).

### Marguerite Duras (1914–96)

Writer and film director, Duras wrote *Hiroshima Mon Amour* for film-maker Alain Resnais in 1959. Originally intended as a documentary on the atomic bomb, the film was a co-production by companies from both Japan and France with one French character (played by Emanuelle Riva) and one Japanese character (Eiji Okada).

### Shusaku Endo (1923–96)

Endo graduated in French Literature from Keio University. A born Catholic, his novels wrestle with the history of Christian Japan and the contradictions of his faith and culture. His books include *Samurai, Silence (Chimmoku), The Sea and Poison (Umi to Dukuyaku), Wonderful Fool (Obaka San), When I Whistle (Kuchibue o Fuku toki)* as well as *Golden Country (Ogon no Kuni)* and *A Life of Jesus (Iesu no Shogai)*. He won the Akutagawa and the Tanizaki Prizes among others.

### Will Ferguson

Will Ferguson was born and grew up in the former fur-trapping settlement of Fort Vermillion in Northern Canada. His works include *The Hitchhiker's Guide to Japan* and a satirical novel, *Happiness*, which has been sold in twenty countries and seventeen languages, including Japanese.

### Mary Crawford Fraser (1851–1922)

Mary Crawford Fraser was the daughter of an American sculptor in Rome. She married the diplomat Sir Hugh Fraser in 1874. Fraser had just been appointed to Peking and Mary travelled with her husband on missions to Vienna, Rome and Santiago in Chile. In 1888 Fraser was sent as Minister to Japan and Mary accompanied him. Mary Crawford Fraser wrote many books on Italy as well as *A Diplomatist's Wife in Many Lands* (1911) and *Further Reminiscences of a Diplomatist's Wife* (1912). She called Japan and Southern Italy, her 'two real homes'.

### Luis Frois (1532–97)

Frois was born in Lisbon and after his entrance into the Society of Jesus arrived in Japan in 1563. For the next thirty-four years he sent letters and news back to India and Europe. He was also the author of the valuable *Historia do Japão*.

### William Griffis (1843–1928)

Griffis was born in Philadelphia, and taught a young samurai Taro Kusakabe at Rutgers University. In 1870 Griffis was invited to teach in Fukui, Japan, moving swiftly on to Tokyo Imperial University. His books on Japan include his translation of *Bushido: The Soul of Japan* (1905) with Inazo Nitobe. He received two orders of the Rising Sun (Third and Fourth).

### Kitahara Hakushu (1885–1942)

Kitahara Hakushu attended the literature department of Waseda University, Tokyo, but never graduated. In 1906 he joined the Shinshisha New Poetry Association, and published poems in its magazine *Myōjō*, (*Bright Start*), which made him famous. He strove for simplicity in *Suibokushu, Collection of Ink drawings* and *Suzume no Tamago, Sparrow's eggs*. Kitahara published about two hundred books in his lifetime including children's songs, nursery rhymes and he also translated English children's stories. He also wrote anthems for high schools around the country and many of his poems remain popular.

### Lafcadio Hearn (1850–1904)

Hearn was born on the Greek island of Santa Maura to a Maltese mother and an Anglo-Irish father. Aged nineteen, he went to Cincinnati, Ohio, where he became a reporter. In 1890 Hearn went to Japan on a commission for *Harper's Weekly*, where he stayed, teaching English in Matsue. He married Setsuko Koizumi there, taking the name Yakumo Koizumi himself. He later became Professor of Literature at the Imperial University of Tokyo and his books include *Glimpses of Unfamiliar Japan, Kokoro, Gleanings in Buddha-fields, Exotics and Retrospectives, In Ghostly Japan, Shadowings, Kwaidan* and *Japan: An Attempt at Interpretation* (1904).

### Henry Heusken (1832–60)

A Dutch translator, Heusken emigrated to the US in 1853 where he lived in New York, he then joined American Commander Townsend Harris on his expedition to Japan arriving at Shimoda in August 1856 and moved with him to Edo in 1857. Returning from dinner on December 5th, 1860, he was assassinated by a member of the Satsuma clan.

### Tobias Hill (1970– )

Tobias Hill spent two years teaching in Japan. He is the author of several poetry books including *The Year of the Dog* (1995) as well as his award-winning collection of short stories *Skin* (1997), based on his experiences in Japan. He has also written three novels.

### Higuchi Ichiyō (1872–96)

Ichiyō entered the Haginoya poetry school at fourteen and, after the loss of her brother and father, she became head of the Higuchi household aged seventeen. She decided to become a writer to support her family and published her first novel, *Otsugomori*, when she was twenty. Three novels followed: *Takekurabe (Child's Play)*, *Nigorie (Troubled Waters)* and *Jusanya (The Thirteenth Night)*. Living near Yoshiwara district in Tokyo, her subject matter was the unconventional lives of the geisha. She died of tuberculosis.

### Hitomaro no Kakinomoto (seventh century AD)
Hitomaro was the greatest poet of *The Man'yōshū*, he came from an old Yamato family and was in service to the court as a composer of poems of praise and lament for the Imperial family. Among his works he wrote poems in praise of Emperor Temmu's construction of his new palace at Asuka in 675; a procession by Empress Jitō, Temmu's widow; a lament for the death of Prince Takechi described the Jinshin War in 696. He also wrote personal poems on themes such as the death of his wife.

### Christopher Pemberton Hodgson (1821–65)
Hodgson was British consul first at Nagasaki, then at Hakodate, where he 'was aggressive towards the Japanese, his servants and the British community, he failed to keep accounts, sometimes drunk but not always so and claimed mitigating circumstances for other faults. It was to no avail and he was dismissed.' [ J. E. Hoare, *Britain's Japan Consular Service 1859–1941*]. But he did write a book on Japan, *A Residence at Nagasaki and Hakodate (1859–60)*.

### Ikkyū (born 1394)
Ikkyū was born in a small suburb of Kyoto, the illegitimate son of Emperor Go-Komatsu. Aged five, Ikkyū became a monk in the Rinzai Zen temple, Ankoku-ji, studying Chinese. In 1414, when Ikkyū was twenty-one, he found a new master, Kaso, at Daitokuji temple, where he became abbot. Anime TV series *Ikkyū san* is named after him.

### Takuboku Ishikawa (1886–1912)
Takuboku was both a *tanka* and free style (*jiyushi* poet). He was a member of the Myojo, a group of naturalist poets (*shintaishi*) and later joined the socialist group. His major works were *Ichiakuno Suna (A Handful of Sand)* and *Kanashiki gangu (Sad Toys)*.

### Kazuo Ishiguro (1954– )
Born in Nagasaki, Ishiguro moved with his family to England when he was six, and grew up straddling two cultures. He graduated from the University of Kent. His Japan-set novels include *A Pale View of the Hills* and *An Artist of the Floating World*.

### Pico Iyer (1957– )

The son of a Tamil philosopher and theosophist Raghavan N. Iyer, Iyer joined *Time* magazine and has since travelled widely and has written many non-fiction books, including *The Lady and the Monk*, set in Kyoto, near where he lives.

### Engelbert Kaempfer (1651–1716)

Kaempfer was born in Westphalia and travelled throughout the East. He settled in Japan for two years, 1691–2 and became a physician to the Dutch East India Company. During these two years, he made many trips through Japan, gathering information such as a drawing of the shogun's castle and reports on daily life from his own observations and those of previous travellers. Engelbert Kaempfer's *History of Japan* was a best-seller from the moment it was published post-humously in 1727.

### Nagai Kafū (1879–1959)

Born Nagai Sokichi, Kafū wrote about life among the geisha, cabaret dancers and other 'low-life' of early twentieth century. The lyrical quality of his work is very apparent in *Sumidagawa* (*The River Sumida*) published in 1909. He also taught at Keio University.

### Kamo no Chōmei (1155–1216)

The son of Kamo no Nagatsu, Kamo no Chōmei was an author, poet and essayist and superintendent of the Lower Shrine of Kamo in Kyoto. His patron, Emperor Go Toba, commissioned him to con-tribute to the Imperial Poetry office by writing for the *Shinkokinshū* (the *New Collected Poems*) although he was then passed over for promotion. In 1204, he retired to Mount Hiei and then to Hino where he spent the rest of his life writing the *Hōjōki* (otherwise known as the *Tales of the Heike*).

### Lady Kasa

Also known as Kasa no Iratsume, Lady Kasa lived in the eighth century and was a lover of Ōtomo no Yakamochi. Her poems were imitated by women poets of the ninth and tenth centuries, such as Izumi Shikibu and Ono no Komachi.

## Yasunari Kawabata (1899–1972)

Born in Ōsaka, Kawabata's novel *Snow Country* written in 1937, won him fame. This was followed by *A Thousand Cranes* and *The Sound of the Mountain* (1949), *The Lake* (1955), *The Sleeping Beauty* (1960) and *The Old Capital* (1962). He became the first Japanese to win the Nobel Prize for Literature in 1968.

## Professor Donald Keene (1922– )

Director of the Donald Keene Centre for Japanese Studies at Columbia University, Donald Keene has received the Kikuchi Kan Prize of the Society for the Advancement of Japanese Culture (1962) and the Order of the Rising Sun (Second Class and Third Class, 1993 and 1975). In 2002, he was awarded Person of Cultural Merit (Bunka Koro-sha), for his distinguished service in the promotion of Japanese literature and culture. He has published about twenty-five books in English and thirty in Japanese.

## Alex Kerr (1952– )

Kerr studied Japanese at Yale University and Chinese at Oxford. His journalism is published internationally and his books include *Lost Japan* (*Utsukushiiki Nihon no Zanzo*) – for which he was awarded the Shincho Gakugei Literature Prize – and *Dogs and Demons* (2001).

## George Kerr (1911–92)

George Kerr started his career as a teacher in Taiwan and continued while a diplomat during World War II as a researcher and analyst on Formosa (Taiwan). In 1944–6 he was the director of the Formosa research unit at the Naval School of Military Government and Administration. In the 1950s he realised his wish to visit Okinawa with a military commission to write *Okinawa: The History of an Island People* (1958). This was translated into Japanese as *Ryūkyū Rekishi*. In his later years he became an author and an academic.

### Rudyard Kipling (1865–1936)

Kipling is best known for his works *The Jungle Book*, the *Just So Stories*, *Puck of Pook's Hill* and his novel *Kim* (1901). He set off to travel the world, including Japan, for *The Times* newspaper, writing *From Sea to Sea* in 1889. He received the Nobel Prize for Literature in 1907.

### James Kirkup (1918–2009)

Kirkup is a prolific English poet, translator and travel writer. He was the first Gregory Poetry fellow at the University of Leeds in 1952 before leaving England in 1956 for Europe, America and the Far East. He has published over thirty books including autobiographies, novels and plays. His poetry collections include *The Sense of the Visit*, *To the Ancestral North*, *Throwback* and *Shields Sketches*. He won the Japan P.E.N. Club Prize for Poetry in 1965, and was awarded the Scott-Moncrieff Prize for Translation in 1992.

### Mantarō Kubota (1889–1963)

Mantarō Kubota was an author, playwright and poet, born in Asakusa, Tokyo. His novels include *Tsuyushiba* (*Dew on the Grass*) and *Shundei* (*Spring Thaw*). In 1926 he joined Tokyo Central Broadcasting Station (NHK) and in 1937 he co-founded the Bungakuza theatre.

### Arthur Lloyd

Arthur Lloyd came to Japan in 1884 as a British missionary and educator working at the Higher Naval College and Tokyo's Imperial University. His books include *The Creed of Half Japan: Historical sketches of Japanese Buddhism* and *In Everyday Japan*.

### Henry Wadsworth Longfellow (1807–82)

One of the most popular poets of the nineteenth century, Longfellow was Smith Professor of Modern Languages at Harvard from 1836 to 1854 and travelled to Europe, often walking by foot and talking to people on the way. In 1839 he published his first book of poems, *Voices of the Night*, and in 1854 he started to write *The Song of Hiawatha*. His home, Craigie House, in Massachussetts became a meeting place for figures such as Ralph Waldo Emerson, Nathaniel Hawthorne, Julia Ward Howe and Charles Sumner. His last book, *In the Harbour*, was published in 1882.

### Pierre Loti (1850–1923)

Born in France, Louis Marie-Julien Viaud (Loti's real name), joined the navy, becoming a captain in 1910. Fellow officers encouraged him to turn his ship journal into a novel, *Aziyade*, part-romance, part-autobiography. Several novels based on his travels followed including *Rarahu* (1880) about Tahiti and *Roman de Spahi* about Senegambia. He also wrote about atrocities leading up to the Sino-French War for the *Figaro* newspaper. In 1887 he wrote *Madame Chrysenthème*.

### Sugawara no Michizane (845–903)

A scholar, poet, and politician of the Heian period, Sugawara no Michizane's father was a man of letters who taught pupils at home in his Heian mansion. He was appointed an ambassador to China in the 890s, but supported the Fujiwara in stopping imperial embassies. He was exiled by Fujiwara no Tokihira to Dazaifu in Chikuzen province and died there. Posthumously, however, he was pardoned and deified as a god of scholarship Tenjin-sama and is still worshipped at shrines known as Tenmangu.

### Yukio Mishima (1925–70)

Mishima wrote eight novels and four plays for Kabuki theatre including *After the Banquet*, *Confessions of a Mask*, *The Sailor who Fell From Grace with the Sea* and *Forbidden Colours*. *The Sound of Waves* won him the 1954 Shinchosha literary prize. He and a colleague committed suicide by *hara-kiri*, or ritual disembowelment.

## A. B. Mitford (1837–1916)

Algernon Freeman-Mitford, 1st Baron Redesdale, was a British diplomat, collector and writer and the grandfather of the Mitford sisters. Entering the Foreign Office in 1858, he was appointed Third Secretary of the British Embassy in St Petersburg and served in Peking. He went to Japan as the Second Secretary to the British Legation at the time of the Meiji Restoration. Here he wrote *Tales of Old Japan* with the help of Sir Ernest Satow. In 1906 he accompanied Prince Arthur to Japan to honour Emperor Meiji with the Order of the Garter.

## Kenji Miyazawa (1896–1933)

Miyazawa graduated from Morioka Forestry College and moved to Tokyo in 1921. Very soon his younger sister became ill and he moved back to Iwate to look after her. He published many collections of poetry (*Spring* and *Asura*), as well as children's stories. A Nichiren Buddhist, he devoted his life to the people of Iwate.

## Chikamatsu Monzaemon (1653–1725)

Born in Echizen, present-day Fukui, as Sugimore Nobumori, Monzaemon became the greatest dramatist in the history of the Japanese theatre with over one hundred plays. His works combine comedy and tragedy, poetry and prose, combat, torture, and suicide on stage in plays written for the Kabuki theatre in Edo. In 1705, Chikamatsu moved to Ōsaka where he became a writer for the puppet theatre, transforming Japanese *bunraku*. He remained in Ōsaka until his death.

## Iso Mutsu (1867–1930)

Iso Mutsu was born Gertrude Ethel Passingham. While Munemitsu Mutsu, a Japanese baron, and the son of the then Japanese foreign minister, was studying at Cambridge, he fell in love with Passingham, his landlord's daughter. She came to Japan to join him in 1901 secretly, disguised as a child's governess, due to his family's disapproval of the affair. She was finally allowed to marry in 1905 with Imperial consent.

## Takashi Nagai (1908–1951)

Nagai wrote twenty books between the time of Nagasaki's atomic bomb blast in 1945 and his death in 1951, including volumes of poetry. He wrote passionately from his sickbed on behalf of the *hibakusha* (A-bomb victims) and against corruption, meeting with many other peace campaigners, such as Helen Keller.

## John K. Nelson

Nelson is an Associate Professor of East Asian Religions at the Department of Theology and Religious Studies at the University of San Francisco. He is also the Director of Asian Studies degree programme. He is the author of two books on Shinto in contemporary Japan, *A Year in the Life of a Shinto Shrine* (1996) and *Enduring Identities: the Guise of Shinto in Contemporary Japan* (2000), as well as documentaries on the Yasukuni Shrine and the Pacific War.

## Princess Nukuda

Little is known about this woman who was Japan's first lyric poet. She may have been of Korean origin (as many of the Japanese elite were at this time), and she was a central figure in the poetry circle which flourished during the reign of Emperor Tenji (661–671). Tenji was an enthusiastic student of Chinese Literature under whose patronage continental scholars came to teach at the Japanese Court, armed with copies of the Chinese Anthology of poetry and prose, the *Wen IIsuan*.

## Kenzaburo Ōe (1935– )

Born in Shikoku, Ōe won the Akutagawa Prize for his novella *The Catch*. His first novel, also published in 1958, was *Nip the Buds, Shoot the Kids*. He travelled widely in the 1960s meeting with Mao in Peking, Sartre in Paris, and wrote *Screams* in 1963. He won the Nobel Prize for Literature in 1994.

## Jun Okamoto (1901–78)

A communist writer, Okamoto founded the jounal *Red and Black* with Tsuboi Shigeji.

### Ōtomono Tabito (Eighth century AD)

Tabito was the son of a chancellor and the descendant of a great family that had begun to decline. In 728, at the age of 64, Tabito became Commmander of the Dazaifu in Kyūshū. The Dazaifu had been established in the late seventh century as the defence headquarters near the Tsushima Straits between Japan and Korea. Tabito stayed for three years until he was made Chancellor and called back to Nara. Many of his poems are contained in the Man'yōshū.

### Chizuko Oyasato (1931– )

An Okinawan islander, Chizuko Oyasato escaped World War II by hiding in the caves and tunnels that riddled the island, and finally crossed enemy lines with her mother and sister while Okinawa was under bombardment. She has devoted her life to peace promotion.

### Marco Polo (1254–1324)

The world-famous Venetian trader and explorer recorded his Asian travels in *Il Millione* (or *The Travels of Marco Polo*, written in Italian, 1310–20). He travelled with his father and uncle, Niccolo and Maffeo, to China through the Silk Road, visiting Kublai Khan, the grandson of Genghis Khan, who founded the Yuan Dynasty in China.

### William Plomer (1903–1973)

A South African novelist, poet and literary editor, who became famous in South Africa for his first novel, *Turbott Wolfe*, which featured a mixed marriage. He spent some time in Japan in the 1920s and '30s and moved to England where he wrote many novels and collections of poetry. He became a literary editor for Faber and was also active as a librettist writing *Gloriana* and *Curlew River* for Benjamin Britten.

### Herbert Ponting (1870–1935)

Born in Salisbury, England, Ponting became a freelance photographer selling illustrations to the *Graphic*, the *Illustrated London News* and *Strand Magazine*. He published his photographs of Japan as a book, *In Lotus-Land Japan*. He joined Scott's Terra Nova expedition in 1911 where he showed a slide show of Japan to entertain the explorers.

## Donald Richie (1924–2013)

Richie first went to Japan with the American occupation force in 1947 as a staff writer for the *Pacific Stars and Stripes*. His books include: *The Japanese Film: Art and Industry, One Hundred Years of Japanese Film, Tokyo Nights, The Inland Sea, Public People, Private People* and *The Japan Journals* (1947–2004). He received the Japan Foundation Award in 1995.

## Joao Rodrigues (1561–1634)

Born in Sernancelhe, Portugal, Rodrigues was fifteen when he sailed to Japan and entered the Society of Jesus there in 1580. He served as *Tsuzu*, an interpreter for *daimyo* Hideyoshi and shogun Ieyasu. His books include *História da Igreja do Japão* as well as *Arte da Lingoa de Japam* and collaborated on *Vocabulario da Lingoa de Japam*. After being expelled from Japan in 1612, he settled in Macao.

## Saigyō (1118–90)

Saigyō was a Buddhist priest, who entered the priesthood at the age of twenty-three after serving the Emperor Gotoba as a warrior and met the leaders of both sides of the wars between the Genji and the Taira clans. His life became the subject of many plays, narratives and *bunraku* puppet dramas. He travelled all over Japan as a priest, working with Taira no Kiyomori and his poems are collected in the anthology *Sankashū*. He belonged to the Shingon or mantra school of Buddhism founded by Kūkai.

## Ihara Saikaku (1642–93)

Saikaku began to compose *haikai* at the age of twenty and became a master. After the death of his wife he decided to become a monk and travel, but he returned to writing novels in 1682 with *The Life of an Amorous Man, The Great Mirror of Beauties* and *The Five Women who Loved Love*. Saikaku wrote *Tales from the Provinces* in 1685.

## Oda Sakunosuke (1913–47)

Sakunosuke is grouped with Dazai Osamu and Sakaguchi Ango as part of the Buraiha, 'the school of irresponsibility and decadence'. An Ōsaka native, in 1940 he published *Meoto Zenzai*, named after an Ōsakan sweet shop. Several of his works were banned during his lifetime.

## Rai Sanyō (1780–1832)

Neo-Confucian historian and author of *Nihon gaishi*, or *Unofficial History of Japan*.

## John Saris (1579–1643)

Saris, a Yorkshireman, arrived in Japan in June 1613 in order to establish a trading post for the East India Company. He stayed in the country for six months. On his return to England, he married a daughter of a former Lord Mayor of London.

## Sir Ernest Satow (1843–1929)

Satow was a Japanologist, diplomat and scholar as well as an exceptional linguist, energetic traveller, and writer of travel guidebooks. He compiled dictionaries and was an avid botanist. He succeeded in coming to Japan after successfully winning a scholarship to learn Japanese and Chinese, and there followed a distinguished career in the foreign office. He advised many British Ambassadors to Japan including Sir Harry Parkes, and later became the British High Commissioner in Peking, 1900–6.

## Edward Seidensticker (1921–2007)

Edward G. Seidensticker was Emeritus Professor of Japanese literature at Columbia University. An ex-marine officer to Iwo Jima during World War II, Seidensticker returned to Japan and translated Murasaki Shikibu's *Tale of Genji* as well as great twentieth century novels such as Junichirō Tanizaki's *Some Prefer Nettles*, Yukio Mishima's *The Decay of the Angel*, and Yasunari Kawabata's *Snow Country* and *Thousand Cranes*. He also wrote non-fiction books, *Low City, High City: Tokyo from Edo to the Earthquake*, *Tokyo Rising: The City Since the Great Earthquake* and a memoir, *Tokyo Central*, published in 2002. He won the National Book Award for his translation of *The Sound of the Mountain* by Kawabata.

### Masaoka Shiki (1867–1902)

Shiki was the pen-name of Masaoka Tsunenori, poet, literary critic, journalist and author. He was the moderniser of Japanese poetry, using the term *haiku* for the first time (as opposed to *hokku*). He was very ill for much of his life and after serving in the first Sino-Japanese war, he returned in 1895 to convalesce at Natsume Sōseki's house. Despite his short life, he is considered one of the great names of Japanese poetry along with Issa and Bashō.

### Murasaki Shikibu (c.975–c.1025)

After the death of her husband in 1001, Murasaki was summoned into the service of Empress Akiko and remained there for about ten years. Her diary gives detailed descriptions of court life. This is also where she wrote the first great novel in the world, *The Tale of Genji*.

### Futabatei Shimei (1864–1909)

Shimei studied Russian at Tokyo School of Foreign languages and translated the work of Ivan Turgenev and other Russian realists. His novel *Ukigumo* (*Floating Clouds*) is Japan's first modern novel. He died while working as Russian correspondent for the Asahi Shimbun.

### Kaori Shoji

Journalist and film critic Kaori Shoji was educated at Columbia University and lives in Tokyo. *Seeing Tokyo* by Shoji and British Ambassador Graham Fry was published by Kodansha International in 2006. She is a columnist for *The Japan Times*.

### Sei Shōnagon (966–1017)

Sei Shōnagon was a Japanese author and court lady who served Empress Sadako, consort of Emperor Ichijo, during the Heian period around the year 1000. Her diary *The Pillow Book* is a gossipy chronicle of lists, seasons, fashion, and observations of court life.

### Natsume Sōseki (1867–1916)

Natsume Sōseki was the pen name of Natsume Kinnosuke, considered to be the foremost novelist of the Meiji Era, best known for his novels *I am a Cat, Kokoro, Botchan, Light and Darkness, Kusa Makura* (*Grass Pillow*) and *Kokoro*. He lived in Clapham, London, 1901–3.

### Prince Shōtoku (573–621)

Also known as *Shōtoku Taishi* was a regent and politician of the Asuka period in Japan. According to the *Nihon Shoki* he established a centralised government in Japan, based on Confucius' teachings and he also established the twelve ranks at court. He was a proponent of Buddhism, composing commentaries on the *Vimalakirti Sutra* and also the *Lotus Sutra*. He also sent an embassy from Japan to China in 607 using the title Nihon, Land of the Rising Sun for the first time.

### Oliver Statler (1915–2002)

Statler began a career as a writer and art researcher in Japan after the Second World War. He was invited to Honolulu in 1977 as Visiting Professor in Asian Studies and published *Japanese Pilgrimage* in 1983, followed by *Japanese Inn* and *Modern Japanese Prints: an Art Reborn*.

### Jonathan Swift (1667–1745)

Swift wrote *Gulliver's Travels* in 1726 to 'vex the world rather than divert it'. When the book was published anonymously in 1726, it was an instant success, and ten thousand copies were said to have been sold in three weeks with translations into French and Dutch and serialisation in weekly journals.

### Junichirō Tanizaki (1886–1965)

Tanizaki was born in Nihombashi, Tokyo. His short story *Shisei* (*Tattooer*) earned him a reputation as a literary novelist. Other works followed including *Kirin, Shonen, Himitsu* (*The Secret*), and *Akuma* (*Devil*), *Chijin no ai* (*Naomi*), *Tade kuu mushi* (*Some Prefer Nettles*) and *Kagi* (*The Key*). His last novel, *Futen Roji Nikki* (*Diary of an Old Man*), continued his favourite theme of erotic obsession.

### Anthony Thwaite (1930– )
Poet, broadcaster, critic, reviewer and academic, Thwaite has worked as literary editor for several national magazines. His collections include *The Stones of Emptiness: Poems 1963–1966* as well as *Inscriptions* and *New Confessions*. He taught at Tokyo University 1955–7 and co-edited with Geoffrey Bownas *The Penguin Book of Japanese Verse* (1964 and 1998). He returned to Tokyo in 1985 as Japan Foundation Fellow, which he explored in *Letter from Tokyo*.

### Shimazaki Tōson (1872–1943)
Tōson was the son of a *shoya* or headman of the village of Magome in the Shinsū mountains, present-day Nagano. He lived in Sendai and published three collections of poetry. In 1899 he moved back to Komoro in Shinshū where he set his novel *The Broken Commandment*, based on the story of Oe Isokichi, a brilliant young *eta* or outcast who became a headmaster but was murdered.

### Ki no Tsurayuki (872–945)
An author, poet and courtier of the Heian period, Ki no Tsurayuki was the son of Ki no Mochiyuki and became a waka poet in the 890s. He was one of the four poets selected to compile the *Kokinshū* (*A Collection of Poems Ancient and Modern*), with an introduction in Chinese. He was governor of Tosa province between 930 and 935. He is mentioned in *The Tale of Genji*.

### Rey Ventura (1962– )
Journalist Ventura was born in the Philippines, and in 1988 he worked for a year as a day labourer in Yokohama, becoming Manila correspondent of Asia Press International, a Tokyo-based news agency between 1996 and 2001.

### Elizabeth Gray Vining (1902–99)
Born a Quaker, in 1946–50 Elizabeth Gray Vining was selected by Emperor Hirohito to be a tutor for the Crown Prince, the future Emperor Akihito. She also taught Empress Nagako and became friends with other members of the Imperial family.

**Angus Waycott**

Waycott is the author of three books – *Sado: Japan's Island in Exile*, *Paper Doors*, *Japan from Scratch* and *National Parks of Western Europe*.

**Oswald Wynd (1913–98)**

Born in Tokyo of Scots parents, Wynd set his novel *The Ginger Tree* in Tokyo. He grew up speaking both English and Japanese and his novel *Black Fountains* won the Doubleday prize in 1947. He also wrote thrillers under the pseudonym Gavin Black.

**Kunio Yanagita (1875–1962)**

Yanagita almost singlehandedly initiated the serious study of folklore in Japan. Acclaimed in his own lifetime and after his death, Yanagita became a cult figure symbolising the mythical elements of Japanese culture. His collected works of thirty-six volumes sold 60,000 copies up to 1973.

**Rika Yokomori (1963– )**

The novelist Yokomori was born in Yamanashi and studied graphic and movie design. She moved to New York becoming a magazine columnist and published her first novel, *New York Night Trip*. *Tokyo Tango* was published in English in 2007.

**St Francis Xavier (1506–1552)**

St Francis was born in the Basque country near Zaragoza, in the Spanish kingdom of Navarre. He was educated in Paris, where he first met St Ignatius Loyola. Responding to the call of King John III of Portugal for Jesuit missionaries to go East, he set sail in 1541, travelling to Mozambique, Goa in India, and The Moluccas. In Malacca he met an exiled Japanese samurai, Anjiro, who invited him to Japan. He arrived there in 1549. He stayed for two years, establishing congregations in Hirado, Yamaguchi and Bungo. He died of fever on the island of Sancian while attempting to enter China.

# Bibliography

**Tokyo**

Bashō, Matsuo, *A Cloud of Cherry Blossoms*, translated in Haiku by R. H. Blyth, Volume One: Eastern Culture, Hokuseido Press, Tokyo, 1952

Bashō, Matsuo, *Narrow Road to the Deep North and Other Travel Sketches*, translated by Nobuyuki Yuasa, Penguin, 1966

Blunden, Edmund, *Wanderings in Japan*, Asahi Shimbun-sha, Tokyo, 1948

Bouvier, Nicolas, *The Japanese Chronicles*, translated from the French by Anne Dickerson, Polygon, 1995

Chichibu, Princess Setsuko, *The Silver Drum: A Japanese Imperial Memoir* translated by Dorothy Britton, Global Oriental, Folkstone, Kent, 1996

Hakushū, Kitahara, on the disappearance of Tsukiji (1923) quoted in *Low City, High City*, translated by Edward Seidensticker (1921 2007), Alfred A. Knopf, 1983

Heusken, Henry, *Japan Journal 1855–1861*, edited by Jeanette C. Van der Corput, Rutgers University Press, New Brunswick, New Jersey, 1964

Kaempfer, Engelbert, *Kaempfer's Japan: Tokugawa Culture Observed*, edited by Beatrice M. Bodart-Bailey, University of Hawaii Press, Honolulu, 1999

Kafū, Nagai, *During the Rains*, translated by Lane Dunlop, Stanford University Press, 1994

Kawabata, Yasunari, *The Scarlet Gang of Asakusa*, translated by Alisa Freeman, University of California Press, 2005

Lloyd, Arthur, *Everyday Japan*, London, 1911

Lyons Danly, Robert (Ed.), *In the shade of spring leaves, the life and writing of Higuchi Ichiyo, a woman of letters in Meiji Japan*, Norton, London, New York, 1992

Mantaro, Kubota, quoted in *Low City, High City*, translated by Edward Seidensticker, Alfred A. Knopf, 1983

Okamoto, Jun, from *New writing in Japan*, edited by Geoffrey Bownas and Yukio Mishima, Penguin, 1972

Richie, Donald, *Tokyo Nights*, Printed Matter Press, Tokyo, 2005

Satow, Sir Ernest, *A Diplomat in Japan*, Oxford University Press, 1968

Shimei, Futabatei, *Drifting Clouds*, 1887, translated by Ryan Marleigh Grayer, Greenwood Press, Westport, Connecticut, 1983

Sōseki, Natsume, *Sanshiro*, translated by Jay Rubin, University of Washington Press, 1977

Statler, Oliver, *Japanese Inn*, Secker and Warburg, London, 1961

Swift, Jonathan, *Gulliver's Travels*, Penguin, Harmondsworth, 1967

Thwaite, Anthony, *Penguin Book of Japanese Verse*, Harmondsworth, Penguin, 1998

Wynd, Oswald, *The Ginger Tree*, Eland Publishing, 1988

Yokomori, Rika, *Tokyo Tango*, translated by Tom Gill, Duckworth Overlook Editions, 2006

**Yokohama**

Plomer, William, *Collected Poems*, London, 1960

Tanizaki, Junichirō, *Seven Japanese Tales*, Tuttle, Tokyo and Vermont, 1977

Ventura, Rey, from *Underground in Japan*, edited by James Fenton, Jonathan Cape, 1992

**Kamakura**

Kawabata, Yasunari, *The Sound of the Mountain*, translated by Edward M. Seidensticker, Secker & Warburg, 1971

Mutsu, Iso, *Kamakura: Fact and Legend*, Tuttle, 1995

Shōji, Kaori, 'Shōnan Beach mystique evaporates upon arrival', *Japan Times*, March 31st 2005

Sōseki, Natsume, *Kokoro* or *The Heart of Things* translated by Edwin
 McClellan 1957, Arena, 1984

Tanizaki, Junichirō, *Naomi*, translated by Anthony H. Chambers,
 Secker and Warburg, 1985

**Izu Peninsula**

Anonymous, *The Man'yōshū* – 'Poem about Mount Fuji' translated
 by Ian Hideo Levy, Princeton University Press, 1981

Chamberlain, Basil Hall, *Things Japanese*, 2nd edn revised, London,
 1891

Fraser, Mary Crawford, *A Diplomat's Wife in Japan*, London, 1899

Kaempfer, Engelbert, *Kaempfer's Japan: Tokugawa Culture Observed*,
 edited by Beatrice M. Bodart-Bailey, University of Hawaii Press,
 Honolulu, 1999

Kawabata, Yasunari, *The Izu Dancer*, from *The Oxford Book of
 Japanese Short Stories*, edited by Theodore W. Goossen,
 translated by Edward Seidensticker, Oxford University Press,
 1997

Saigyō, *Zen Poems*, translated with an introduction by Geoffrey
 Bownas and Anthony Thwaite, selected and edited by Peter
 Harris, Alfred A. Knopf, 1999

Statler, Oliver, *Shimoda Story*, Charles E. Tuttle, Tokyo and Vermont,
 1969

**Gifu and Nagano**

Bashō, *The Sarashina Diary*, *The Journey to Sarashina*, from *The
 Pleasures of Japanese Literature*, translated by Donald Keene,
 Columbia University Press, 1988

Booth, Alan, *The Roads to Sata: a 2000-mile walk through Japan*,
 Penguin Putnam Books, 1985

Downer, Lesley, *The Last Concubine*, Bantam Press, Transworld, 2008

Fraser, Mary Crawford, *A Diplomat's Wife in Japan*, London, 1899

Gray Vining, Elizabeth, *Windows for the Crown Prince Akihito of
 Japan*, Tuttle Publishing, Tokyo and Vermont, 1952

Griffis W. E., *The Mikado's Empire*, Kegan Paul, 2002

Tōson, Shimazaki, *Komoro Castle*, translated by Harry Guest from *The Elek Book of Oriental Verse*, edited by Keith Bosley, 1994

Tōson, Shimazaki, *The Broken Commandment* translated by Kenneth Strong, University of Tokyo Press, 1974

**Kyoto**

Bouvier, Nicolas *The Japanese Chronicles*, Polygon, Edinburgh, 1995

Frois, Louis, from *They Came to Japan: An Anthology of European Reports on Japan, 1543–1640*, edited by Michael Cooper, University of California Press, Berkeley, 1965

Ikkyū, *Ikkyū and the Crazy Cloud Anthology, A Zen poet of Medieval Japan*, translated with an introduction by Sonja Arntzen, University of Tokyo Press, 1986

Iyer, Pico, *The Lady and the Monk: Four Seasons in Kyoto*, Black Swan, 1991–2

Kerr, Alex, *Lost Japan*, Lonely Planet, London and Melbourne, 1996

Kipling, Rudyard, *From Sea to Sea*, 1889, e-text from http://whitewolf.newcastle.edu.au/authors/K/KiplingRudyard/prose/FromSeatoSea/index.html

Polo, Marco, *The Travels of Marco Polo*, edited by Hugh Murray, Oliver and Boyd, Edinburgh, 1844

Princess Nukuda, from *Women Poets of Japan*, translated and edited by Kenneth Rexroth and Ikuko Atsumi, New Directions, New York, 1977

Rodrigues, Joao, *Historia do Japao*, from *They Came to Japan: An Anthology of European Reports on Japan*, edited by Michael Cooper, University of California Press, 1965

Saris, John, *The Voyage of John Saris*, edited by Sir E. M. Satow, Hakluyt Society, 1900

Shikibu, Murasaki, *The Diary of Murasaki Shikibu*, translated by Annie Shepley Omori and Kōchi Doi, from *Anthology of Japanese Literature*, edited by Donald Keene, Penguin 1968

Shōnagon, Sei, *The Pillow Book of Sei Shōnagon*, *c*.1002 edited with
    introduction and translation by Ivan Morris, Oxford University
    Press, 1967
Tanizaki, Junichirō, *The Makioka Sisters*, Vintage Books, London,
    1995

**Nara**
Anonymous, 'On the move from Asuka to Nara', *The Man'yōshū*,
    translated by Ian Hideo Levy, University of Tokyo Press,
    Princeton University Press, 1981
Hitomaro, from *The Man'yōshū*, translated by Ian Hideo Levy,
    University of Tokyo Press, Princeton University Press, 1981
Ponting Herbert, *In Lotus Land Japan*, London, Macmillan, 1910
Shiki, Masaoka, *Selected Poems*, translated by Burton Watson,
    Columbia University Press, 1993
Shōtoku, Prince, *The Man'yoshu*, translated by Ian Hideo Levy,
    University of Tokyo Press, Princeton University Press, 1981
Tabito, Ōtomo no, *The Man'yōshū*, translated by Ian Hideo Levy,
    University of Tokyo Press, Princeton University Press, 1981

**Ise**
Craig McCullough, Helen, edited by Ise Monogatari, *The Tales of Ise*,
    Stanford Press, 1968
Hill, Tobias, *Year of the Dog*, Salt Publishing, 1995
Lloyd, Arthur, *Every Day Japan*, London, 1911
Mishima, Yukio, *The Sound of Waves*, translated by Meredith
    Weatherby, Secker and Warburg, 1957

**Ōsaka**
Barr, Pat, *The Coming of the Barbarians: The Story of Western Settlement
    in Japan 1853–1870*, Macmillan, 1967
Kerr, Alex, *Lost Japan*, Lonely Planet, London, Melbourne, 1996
Mitford, Algernon Bertram, *Mitford's Japan: The Memoirs and
    Recollections 1866–1906*, Kodansha International, 1985

Monzaemon, Chikamatsu, from *The Love Suicides of Sonezaki* (1703), from *Four major plays of Chikamatsu*, translated by Donald Keene, Columbia University Press, New York and London, 1961

Monzaemon, Chikamatsu, *The Love Suicides of Amijima*, translated by Donald H. Shively, University of Michigan Press, 1991

Sakunosuke, Oda, *Stories of Ōsaka Life*, translated by Burton Watson, Weatherhill Inc, New York, 1994

**Hiroshima and Chūgoku**

Booth, Alan, *The Roads to Sata: a 2000-mile-walk through Japan*, Penguin Putnam Books, 1985

Chōmei, Kamo no *Ten Foot Square Hut and the Tales of Heike*, translations of the *Hojoki* and the *Heike Monogatari* by A. L. Sadler, Greenwood Press, Westport, Connecticut, 1970

Hearn, Lafcadio, *Writings from Japan (1850-1912)*, anthology, edited with an introduction by Francis King, Penguin, 1994

Ōe, Kenzaburo, *Hiroshima Notes*, translated by Toshi Yonezawa, YMCA, Tokyo, 1981

**Shikoku and the Inland Sea**

Kasamaro, Tajihi, *The Man'yōshū* , translated by Ian Hideo Levy, University of Tokyo Press, Princeton University Press, 1981–

Ki, Tsurayuki, *The Tosa Diary*, translated by William N. Porter, London, 1912

Richie, Donald, *The Inland Sea*, Weatherhill Inc, New York, 1971

Shiki, Masaoka, *Selected Poems*, translated by Burton Watson, Columbia University Press, New York, 1993

Statler, Oliver, *Japanese Pilgrimage*, Pan Books, London, 1984

**Kyūshū**

Longfellow, Henry Wadsworth, from *Kéramos*, 1878, reprinted Lightyear Press, 1993

Endo, Shusaku, *The Oxford Book of Japanese Short Stories*, translated by Van Gessel, edited by Theodore W. Goossen, Oxford University Press, 1997

Michizane, Sugawara no, from *The Nobility of Failure: Tragic Heroes in the History of Japan*, translated by Ivan Morris, Secker and Warburg, 1975

Saikaku, Ihara, *The Umbrella Oracle*, translated by Richard Lane, from *Anthology of Japanese Literature*, edited by Donald Keene, Penguin, 1968

Xavier, St Francis, *Excerpts from a letter to the Society of Jesus in Rome from St. Francis Xavier about his activities in Japan, 1552*, http://www.artsales.com/ARThistory/Xavier/Xavier-2.html

### Nagasaki

Ishiguro, Kazuo, *A Pale View of the Hills*, Faber, London, 1991

Loti, Pierre, *Madame Chrysanthème*, translated from the French by Laura Ensor, T. Werner Lorrie, London, 1916

Nagai, Takashi, *The Bells of Nagasaki*, edited by William Johnston, Kodansha International, Tokyo, 1984

Nelson, Richard K., *A Year in the Life of a Shinto Shrine*, Washington Press, 1996

Sanyo, Rai, *Dutch Ships, Penguin Book of Japanese Verse*, translated by Geoffrey Bownas and Anthony Thwaite, Penguin, 1998

Thwaite, Anthony, *Letter from Tokyo*, Hutchinson, 1987

### Okinawa

Nabe, Onna, and Captain Hall, from *Okinawa, the History of an Island People* by George Kerr, Charles Tuttle, Tokyo and Vermont, 1958

Oyasato, Chizuko, *Okinawa 1945*, translated by Kimiko Iha, Naha-shi, 1994

### Hokkaidō

Arashima, Takeo, *Kansoroku, Boyhood diary*, in *The Columbia anthology of modern Japanese literature*, edited by J. Thomas Rimer and Van C. Gessel, Columbia University Press, New York, 2005

Batchelor, Sir John, *Ainu Life and Lore*, Kyobukwan, Tokyo, New York and London, 1971

Ferguson, Will, *Hokkaidō Highway Blues*, Canongate, 1998

Ishikawa, Takuboku, translated by Alan Booth from *The Roads to Sata* by Alan Booth, Viking Penguin, 1986

Matsuura, Takeshiro, *Modern Japanese Diaries: The Japanese at Home and Abroad as Revealed hrough their Diaries*, edited by Donald Keene, Henry Holt, New York, 1995

Miyazawa, Kenji, *Spring and Asura Poems*, translated by Burton Watson, Chicago Review Press, 1973

### Northern Honshū

Bashō, Matsuo *Narrow Road to the Deep North*, translated by Nobuyuki Yuasa, Penguin, 1966

Bird, Isabella, *Unbeaten Tracks in Japan*, John Murray, London, 1880

Downer, Lesley, *On the Narrow Road to the Deep North*, Jonathan Cape, 1989

Endo, Shusaku, *Samurai*, translated by Van C. Gessel, Owen, 1982

Kawabata, Yasunari, *Snow Country*, translated by Edward Seiden-sticker, Alfred A. Knopf, New York, 1956

Kirkup, James, *These Horned Islands: a Journal of Japan*, Collins, London, 1962

Miyazawa, Kenji, *Spring and Asura Poems*, translated by Burton Watson, Chicago Review Press, 1973

Yanagita, Kunio, *The Legends of Tono*, translated and introduced by Toda Shizuo, Shohan, Japan, 1983

### Niigata and Sado

Saikaku, Ihara, *The Life of an Amorous Man*, translated by Kengi Hamada, Tuttle, Tokyo and Vermont, 1964

Waycott, Angus, *Sado: Japan's Island in Exile*, Stonebridge Press, Berkeley, California, 1996